D1061765

STATEMENT CONCERNING PUBLICATIONS OF RUSSELL SAGE FOUNDATION

Russell Sage Foundation was established in 1907 by Mrs. Russell Sage "for the improvement of social and living conditions in the United States of America." While the general responsibility for management of the Foundation is vested in the Board of Trustees, the responsibility for facts, conclusions, and interpretations in its publications rests with the authors and not upon the Foundation, its Trustees, or its staff. Publication under the imprint of the Foundation does not imply agreement by the organization with all opinions or interpretations expressed. It does imply that care has been taken that the work on which a manuscript is based has been thoroughly done.

INTEGRATING SOCIOLOGICAL AND PSYCHOANALYTIC CONCEPTS

An Exploration in Child Psychotherapy

By OTTO POLLAK

1956

Russell Sage Foundation / New York

Printed in the United States
of America

Library of Congress
Catalog Card Number: 56-7934

Foreword

THE ESSENTIAL HYPOTHESIS which Dr. Pollak and his collaborators at the Child Guidance Institute of the Jewish Board of Guardians have been testing is that the diagnostic and therapeutic capabilities in a psychiatric child guidance agency are substantially increased by the effective application of selected social science concepts and approaches. In an earlier phase of their work they found this hypothesis to be of sufficient plausibility to warrant an exploratory systematic employment of these concepts in the diagnosis and treatment of cases assigned to a special therapeutic team which included Dr. Pollak. A major portion of the present work is devoted to a detailed presentation of some of the cases dealt with by this team.

The weight of evidence seems by and large to support the hypothesis, but of far greater interest and challenge is the finding that what is involved is much more than a mere addition of social science ideas to those of psychoanalysis. Efficient integration, the report shows, will entail substantial modification of both orientations and further theoretical reformulations.

In their experimentation up to the present Dr. Pollak and his colleagues have arrived at a theoretical position which, while accepting the conception of social interaction, also requires that the intrapsychic character of the participants in the interaction be determined. This position calls for an operation in which, ideally, the significant participants in the child's social world will be examined to determine their intrapsychic structure, and then to study the problems occasioned by the interaction among these intrapsychic characteristics. While the position taken accounts in part for the relatively heavy dependence upon psychoanalytic theory, it also opens up a field of clinical study which could well lead toward a more thorough-going interactional type of theory and explanation.

This intermediate condition may offend some readers. For example, the orthodox Freudian may deplore the heterodox departures he can detect, and the radical interactionist may decry what to him is the failure to identify the interactional character of behavior described in psychoanalytic terminology. On the other hand, the less orthodox psychoanalytically oriented reader will find significant and constructive evidence of the potentialities of the situational-interactional approach. And even the hardened interactionist will probably have to yield to some extent in the direction of the position taken by the team although he may resist the use of psychoanalytic interpretation. In seeking for explanations of the behavior of a participant in a given interacting situation in terms of the interaction itself, he would certainly have to take into account the previously established self-conceptions and expectations of others which the participants bring to that situation.

While this work is a study of cases, it is itself a case study which makes an important contribution to our understanding of problems which transcend those of immediate clinical concern. Sharpening as it does our recognition of essential issues in the development of a more adequate theory of human behavior, it is published in the expectation that it will stimulate further integrative efforts among the behavior sciences and between theory and practice.

LEONARD S. COTTRELL, JR.

Acknowledgments

MANY PERSONS have helped in the venture on which this book reports. They represent several disciplines and organizations. Outstanding among them is Mr. Herschel Alt, executive director of the Jewish Board of Guardians. His contribution to the clarification of concepts and perspective of the field proved a never failing source of assistance. Closest in collaboration, enabler and co-worker was Dr. Maurice R. Friend, at that time clinical director of the Madeleine Borg Child Guidance Institute and co-leader of our experimental team. His interest and dedication provided an invaluable contribution to the project.

It is pleasure as well as duty to mention the staunch friendship, enthusiasm, and therapeutic skills of Mrs. Bettina Lehnert, Miss Herta Mayer, Miss Betty Klein, and Miss Louise Schiddel who gave of themselves unsparingly in the treatment ventures and the team discussions. Miss Frederika Neumann lent great assistance through her critical comments and constructive scrutiny of the manuscript. Dr. Leonard S. Cottrell, Jr., of Russell Sage Foundation and Dr. Eleanor Boll of the University of Pennsylvania provided the author with the understanding assistance of fellow sociologists to a colleague engaged in a psychodynamic adventure. The author is greatly indebted to Miss Margaret R. Dunne of Russell Sage Foundation for her patience and excellent editorial work.

Thanks are also due the project secretaries, Mrs. Libby R. Friedberg and Miss Rose Farkas, who were always cheerful during our sometimes turbulent discussions and exceedingly efficient in recording the minutes of meetings. All these persons and many others helped. The mistakes, however, are as always entirely the responsibility of the writer.

OTTO POLLAK

Contents

PART FOUR
THE AGENCY LOOKS AT THE PROJECT

I. History of the Project and Outlook

THE WORK WHICH THIS BOOK describes had its beginning in the year 1949 when Russell Sage Foundation and the Jewish Board of Guardians entered into an agreement to conduct a joint project to explore whether cooperation between social scientists and clinicians in child guidance practice could prove to be of mutual benefit. More specifically, it was visualized at the time that two areas of interest would be investigated: (1) the contribution potential of the existing funds of social science knowledge to child guidance practice, and (2) research needs encountered by child guidance workers which could be met by social scientists. Under the arrangement the writer was made available to the Board by the Foundation as consulting sociologist. Begun cautiously for an eleven-month period only, the project showed its vitality by being twice renewed. At first, it was continued another year for the purpose of collaboration between the senior staff of the agency's Child Guidance Institute and the consulting sociologist on a symposium volume, which might show in what areas and in what ways social science thinking could be applied in child guidance practice. That symposium volume appeared in 1952, under the title *Social Science and Psychotherapy for Children.*[1]

THE TWO MAJOR PHASES OF THE PROJECT

A short history of this collaborative effort seems in order at this point. After having spent roughly seven months in the agency, familiarizing himself with the nature of the work of

[1] Pollak, Otto, and Collaborators, *Social Science and Psychotherapy for Children.* Russell Sage Foundation, New York, 1952.

the Child Guidance Institute, with the terminology utilized in carrying it out, and the theory underlying it, the consulting sociologist met with the borough supervisors, the director of group therapy, and the director of the volunteer department, as well as with the director of casework services in a series of conferences. In these meetings he reported to this group of line executives of the agency his observations and proposals. He pointed out what to him seemed gaps in the consideration of pertinent phenomena in the course of diagnosis and therapy as practiced, and conceptualizations of these phenomena in the social sciences which might aid in securing their consideration by the therapists. This was done with the express purpose of having the group check on the correctness of these observations and evaluate the promise of an incorporation of these concepts into the theory underlying child guidance practice. The group undertook this task of checking and evaluating with care and concern. It saw sufficient merit in the observations of the consultant sociologist and his proposals not only to endorse the writing of the report but also to undertake the task of collaboration in its preparation.

Taking observations of practice rather than theoretical statements about it as a baseline for its propositions, the symposium stressed the importance of a total situational approach for psychotherapy in child guidance work and of special social science concepts as perceptual tools and ordering devices for the consideration of factors which seemed important for diagnosis and therapeutic planning. "It analyzed the implications of family structure and of social interaction for diagnosis and therapeutic planning in terms of patient selection, collateral contacts, and prognosis. It contained an examination of extrafamilial influences in pathogenesis. Special emphasis was put on the socializing influences of nonmorbid anxiety. Indications of shifting from complete permissiveness to a measure of activity and direction on the part of the therapist in the later phases of the treatment process were discussed in terms of learning psychology. The problem of culture conflict between therapists and persons of power in the life space of the child was analyzed in terms of communication difficulties and the setting of treatment goals. Age and sex factors of the patients were pointed out in their impact upon the solution of the question whether outpatient treatment or treatment in a controlled environment seemed to be indicated in cases of adolescents. Finally, the effective use of volunteers in treatment and the occasional necessity of setting limited treatment goals were discussed with specific suggestions for therapeutic planning. The findings presented in that book were based on deductive reasoning, illustrated by case material available in the agency's files, and evaluated by the clinical director, Dr. Maurice R. Friend, from the psychiatric point of view.

"The findings of a research effort conducted along such lines required by their very nature the testing of their usability in treatment practice. Arrived at by logical thought processes and illustrated by cases analyzed with hindsight, they could not be considered to be of established value before they had been tried out and found useful in diagnostic and therapeutic practice, where they have been applied to cases from the beginning. For this reason, Russell Sage Foundation and the agency entered upon a second two-year project devoted to such practice testing."[1]

The practice testing was undertaken by a treatment team in which for the first time a social scientist functioned as a regular member. The team was composed of the clinical director as the psychiatrist, the director of casework services, a senior supervisor, five experienced caseworkers who carried cases in treatment, the writer as consulting social scientist, a social science associate, and two caseworkers who did not carry cases in the child guidance clinic. A clinical psychologist was foreseen as a member of the team but for reasons of illness had not been able to join the team sessions regularly. However, where psychological tests were given, the clinical psychologists who administered them participated in the seminar discussions of the test results. Other social scientists were drawn in for occasional

[1] Pollak, Otto, "Exploring Collaboration Between Casework and Social Science in Practice," *Social Work Journal*, vol. 33, October, 1952, p. 177.

consultation. In the second year two social science associates participated in the discussions of the team.

"As to procedure, the treatment team decided to aim at coverage of ten cases. This immediately raised a number of questions with theoretical and practical implications beyond the purely formal ones of methodology. Administratively speaking, the workers were accustomed to think of a case in terms of their giving therapy to one patient. Thus, if one worker saw the child and another worker the mother in regular treatment procedure, the workers were considering this situation as presenting two cases. In consequence, they saw their responsibility for the integration of their diagnostic and therapeutic work in these 'two' cases confined to occasional conferences. Under the situational approach of social science, however, such a constellation had to be considered as one case because of the interlocking of meaningful relationships between the patients. . . .

"The limited number of ten cases required clarification from the beginning that the test project was not meant to be statistically meaningful. All that was meant to be investigated by the test team was whether the situational approach and social science concepts introduced could result in changes of diagnostic and therapeutic procedures in individual cases to such a degree that the testing of their effectiveness on a statistical basis seemed indicated. . . . Research of the latter type, however, had to be left to a third stage of the project, if indeed the outcome of the second phase should suggest its desirability." Actually, only eight cases were considered by the seminar on a sustained basis because of the workload of two seminar members, which made it impossible for them to take on two new cases each.

"In view of the test purpose to see what a special emphasis on the situational approach and the introduction of specific social science concepts would do when applied with foresight rather than with hindsight, it was decided to use primarily cases which were still in the intake stage. . . .

"The procedure decided upon by the team was that every case was to be presented as far as possible for the first time while it still was in the early stage of the diagnostic process, and then at more or less regular intervals as treatment proceeded. Thus, it was arranged that the impact of the social science approach and the new conceptualizations could be maintained upon the whole course of therapy in the test cases."[1]

The two years of practice testing which constituted the project's second phase brought about a number of reorientations in our thinking and practice which seem significant. We received proof in all cases that were included in the seminar of the value of reiterating the importance of a situational approach to the problems of diagnosis and therapy. This approach increased recognition by the workers of the fact that a much wider field of forces determines the difficulties of a child than was, and frequently still is, routinely considered in the practice of child guidance clinics and psychiatric clinics for children. It increased realization of the need to widen correspondingly the scope of diagnostic inquiry. It brought about better recognition of the importance of relating treatment to this wider field of forces either by limiting treatment goals or by making adaptations to the situation through increasing the number of family members who were accepted for treatment. In this respect our experience ran parallel with a current trend that has been pinpointed in the Editorial Notes of the October, 1953, issue of *Social Casework* as follows: "The papers in this issue, all presented at the 1953 National Conference of Social Work, in one sense constitute a symposium on the family or, in another sense, a symposium on mental health. The authors, representing the social sciences, psychiatry, and casework practice, examine various aspects of human relationships and social functioning with particular emphasis on the role of the family in furthering healthy personality development.

"Of the various threads running through the articles, the dominant one seems to be the recurrent reference to the 'person-situation' entity. . . .

"This emphasis on the interaction of forces is, of course, not new to caseworkers. Mary Richmond recognized the principle and reiterated it in her various formulations of casework theory

[1] *Ibid.*, pp. 178–179.

and method. The point that seems worthy of mention, however, is that casework is currently re-emphasizing the principle. As Mrs. Scherz points out, casework in recent years took excursions into psychiatric bypaths which led to an underemphasis on social and cultural factors. She notes that the caseworkers' interest in adding to their knowledge of psychological manifestations and pathology, and the necessity to understand, and to learn to utilize, the dynamics of the helping relationship, resulted in some neglect of the situational aspects of client problems. Dr. Gomberg, in his article, indicates that this imbalance, to whatever extent it has existed, is currently being redressed, and that caseworkers, through their increased understanding of ego psychology, have learned to focus attention on ways to help clients with their struggles to master difficult life situations. Casework, as a result, has come to be more truly psychosocial."[1]

We developed this same theme along the lines of an integration rather than of a twosided consideration. From viewing the client in the situation and distinguishing between psychological manifestations and the situational aspects of the client problems we utilized our understanding of psychodynamics and our concern with a wider consideration of the environment in order to see psychological manifestations in the situation and situational manifestations in the intrapsychic. During this effort we came to realize more and more that *what appears to be the social environment of one person is a combination of the intrapsychic problems of others. Correspondingly we found that the intrapsychic problem of one person is part of the social environment of other persons.*

CONCEPTS THAT PROVED TO BE USEFUL

Of the numerous social science concepts proposed for incorporation into child guidance practice in the symposium volume so far only four have proved to be highly fruitful in practice. These concepts are the *family of orientation* as distinguished from the family of procreation along the lines developed by

[1] "Editorial Notes," *Social Casework*, vol. 34, October, 1953, p. 354.

Bossard,[1] *social interaction* as defined by Bloch,[2] *social role* as utilized for theorem construction by Cottrell,[3] and *culture conflict* resulting from social differentiation as analyzed by Sellin.[4] For the convenience of the reader, some statements about these concepts and the reasons for the proposal of their incorporation into the theory underlying child guidance practice are inserted here. This is done with apologies to those who are acquainted with them either through their own professional training or through perusal of the first report.

One of the outstanding characteristics of child guidance practice in the agency and also—as will be shown later on by an analysis of the literature—of the practice in many other child guidance clinics in this country was, and still is, the emphasis on the mother of the child. She is practically the only factor besides the child's personality structure to which attention is paid in treatment if not in diagnosis. Only sporadically are fathers included in diagnostic and even less so in therapeutic contacts. The disregard of parent substitutes is still greater. Where a mother is working or simply emotionally absent and a grandmother, for instance, exerts a harmful influence upon the child, great effort is expended to bring the biological mother to fulfill her mother functions while the grandmother's continued harmful influence is not directly attacked. Although authorities from the field of social casework and child psychiatry had pointed out that such neglects might lead to failures in therapy, no quantitatively significant changes in this practice had occurred when the project was started. This presented a problem which suggested the possibility that the introduction of the concept of the *family of orientation* might be helpful in redistributing the perception of the workers. The concept designates the sum

[1] Bossard, James H. S., *The Sociology of Child Development.* Harper and Bros., New York, 1948, p. 55.

[2] Bloch, Herbert A., "A Synthetic View of the Social Individual as a Primary Datum in Sociology," *American Sociological Review*, vol. 8, October, 1943, p. 506.

[3] Cottrell, Leonard S., Jr., "The Analysis of Situational Fields in Social Psychology," *American Sociological Review*, vol. 7, June, 1942, pp. 370–387.

[4] Sellin, Thorsten, *Culture Conflict and Crime:* A Report of the Subcommittee on Delinquency of the Committee on Personality and Culture. Bulletin 41, Social Science Research Council, New York, 1938, pp. 66–67.

total of persons who form continuous members of the household and, because of this long-term association, exert an influence upon the development of the child who grows up within their group. Thus, it puts emphasis on the plurality of persons in the household environment of the child and provides an appropriate context within which to interpret the behavior of any particular individual.

Another key concept considered from the angle of its potential power to aid an integration of sociological and psychoanalytic thinking in child guidance practice was *social interaction.* This concept designating the phenomenon that the behavior of one group member is simultaneously cause and effect of the behavior of the other members refers, of course, to situations with which every psychotherapist or caseworker is familiar. Although this was recognized, it seemed useful to introduce the concept into the theoretical basis of child psychotherapy because some of its ramifications appeared to be less emphasized than others. The consultant sociologist and the senior staff of the agency agreed that in actual practice the phenomenon was better perceived with regard to its operation in the past than its operation in the future, better with regard to its negative aspects than its positive aspects, and better with regard to its manifestations between worker and patient than its manifestations between worker and family members of the patient. Care was taken to point out that particularly in psychotherapy with children the patient is not free to utilize therapeutic gains when these gains stimulate negative reactions on the part of adult persons upon whom he is dependent. It was expected that the concept of social interaction would aid in the perception of the fact by the workers that such negative reactions to the temporary or permanent changes in the patient resulting from therapy may occur not as only occasional obstacles to treatment but as frequent phenomena which have to be considered in the preparation of the case for treatment, in determining the selection of family members who would have to be included in the therapeutic effort, and in the utilization of collateral contacts.

In the first phase of the project cases had been encountered which suggested that on occasions childhood and adolescence were regarded only as specific stages of psychodynamic development. Therapeutic planning apparently did not always take into account that these stages of the growth process also determine societal expectations of specific behavior patterns. In consequence, acting out was sometimes endangering the continuation of the therapeutic process because it took forms which seemed incompatible with the behavior demanded from children by adults in our society. Since psychotherapy cannot be expected to be free from social repercussions to the development of the patient during and after treatment, it was proposed to secure the consideration of such possible repercussions by the introduction of the concept of *social roles* into the theory underlying therapeutic planning. It was expected that this concept would prove to be useful particularly in the cases of adolescents, because it would draw attention to the social limitations of behavioral experimentation in this physiologically mature but socially dependent age group.

The concept of *culture conflict* was thought to have value for psychotherapists in child guidance clinics because of its potential usefulness in clarifying the phenomenon of a professional subculture. Such a subculture may follow value orientations other than any of the subcultures from which clients are likely to come whether they are native Americans or not. In other words, culture conflict was not so much seen in its traditional application to the conflict between the values and attitudes of parents and children of immigrant stock, but in terms of the conflict which the discoveries of psychoanalysis and the therapeutic experience of the practitioners might have created between the values and attitudes of social workers and psychiatrists practicing child psychotherapy in an agency setting and the values and attitudes which surround the child patient outside the therapeutic situation. It was pointed out that this phenomenon of culture conflict between therapist and patient, or therapist and patient's family, could create difficulties in diagnosis, application of treatment techniques and setting of treatment goals, and particularly in communication in all these phases of the helping process.

It was felt that it was a characteristic of the professional subculture of psychotherapists to consider in practice, if not in theory, cultural and intrapsychic phenomena as separate entities. An attempt was made, therefore, to show that these phenomena were actually intertwined. A lack of awareness with regard to cultural differences might lead to the diagnostic evaluation of a patient's behavior as a deviation, while this might not be the case in terms of his culture. On the other hand, an apparent conformity with cultural norms might give an impression of normality, while its very intensity might be an expression of pathology.

Special emphasis was put on the communication value of cultural material for purposes of conveying psychodynamic information. It was pointed out that in their attempt to apply the principles of psychodynamics to child guidance practice, many workers have become accustomed to look for direct expressions of the emotional reactions of their patients to the key people in their family. In this quest they frequently have developed a tendency to regard production of cultural material by the patient as diagnostically and therapeutically insignificant. Such production is therefore frequently not utilized and remains more or less unrecorded. A sharp distinction is frequently made between the immediate family environment of the patient and his larger cultural environment and only the former is considered of significance for an understanding of pathogenesis. In view of the development of this characteristic of the professional subculture it was considered necessary to demonstrate that "in producing cultural material the patient engages in a process of self-revelation which may be diagnostically and therapeutically of high significance."[1]

In relation to therapeutic planning it was pointed out that the absorption of a professional subculture by child therapists was likely to lead them on occasion to pursue treatment goals that were opposed to the wishes of the parents. Attention was drawn to the fact that "such goal setting may present an important source of therapeutic failure because of the familial

[1] Pollak, Otto, and Collaborators, *Social Science and Psychotherapy for Children*, p. 110.

and societal reactions to which it exposes the patient who is experiencing personality change in the course of therapy unless the worker is aware of this possibility."[1]

In review, it appears that utilization of the four concepts of *family of orientation, social interaction, social role,* and *culture conflict* between therapist and client had the following results. The concept of the family of orientation helped effectively in introducing the father into the framework of clinical concern. It helped in recognizing him as an important factor in the decision whether therapy should be undertaken; in utilizing him as a source of diagnostic information; in recognizing him as a factor in determining the pathology not only of the child but of the family as such; and in visualizing him as a legitimate and sometimes essential recipient of child welfare focused[2] family therapy. We were aware of the fact that lip service had been paid before to the demand for more consideration of the father in child psychotherapy, but we found that such consideration in the reality of practice required continuous conceptual reiteration, continuous prompting, and as a necessary by-product, continuous clarification of content and techniques in handling father contacts. This new emphasis was accompanied by considerable discomfort in terms of an increased complexity in diagnostic and therapeutic work. Our results, however, were rewarding as will be seen from the cases presented in the following chapters. In essence, we found that children show similarity in symptomatology with their fathers to a degree that suggests that the emphasis on the mother-child relationship, which is the dominant theme in psychodynamic case discussions and clinical research, presents a potential source of serious omission in the diagnostic process as well as in the therapeutic effort.

The concept of family of orientation sharpened further our perception for sibling pathology, not as a reason for opening "another case"—if the parents so desired—but as an essential part of the case already at hand. We found situations in which all the children of a family showed severe disturbances and

[1] *Ibid.*, p. 119.
[2] For an explanation of this terminology, see pp. 33–34.

there were cases in which the disturbance of the child who had been referred to us was less frightening to the parents than that of another child whom they had not referred. Furthermore, we found that a therapist by seeing a sibling in therapeutic sessions gained more access to family dynamics than he had gained previously in contact with both parents and the child referred.

Taking stock of these results, our experience suggests that our hypothesis presented in the first report to the effect that this concept would widen the area of diagnostic and therapeutic perception has been significantly strengthened. Essentially, this gain seems to have resulted from the power of the concept to serve as a corrective for certain failures in perception that were anchored not only in routinized practice but also in a onesidedness of theoretical concern and clinical research, which seems to characterize much of current child guidance practice.

The concept of social interaction proved its value in really making the concept of the family of orientation serviceable in a theoretical framework of psychoanalytically oriented child guidance. The concept of the family of orientation alone might have pointed up the importance of widening the field of diagnostic and therapeutic perception. But it might have failed to show how the factors perceived have to be evaluated in terms of disturbance formation and in terms of disturbance alleviation. If we had used it without the concept of social interaction we might have perceived the existence of pathology or health in family members other than the mother and the child, without advancing either our understanding of the etiology of disease or our understanding of the etiology of cure. At best, it might have produced additive effort to attack the foci of pathology newly perceived but not a specific orientation for using this perceptual enrichment constructively. Actually, it might have increased the burden of therapeutic effort but not the availability of therapeutic techniques for carrying this burden. We might have been left with the task of doing more of the same with the temptation of doing it less adequately because of the very increase of the burden.

Of course, the phenomenon of social interaction is inevitably referred to in the theory of the nature and impact of the mother-child relationship. However, the extension of its perception to other family members, to persons of power in the environment of the child who are not family members, and to the interplay between their personalities and the therapist seemed to have promising theoretical and practical consequences as well. Limited to the family as such, it explained, for example, the similarity of symptoms between the child and persons other than the mother. Actually, it proved its power in that respect by permitting the pathogenetic explanation of this phenomenon along dynamic lines which until then had been largely confined to the mother-child relationship. It aided equally in explaining differences in symptomatology and pathogenesis among siblings and between parents. In essence, it proved to be the connecting link between the various syndromes which we encountered in our widened field of perception.

In practice, it led to a significant turning away from the principles of dividing cases as stated in the literature. According to Gordon Hamilton, "whenever the 'client' moves out of the social resource and counseling context and he becomes a 'patient,' he is likely to require a worker for himself. Whenever there is antagonism between marital partners or between child and parent, whenever emotional separation is the chief aim of treatment, whenever a worker finds himself identifying with or being more interested in one partner than in the other (and this is a natural circumstance)—more with the adult than the child, or the reverse—it is better to have two or more workers closely collaborating."[1] Our experience raised a number of questions about the validity of this principle. Even in a situation where emotional separation between parent and child was our aim of treatment we found that to leave the case undivided could be a treatment aid rather than an obstacle. The gain from avoiding a parceling out of perception of human factors which are interrelated in a situation and the establishment of a stra-

[1] Hamilton, Gordon, *Theory and Practice of Social Case Work*. 2d ed., rev. Columbia University Press, New York, 1951, pp. 48–49. For a similar expression see Schmidl, Fritz, "On Contact with the Second Partner in Marriage Counseling," *Journal of Social Casework*, vol. 30, January, 1949, pp. 30–36.

tegical center for the marshaling of all relevant perceptions without the artificiality and time lag of integration conferences proved to be a very great asset. It also gave body and dynamic meaning to the child welfare focus in our work. If there is one theorem that is unquestioned in modern thinking on child development, it is the importance of the total family unit for the growth process. The proposition that in a child guidance case in which a parent is also treated as a patient, division of the case is likely to be better than stressing the essential unity by having all patients in the family treated by the same therapist was not borne out by our experience. It appeared to us the essence of a child welfare focus in the clinical field that a common family problem was guiding therapeutic technique and that conflict in the family was something to be resolved by a concerted and centralized effort. Dividing a case seemed to us to increase the danger of incorporating conflicts into the structure of the therapeutic process rather than of resolving it. Of course, our psychodynamic orientation prevented us from becoming inflexible in this respect. We recognized that specific personality structures and pathologies in patients might indicate division of a case. Even more so did we recognize that for some therapists the emotional demands of seeing more than one member of a family as a patient may be too great. However, we shifted the emphasis of the principle from the assumption of an indication of dividing cases for the reasons mentioned by Gordon Hamilton to an assumption of the desirability of keeping cases undivided in spite of these reasons until the appearance of really negative reactions on the part of the patients and workers. We found that by keeping our child welfare focus paramount such negative reactions occurred only very rarely. They did not occur in a case in which the parents were in intensive personal conflict with one another and prevented the child from achieving a measure of independence, although one worker saw all three of them as patients. And we did not find them in another case where the worker saw both parents and two siblings as patients, although interpersonal conflict existed among all four of them.

In this framework of thinking, our child welfare focus became an indicator of the nature and intensity of therapy rather than an indicator of the person of the patient. It became a principle of unification, coordination, and direction of the diagnostic and therapeutic effort rather than a principle of limitation as our case presentations will demonstrate. It is true, however, that we could realize these gains only because the workers involved in this type of undivided treatment of several family members were able to resist the temptation of identifying more with one member of the family than another and were more interested in our integrated approach to pathological situations than in an exclusive approach to the pathology of any one person. Our experimentation with undivided treatment also was facilitated by the fact that over a number of years general agency practice had indicated a development in that direction.

The concept of social interaction proved its usefulness also in the psychodynamic application of the situational approach beyond the field of the family of orientation. No family is an island unto itself, and in our civilization with its specialization and its division of labor, the representatives of institutions other than the family have a more and more pronounced impact on the growth process of the child. Our efforts of integrating psychodynamic and sociological concepts aided us in making this theoretical truism a practical consideration in child psychotherapy. Extension of clinical concern beyond the family to the whole field of dynamic forces which determine the difficulties of a child—and of the clinician who wants to help a child—aided us particularly in preparing cases for treatment. In our experience, it changed the consideration of family doctors and other persons of power in the environment of the child as potential sources of information into a consideration of these persons as potential aids or obstacles to therapy because of the dynamic meaning of their social interaction with the child or members of his family. In two cases we encountered situations where the social interaction of a professional person with one of the parents presented a negative force which threatened the chances of the children's ever being brought in for treatment although the referrals had been made. In one situation it was social interaction between physician and mother, in the other social interaction between a lay therapist and father. Traditionally, these two persons might have been viewed only as sources of collateral information and their negative attitudes toward psychotherapy for the children involved might have led us into an attempt to start the helping effort without further concern about their meaning and role in the situation. Or worse, it might have tempted us into rationalizing a decision to discontinue efforts directed toward getting these children into treatment. Viewing them as dynamic factors in the environment of the child, however, helped us incorporate consideration of their social interaction with the parents into our preparation of the case for treatment.

The concept of social role proved to be especially helpful in a way we had not foreseen. Intended to strengthen realism in our goal setting, particularly in the treatment of adolescents, it unexpectedly proved helpful in facilitating a family diagnosis in a highly complex situation. And it happened to do this not simply by its own strength, but by the strength of a theorem derived from it. According to a proposition made by Leonard S. Cottrell, Jr., contradictory roles create internal stress in all personality systems and the intensity of this stress is likely to be correlated with the number of incompatible roles which a person feels he has to fulfill.[1] Since it is easier to collect data regarding role contents than data regarding intrapsychic mechanisms, this theorem made it possible for us to base a family diagnosis on role analysis where data sufficient to formulate a family diagnosis based on interaction analysis would have been unobtainable. Thus, the concept happened to furnish a diagnostic tool of as yet hardly visualized promise.

The concept of culture conflict between the professional subculture of child therapists and the culture of the clients found also considerable expression in our discussion of the cases. It expressed itself, however, not so much as an aid in diagnosis

[1] Cottrell, Leonard S., Jr., "The Analysis of Situational Fields in Social Psychology," p. 377.

and therapy directly but as a conceptual tool in identifying values and attitudes held by the therapists which interfered with the application of a truly situational approach in clinical practice. It was, for instance, an ever-recurring concern that the comprehensive and involved intake procedure which this approach requires might interfere with the establishment of a relationship. Since the value of a relationship between therapist and patient or worker and client is beyond the realm of dispute, this concern and the resulting reluctance to undertake the necessary steps in intake is an excellent demonstration of the theorem that a professional culture like other cultures by solving problems can create problems as well.

Our utilization of the concept of culture conflict for purposes of gaining perspective, not only regarding the patient but regarding professional beliefs and developments helped us also recognize a tendency of so extending the concept of client self-determination that our patients were sometimes exposed to the danger of having control over diagnostic measures at the price of excluding the therapist from information which was considered desirable for the treatment effort.

We also spotted some indications of culture conflict as an obstacle to effective communication between therapist and patient in line with our deductions in the first report on the project. The well-established method of helping a patient get insight or of learning about the content of his fantasies and the nature of his feelings by way of turning his questions back to him or asking him other questions proved to be in some instances a block in communication and consequently in the establishment of a relationship. The application of this method to situations in which a substantive answer would meet a reality need for information may well interfere with the establishment in the client's opinion of the caseworker as a professional person with special skills or may give, particularly in child guidance cases, the inquiring parent a feeling of disapproval where no value judgment is intended. In a surrounding culture in which questions from laymen to professionals generally lead to answers, it seems necessary to be aware of the conflict of a profession which has learned that in its field answers usually do not produce therapeutic results. Such a profession is particularly in danger of encountering misunderstanding by an overall application of this specific form of therapeutic reaction.

UNEXPECTED DEVELOPMENTS

Somewhat unexpectedly, we experienced a difference in the evaluation of the importance of these four concepts between the agency and the casework profession outside the agency. While the team was primarily concerned with the impact of the concepts of the family of orientation, social interaction, and social roles upon diagnosis and therapy, the concept of culture conflict between social workers and their clients was found much more provocative and potentially useful by social workers at large. In January, 1952, the writer on invitation of the New York District Branch of the American Association of Psychiatric Social Workers prepared a paper on "The Culture of Psychiatric Social Work."[1] The presentation of this paper was followed by a number of developments which indicate that the profession found the concept of a professional subculture and of conflict between it and the subculture from which the clients, cooperating professions and donors come, a useful stimulus for self-study. Three subsequent meetings of the New York Branch of the Association were devoted to some aspects of psychiatric social work culture. One, on supervision, was accompanied by the almost simultaneous establishment of a workshop committee, which undertook to reexamine the profession's basic hypotheses on supervisory practice and its cultural impact. The second, on ethics, concerned itself with the philosophy which governs the professional behavior of psychiatric social workers and shouldered the task of formulating a more realistic code of ethics. The third was devoted to social work education for psychiatric social workers.[2] The Baltimore Branch of the Association also found the concept useful in

[1] Pollak, Otto, "The Culture of Psychiatric Social Work," *Journal of Psychiatric Social Work*, vol. 21, June, 1952, pp. 160–165.

[2] Frechtman, Bernice Wolf, "Discussion," *Journal of Psychiatric Social Work*, vol. 21, June, 1952, p. 166.

providing a new approach to problems that had represented a concern of the profession for considerable time such as salaries, professional status, place of the untrained worker, research, and private practice. Two workshops were established for a study of these questions from a cultural viewpoint, and the results of the deliberations of one of these workshops have appeared in the *Journal of Psychiatric Social Work,* and created a good deal of discussion.[1] The professional response to this conceptual approach did not remain confined to psychiatric social workers. It came also from family caseworkers and medical social workers. The Annual Meeting of the Massachusetts Conference of Social Work in 1952, Institutes of the Schools of Social Work of the University of Michigan, the University of Louisville, and Atlanta University, and the Kentucky Welfare Conference in 1953 devoted sessions to this topic.[2] For 1954 and 1955 the Southern Regional Institute of the Family Service Association of America scheduled a course on cultural concepts in casework, intended to show the implications of cultural factors in the client, the worker, and the community in relation to casework diagnosis and treatment.

Another unforeseen development was the necessity of facing three tasks which crystallized slowly and came into focus only when the writing of this report was undertaken. Two of these tasks resulted from the work of the project team. The third one resulted from a puzzling divergence between theory and practice which required clarification, if the place of this project in the development of child guidance work was to be fully understood.

During the team sessions themselves phenomena were considered and procedures agreed upon which were not immediately conceptualized. Apparently, the atmosphere of a treat-

[1] Padula, Helen, and others, "Some Thoughts About the Culture of Social Work," *Journal of Psychiatric Social Work,* vol. 23, April, 1954, pp. 172–176; Freudenthal, Kurt, "Our Culture: How to Integrate It into That of Our Community," *Social Work Journal,* vol. 36, January, 1955, pp. 11–12; Letters to the Editor regarding Helen Padula's paper, *Journal of Psychiatric Social Work,* vol. 24, October, 1954, pp. 56–60.

[2] Pollak, Otto, "Cultural Dynamics in Casework," *Social Casework,* vol. 34, July, 1953, pp. 279–284; "Cultural Factors in Medical Social Work Practice," *Medical Social Work,* vol. 3, July, 1954, pp. 81–89; October, 1954, pp. 139–152.

ment seminar composed of such a relatively large group as the one which we established was not conducive to that task. On rereading the minutes of the team discussions, however, it appeared to the writer that certain connections between the concepts introduced and corresponding concepts which already had been established required identifications which had not been carried out in the discussions. It appeared to him also that social science concepts which had not been utilized in the discussions might prove to be useful in further clarifying the diagnostic and therapeutic thinking which the team had followed in response to the stimulation of the concepts applied. These considerations posed the problem whether a progress report such as this should include the identification of these conceptual connections and further conceptualizations. It was felt that this should be done, but that care should be taken in the presentation to help the reader distinguish between expressions of group thinking and expressions of the writer's own further efforts in the direction indicated above. Wherever a postproject conceptualization is presented, the responsibility for it rests entirely with the writer.

A short preview might help in clarifying the discussion of this special part of the report. During the team discussions continuous reference was made to the concepts of the family of orientation and of social interaction. The need for their integration with psychodynamic concepts was continuously stressed. During that phase of our thinking they were considered as having potentially direct impact upon diagnosis and therapy as traditionally formulated. In reviewing the material it appeared that this was not so. What these concepts really had done was to enrich the theoretical basis for the concepts of "family diagnosis" and "family therapy." These concepts were introduced into professional terminology about the same time by a small group of professional leaders. Their formulation reflected the same trend of reorientation as our own project. It was natural, therefore, that the two lines of effort should converge.

A further analysis of the diagnostic and therapeutic thinking which the introduction of the concepts of family of orientation and social interaction had stimulated produced recognition that they had to be supplemented by other social science concepts in order to help provide a sufficient theoretical substructure of family diagnosis and family therapy. It appeared that the concept of "family balance" which is referred to in the casework and psychiatric literature does not sufficiently clarify the dynamic tendencies of interpersonal relationships in families with children. In such families the relationships between the spouses on the one hand and the relationships between the parents and the children follow different tendencies which are conceptualized in the social sciences as *association* and *dissociation.* Unless the adjustive process between the spouses is associative and the process of child development leads from dependency to a measure of independence, that is, dissociative, "family balance" is unlikely to occur. In situations of family pathology both processes may be interfered with by the intrapsychic needs of the family members or may be reversed. The interactive processes in the family which we considered in our team discussions, thus, seemed to stand in need of postproject conceptualization. Other examples could be given at this point, but these illustrations may suffice to show the need for further conceptual analysis which arose after the immediate task of preliminary practice testing through the experimental team had come to an end.

The second task which the writer had to assume as a result of the practice test concerns research. The team members were very much aware of the fact that they were engaged in research work. Research questions were frequently raised and even more frequently implied without clarification on the spot. Other research questions became apparent only upon restudying the material developed in the team discussions. Most of all, the question whether our experience in practice testing justified a research effort geared to quantification and controls had to be answered. It is a frequent source of failure in current research that statistical investigations, and particularly investigations using control groups, are undertaken without sufficient exploration of their theoretical foundation and potential or practical impact. Another danger of equal strength is the temptation existing in the clinical field to remain satisfied with theoretical thinking and practice exploration on a case-by-case basis and never to put the fruitful suggestions of such theoretical thinking and practical case exploration to the test of research which uses rigorous methodology in terms of quantification and controls.

The liaison project between social science and child psychotherapy certainly cannot be considered as having succumbed to the first of these dangers. Four years of theoretical and practical exploration have preceded research confirmation of a quantitative nature. However, this strength on the first count could easily lead to weakness on the second. Our culture puts a premium on quick results and on newness in planning. These cultural pressures threaten the chances of continuing support for any project that has been going on for a number of years. Therefore, it is doubly necessary to stress in this follow-up report that we have not yet reached the end of our road. The efforts expended in deductive thinking, in practice testing, in reconceptualization and refinement of the propositions made in the summary of the findings of the first phase will pay off only if the task of quantified and controlled research is ultimately faced. Questions such as the contribution of conceptual refinement to diagnostic perception, of the existence of a specific professional subculture of child guidance work, of the existence of specific pathological constellations of family dynamics, of merits of child welfare focused family therapy versus family therapy as such, of dividing cases as a principle versus keeping them undivided must be decided ultimately on a level different from that of individual case analyses, or the disputed or undisputed impressions of an individual observer. Very likely they will have to be decided by quantified and controlled research going beyond the framework of any one agency. These considerations necessitated assumption by the writer of the task of analyzing the implications of the project's second phase for further research. The outlook that can be gained from the project's second phase, thus, is a research outlook.

The third task with which the writer had to wrestle during the process of writing this report was the clarification of a phenomenon of crucial significance for the role which social casework plays in modern child guidance work. It is the opinion of the writer that this phenomenon has been continuously oversimplified by the members of the casework profession. This oversimplification has led them into self-deprecatory explanations which on closer analysis appear completely unnecessary. As already indicated, the problem involved is one of divergence between theory and practice. In theory, social casework is essentially concerned with the total family unit. In practice caseworkers see individuals and involve one or the other member of the family in an intensive helping relationship. Only very infrequently do they extend their helping relationship directly to all members of the family unit. This disparity, quite naturally, gave rise to the question whether the social science concepts proposed for integration into the body of theory underlying child guidance practice were really needed. Our own experimental team had among its membership persons who had such questions. They felt that the concepts would not have been needed, if only social caseworkers had contributed their knowledge of the environment to diagnosis and therapy. Some team members felt that it was mostly a fascination with the substantive matter of dynamic psychiatry that had caused social caseworkers to forget their real professional heritage, which consisted of an emphasis on the family as a totality and of their knowledge of the environment.

On reviewing the minutes the writer felt compelled to devote special effort to a study of these doubts and self-accusations. Actually, a review of the literature led him to the conviction that social caseworkers never forgot what they already knew, because their concern with total families goes back to a time when social service effort was not concerned with intrapsychic phenomena and not even so much concerned with interpersonal problems as with group aspects of needs which obviously affected total families. This point was made some time ago by Helen Witmer who, in discussing the influence of the psychological orientation on family casework, stated the problem as follows: "The work of family welfare agencies was modified only slowly by this new point of view. Throughout the 1920's most family case workers were absorbed in refining the techniques of investigation and analysis of problems that had earlier engaged their attention. The development of the implications of the psychological theories for case work was carried on largely in child guidance clinics. . . .

"Another effect of the new knowledge was to force family case workers to relinquish what had been one of their main tenets: that the family is the unit of their work. Betsey Libbey had voiced in 1924 the predominant opinion when she said: 'The family—the problems that are common to all its members, their relations to each other, the needs of each of them individual by individual—this is the field of the family agency. The approach to problems that are individual is indirect through the problems that are common to all. It is some combination of circumstances that is affecting every member of the family that brings the family case worker into the situation.'

"This point of view could be maintained as long as family case work was conceived as being concerned chiefly with bringing families into effective relationship with other organized groups in the community: that is, when ignorance, neglect of duties, and lack of material resources were regarded as the main factors hindering social adjustment. But when the importance of psychological factors became recognized, a subtle shift occurred in the whole basis of family case work and individuals rather than families came to be regarded as clients."[1]

Thus, social caseworkers did not forget what they had practiced but discovered a new practice. That this practice was focused on individuals and not on families in their totality was not their fault. Caseworkers did not wilfully give up their concepts for those of psychiatry. They were forced to abandon the use of their own concepts in the new practice because they had been geared to different types of problems.

This new practice, it is true, required the mastery of a new

[1] Witmer, Helen Leland, *Social Work:* An Analysis of a Social Institution. Rinehart and Co., Inc., New York, 1942, pp. 174–175.

set of concepts which were taken from the funds of knowledge accumulated by dynamic psychiatry. But the social workers who absorbed these concepts did not give up their own concepts in what is now sometimes presented as a losing sight of their own heritage. They tried to maintain their own concepts without really being able to do so. This appears with great clarity in an authoritative publication of recent date.

In 1953 the Family Service Association of America published a report on the scope and methods of casework in family welfare agencies with a diagnostic orientation. In this report the theoretical concern with the total family is expressed as follows: "The focus of casework in the family agency is on the family as a unit. The family's values, its patterns of behavior, the interplay of social, economic, and cultural forces, and the role each member plays within the family and in the outside world are major considerations in family casework. Out of its long experience, the family agency has developed a special knowledge about family interrelationships and their effects on behavior and social functioning. Family casework has a considerable fund of specific knowledge about the role of the family in furthering optimal development of its members, by providing both emotional security and suitable growth experiences for its members. Casework treatment by a family agency may be described as 'composite' or 'family oriented'; it takes into account family interrelationships as well as the needs of individual members of the family."[1]

This theoretical emphasis, however, apparently could not be transferred to the methods of social casework practice. The descriptions of the actual casework process in the same report indicate the existence of this difficulty. The discussion is consistently in terms of the individual client[2] rather than in terms of his social situations and multiple relationships. That the use of the singular in this discussion is deliberate, reflecting the reality of practice, becomes apparent in the second part of the

[1] Family Service Association of America, *Scope and Methods of the Family Service Agency*. The Association, New York, 1953, p. 4.
[2] *Ibid.*, p. 5.

report. "Social casework is a professional method of helping people. Its aim is the mobilization of the 'capacities in the individual and [of] resources in the community appropriate for better adjustment of the client and all or any part of his total environment.' The mobilization of both inner capacities and of environmental resources is achieved primarily through communication, that is, through the relationship between caseworker and client, and caseworker and other individuals. Through the medium of the relationship, which is handled and directed by the worker in accordance with technical principles and procedures, the client is enabled to work toward appropriate solutions of his problem."[1]

This passage suggests strongly that the reiterated concern about service to total families, about viewing persons in their situations, about family balance, and so forth, somehow does not carry over into practice.

An application of the principles of Gestalt psychology will strongly suggest that the conceptualizations of dynamic psychiatry as well as those of casework were likely to enforce fractional perception in practice rather than to safeguard total perception. Social caseworkers were served by their concepts as long as the level of abstraction expressed by them was appropriate for the consideration of the phenomena to which they originally referred. When their concern shifted to other phenomena, their concepts became too abstract, or too concrete. The exasperation created by this conceptual inadequacy led social caseworkers into the ever-repeated affirmation that every case was different. It led them into embracing more and more the concepts of dynamic psychiatry and into confining their adherence to social casework concepts to statements of theory. In practice, however, they were forced to disregard their traditional casework concepts, no matter what theoretical and programmatical pronouncements regarding the contribution of social casework to interprofessional teams might say about their value. The fascination with the discoveries of psychoanalysis and the high status of the profession of psychiatry may have had

[1] *Ibid.*, p. 15.

much influence on this development. It is, however, very likely that this was not the only influence that was at work. When a concept of great specificity such as oedipal involvement, reaction formation, or infantilization is brought together with a concept of a much higher level of abstraction such as family constellation or parent-child relationship, the concept of greater specificity is likely to capture perception. When one concept combines elements of specificity with elements of generality such as "person in situation," the specific part, the person, will be singled out and the general part, the situation, will remain relatively unperceived.

This law of perception which is presented here as a hypothesis central to the relationship between dynamic psychiatry and social casework, may point the way to the solution of one of the great problems of interdisciplinary integration in general. It has been recognized as such by Dr. John P. Spiegel in his evaluation of the recently published symposium on *Mid-century Psychiatry*. Reviewing the growth of interdisciplinary effort and the widening of the area of perception to which that symposium testified, he said: "All these efforts at collaboration lend an excitement and a ferment to the field of psychiatry which only partially conceal the existence of the basic, serious problem whose solution is necessary before a real consolidation of the current gains can take place. This problem is the lack of a conceptual scheme, pitched at a level of abstraction from human behavior appropriate to the unification of the various points of view. What exist currently are patchworks of concepts loosely basted together by naive operations which do not satisfactorily achieve multilevel correlations much less their integration. Undoubtedly there is virtue in the mere accumulation and matching of concepts derived from the various levels of abstraction. But this is only a beginning. . . ."[1]

In our practice testing an effort was made to overcome this basting together of concepts. In the postproject conceptualiza-

[1] Spiegel, John P., "Critique of Symposium" in *Mid-century Psychiatry:* An Overview, edited by Roy R. Grinker. Charles C. Thomas, Springfield, Ill., 1953, p. 181.

tion presented in this follow-up report, an attempt will be made to point the way to a clarification of what an integration between social science and psychodynamic concept seems to imply. In order to do so, we shall have to see what our practice testing suggested and achieved; we shall have to devote our effort to the realities of practice and theory as they are revealed by the literature; we shall have to pay special attention to the laws of perception; and we shall have to delineate the vistas of *further* research which our work has opened up.

PART ONE

FAMILY PATHOLOGY, FAMILY DIAGNOSIS, AND FAMILY THERAPY WITH CHILD WELFARE FOCUS

PART ONE: FAMILY PATHOLOGY, FAMILY DIAGNOSIS, AND FAMILY THERAPY WITH CHILD WELFARE FOCUS[1]

THE CONCEPT that proved to be most useful in our attempt to integrate sociological and psychodynamic thinking in child guidance practice was the *family of orientation.*[2] It had the effect of extending diagnostic perception and therapeutic planning to all members of the household in which the child who was referred to the Clinic was growing up. It helped us to free ourselves from the perceptual trap presented by the dichotomy of patient and environment and actually to see the total family as a unit of diagnostic and therapeutic concern. It provided a permanent challenge to strive for a psychodynamic understanding of all the members of the family, to see the social interaction among them as based on these individual psychodynamic pictures, and to base therapeutic planning on such understanding. In essence, it helped us shift our orientation from child psychotherapy to family psychotherapy with child welfare focus and to experiment with procedures which such an orientation demanded. In response to this challenge of reorientation we attempted wherever possible to perform three tasks. First of all, we tried to formulate a clinical, a genetic, and a dynamic diagnosis[3] of every family member in whom we encountered pathology. Essentially this was only an accumulation of individual diagnostic procedures which had been practiced before regu-

[1] The replacement of the term "child focus" by the term "child welfare focus" is explained on pp. 33–34.

[2] Bossard, James H. S., *The Sociology of Child Development.* Harper and Bros., New York, 1948, p. 55.

[3] Hollis, Florence, "The Relationship Between Psychosocial Diagnosis and Treatment," *Social Casework,* vol. 32, 1951, p. 68; Levine, Maurice, "Principles of Psychiatric Treatment" in *Dynamic Psychiatry,* edited by Franz Alexander and Helen Ross, University of Chicago Press, 1952, pp. 309–332.

larly as far as the mother and the child were concerned. To be sure, the extension of this procedure to other members of the family as well was burdensome because of its demand on the worker's time. It also proved technically difficult because of the concern that such an extension of the diagnostic inquiry might on occasion interfere with the establishment of a relationship between the worker and the individual patient. Still, this was from the point of view of theory simply an additive process of gaining information.

The next step in our team thinking, however, presented theoretical difficulties which we did not fully overcome and which suggest a fruitful field of further research. To identify pathology in the various members of a family on an individual basis and even to gain an understanding of pathological interaction between two of them is one thing. To gain and formulate an understanding of pathological interaction patterns among three, four, or even more members of a household on which to base therapeutic planning on such an understanding is more difficult, because this presents problems of another order, namely, problems of formulating a family diagnosis and planning a family therapy. The solution of these problems requires specific conceptual tools and specific therapeutic practices which have been hardly yet developed, although the need for advance in that direction has been recognized and some promising beginnings have been made.[1]

Thus, our own attempts at formulating a family diagnosis represent only one phase in a development of thought which apparently goes in this direction. They were characterized not only by an effort to keep a balance between our psychodynamic understanding of individuals and the observation of interactional patterns but by an effort to achieve an integration between these two orientations. We tried to see how the intrapsychic difficulties of the individuals involved determined their interaction patterns and how these interaction patterns in turn determined the development, persistence, or abating of their

[1] For a detailed analysis of the development of theory and practice in this regard see Chapter IX, Trends of Practical and Theoretical Reorientation.

intrapsychic difficulties. Furthermore, we attempted to make these analyses not on a two-person but on a real family basis, which always involved more than two persons. Finally, we evaluated the nature and effect of the interaction patterns which we found operating in a family in terms of family functions and family tendencies as seen from an institutional angle.

Our third effort was concerned with the development of a family treatment plan. Owing to the very nature of our family diagnoses, these treatment plans had to express concern with pluralities greater than dualities. They had to be directed at the change of more than one interaction pattern. In consequence, frequently more than two persons had to be considered for treatment. Furthermore, because of trying to think in terms of families rather than in terms of two-person fragments thereof, we had to be reluctant about dividing cases. While it still may be possible to keep treatment procedures pursued by two workers integrated, the chances for maintaining such an integration where three workers are involved obviously are slight. In consequence, we found it fruitful to have the same worker see all the members of the family as actual or potential patients to be treated by herself until such time as special counterindications became apparent. The latter actually happened very infrequently.

Our attempts to treat families as totalities rather than only in terms of two-person fragments also strengthened our awareness of the limitation of goals. We became better aware of the fact that such limitations are determined not only by the intensity of intrapsychic difficulties in one or the other member of a family, but also by the nature and the level of common concern in the family unit. In this respect the child welfare focus of the agency proved to be helpful in keeping the various courses of therapy with the individual members of the family on a concerted plane.

It will be noticed that in this report the term "child focus" is replaced by the term "child welfare focus." This substitution of terms represents a postproject conceptualization. In our actual team discussions we had retained the term "child focus."

In retrospect it appears, however, that the use of this term created a number of difficulties. It failed to express conceptually the reorientation which our situational approach implied. For this reason, it caused perceptual pitfalls and logical inconsistencies with which we had to struggle a great deal and against which the term "child welfare focus" promises to furnish a measure of protection.[1]

By focusing upon the child as an individual, perception is likely to be restricted and the dynamic forces in his environment are likely to be blurred. Under the impact of such a terminology clinical consideration of the mother on an equal footing with the child is indeed an advance. By focusing on the welfare of a child, however, the perception of the plurality of factors involved is promoted and clinical emphasis upon the mother-child relationships as encountered in routinized practice appears to be fragmentation rather than comprehensiveness. Child welfare focus, furthermore, makes it difficult to single out one child from a number of siblings as the only receiver of clinical concern. It directs attention to the siblings rather than to a sibling. By doing so it is likely to enhance effectiveness in the prevention function of child guidance work. The concept of child welfare focus also promises to keep family therapy from disintegrating into a number of treatments which serve only the individuals involved for their own sake rather than gearing the therapeutic efforts to a common social interest. Thus, the concept may serve as an orchestrating principle in the management of the various individual lines of therapy which compose the family treatment, and it seems to anchor the clinical effort in a recognized area of social concern.

It seemed desirable, therefore, to introduce the concept of "child welfare focus" into the account of those cases in which the guiding principle of diagnostic and therapeutic thinking which we finally achieved is appropriately expressed by this concept. It must be made clear, however, that this is a post-project conceptualization formulated by the writer.

[1] The credit for having stimulated the writer to coin this new terminology belongs to Mr. Herschel Alt, whose concern with child welfare as a mandate for the agency accompanied the writer's work in the agency through all its phases.

II. The Family of Peter S.

PRESENTING SYMPTOMS

PETER WAS REFERRED to the Clinic at the age of seven years on suggestion of a Neighborhood Center, because he wanted to use only his home bathroom for bowel movements, dawdled in dressing to the degree of changing his trousers often five times before going to school, made no friends, and did unsatisfactory school work.

The mother added to this description that Peter used his toys to bribe other children into playing with him, but was unsuccessful in his efforts. Further information elicited from her showed that he was constantly nagging his parents for entertainment, was disobedient, and had severe temper outbursts in which he called his mother derogatory names. The mother mentioned that in the latter respect he was imitating his father's behavior toward her. In Peter's hostile outbursts he sometimes destroyed his most cherished possessions. On occasion he showed feminine mannerisms. He suffered from nightmares; he dreamt that wolves were chasing him; and he also had fears of animals, particularly dogs.

FAMILY COMPOSITION AND THERAPEUTIC CONTACTS

The family consisted of Peter, his parents, and a sister, Louise, who at the time of referral was three and a half years old. The marital relationship was disturbed. The father continually quarreled with the mother, blaming her for everything that did not turn out according to his wishes. The parents were afraid that Peter was "insane." Louise also had many fears and violent fits of anger, and when she had a tantrum destroyed her own toys as well as household goods. The mother understood from the beginning that contacts between her and the worker would be part of the Clinic's therapeutic procedure. Following our orientation, the father was also brought into contact with the Clinic and expressed an interest in being seen regularly by the worker. This led to the arrangement that Peter and his mother would be seen weekly and the father biweekly.

FRAMEWORK OF DIAGNOSTIC STUDY

Six weeks after this procedure had been agreed upon, Dr. Leonard S. Cottrell, Jr., social psychologist of Russell Sage Foundation, attended one of the discussions of the case as special consultant. He related the team's interest in family dynamics to his work on the prediction of marital adjustment as a result of the harmony or conflict of expected response patterns which the spouses had developed on the basis of their past experience.[1] On that basis he suggested a scheme of blocking out diagrammatically the three social situations from which the disturbances in the family seemed to have resulted. This scheme, which is conventional practice in genetics, anthropology, and genealogy proper, helped to extend diagnostic perception from the child's family of orientation to the families of orientation of the parents. Since agency practice has always been concerned with material necessary for a genetic diagnosis of the mother's difficulties, this diagram helped particularly to focus attention also upon material which would be useful in formulating the genetic diagnosis of the difficulties of the father. It also helped to produce awareness of missing information in regard to the total family situation in both parental background families. The diagram for the case of Peter, in which triangles represent males and circles females, is reproduced herewith.

In his discussion Dr. Cottrell superimposed on this scheme an analysis of the particular role patterns of self-conception and expectation of others which emerged in the parental families of the marriage partners and with which they were

[1] Cottrell, Leonard S., Jr., "Roles and Marital Adjustment," *Publications of the American Sociological Society*, vol. 27, May, 1933, pp. 107–115; and Chapter XI of *Predicting Success or Failure in Marriage*, Prentice-Hall, Inc., New York, 1939 (with E. W. Burgess).

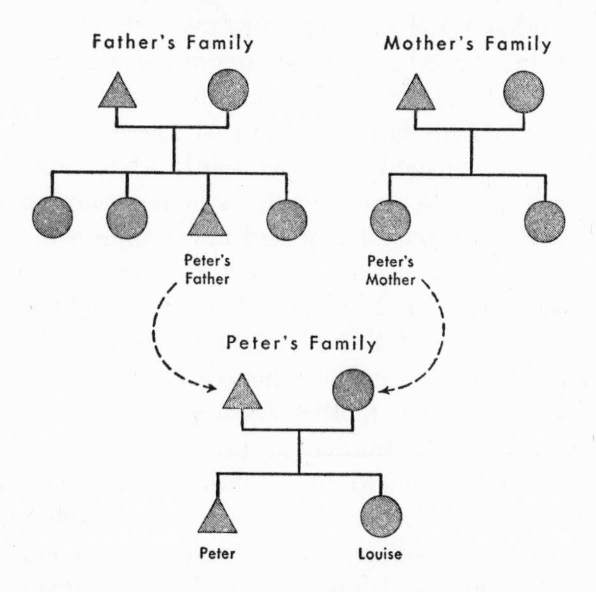

equipped to operate in their own marital and parent-child relations. He indicated that this procedure could be used as self-sufficient or be used as a framework for any type of psychology.

The group found this diagram of considerable assistance in achieving a coverage of the diverse genetic factors operating in the case and proceeded to integrate this mapping out of the three family situations with the psychodynamic information which the worker obtained as the case continued.

DIAGNOSIS OF FATHER

The father, a man of brilliant intellect, suffered from a number of symptoms which suggested the diagnosis of psychoneurotic disorder, mixed type, with phobic reactions, obsessive-compulsive reactions, and depression. His outstanding personality traits were dependency and passivity strivings. He was constantly worried about his own health as well as the health of his children. He felt a great deal of anxiety about economic security and about threats of world conditions, especially war in an atomic age. He had fears of animals, worried about where to draw the line between courage and prudence in the avoidance of danger. He had temper outbursts which he felt unable to control and suffered severely from fears of self-destruction. On occasion he showed an unusual amount of regression.

He had had an exceedingly difficult childhood. When he was only one year old his father committed suicide. At that time his mother was pregnant with her fourth child. Since all his siblings were girls, he grew up in a home composed of his mother and three sisters. There had never been a male figure with whom he could have established a relationship of formative influence. He had developed, however, an identification with the image of his father concerning whom he knew only that he had committed suicide. Severe economic deprivation existed in his home. His mother resented having been left by her husband with the burden of bringing up four children under such conditions and the children had to earn money through odd jobs from the early years on. He felt, probably correctly, that he had never received sufficient love in his childhood. In spite of all these difficulties, he had managed to graduate from college summa cum laude. Though his interest in accordance with his intellectual gifts would have made a professional career appropriate for him, economic conditions forced him to start out and later on to stay in commercial jobs which he did not do badly but which failed to give him personal satisfaction. At the time of the Clinic contact he was manager of a garment factory. Since he was mentally superior to the other members of the family and always treated by them with a certain degree of deference, he developed an attitude of superiority toward women generally. He expected them to make his life smooth and comfortable, but not to be his equals intellectually. Not having had any positive experiences with authority in his childhood and having found a certain amount of defense against his own feelings of insecurity in considering himself intellectually superior, it was difficult for him to accept authority in adult life.

The dynamic burden which the economic insecurity, the emotional deprivation, and the lack of an opportunity of healthy identification with a male figure had put upon him was counteracted to a degree by a number of compensatory defenses which, however, created difficulties in his life as wage-earner, husband,

and father. His economic concern, although enabling him to persevere and make a go of jobs which he basically did not enjoy often made him worry that some day he might be unable to support his family and anticipate all types of financial difficulties which his wife considered unrealistic. The lack of emotional warmth which he had experienced in childhood made him ever eager for demonstrations of affection on the part of his family and made it particularly difficult for him to remain undisturbed when they were not forthcoming, or when he encountered expressions of aggressiveness from his wife or opposition from his children. His efforts to overcome his own basic lack of aggressiveness, on the other hand, made him feel threatened when he saw lack of aggressiveness in his son. His own compensatory mechanism of intellectual achievement in turn made him demanding of school achievement on the part of Peter. On the other hand, it prevented him from appreciating the intellectual caliber of his wife.

DIAGNOSIS OF MOTHER

The mother was equally a neurotic personality. The diagnosis of her condition was psychoneurotic disorder, mixed type, with conversion reactions. She had been a stammerer in her youth. Between thirteen and fourteen years of age she had had hypertension and until her first pregnancy she had suffered from continuous headaches. She had a great need for sleep, requiring nine hours and more every night, but had occasional periods of insomnia. In consequence, she found it difficult to rise in the morning and was inclined to stay in bed while her husband and son had to get themselves ready for leaving the home. She also had sensations of tension in her legs which usually accompanied her periods of insomnia. Like her husband she had had a college education, and then had become a public health nurse. Although she was successful in her jobs and in organizing community activities, the household was frequently too much for her and she was aware of having remained a relatively inefficient housekeeper even after she had given up going out to work.

From the point of view of a genetic diagnosis it had to be

considered that her sister had always been preferred to her. Her mother had been a domineering and nagging woman. Her father had been relatively withdrawn but had occasional outbursts in which he subjected her to severe physical punishment. In financial matters he had been a miser and concerned about money somewhat like Mr. S. Another similarity between her father and her husband was the former's intellectual brilliance. She had been led into the marriage with her husband through the managerial influence of her mother. All during her childhood and youth she had been made to feel that she could be accepted only if she was successful in whatever she was supposed to do. She also had difficulties in making friends.

Dynamically she still felt that she had to be successful in order to be loved, and suffered, therefore, under her husband's attitude of mental superiority, although she was impressed by his brilliance. For the same reason she was unable to accept his criticism of her housekeeping and child care, although she felt them to be justified. With Peter, she always insisted upon achievement in performance. This expressed itself particularly in her supervising his drawings, which she compared in quality with what she thought she had been able to do when she was a child. Since she had suffered from loneliness as a child, she tried to maneuver Peter into friendships and was upset when he resisted her efforts. Being somewhat inclined to be dilatory herself, she objected particularly to the boy's dawdling in the morning. In order to make up for her feelings of inferiority she had a tendency to throw herself into outside activities but then suffered under the conflicting demands of these activities and the demands of her household.

DIAGNOSES OF CHILDREN

Peter's clinical diagnosis was the same as that of his father. The contact with him had revealed that he had a recurrent dream of something big falling upon him and pressing on his chest. When he was worried about something, his right eye started to twitch. He expressed extreme concern about not doing well in school, although his actual school record did not justify his self-estimate. Like his father he was preoccupied with the thought of gloomy events about to happen and particularly about explosions of atomic bombs. On psychological testing he proved to be of average intelligence.

Genetically, of course, little can be added to what is already presented, at least by implication in the individual diagnoses of his parents. Essentially Peter had been influenced by his father's need to see him aggressive and yet judicious, as well as by his mother's concern about achievement as a condition of being accepted by others and by her desire that he should be popular. Furthermore, he had been subjected to the persistent demands of both his parents for school success, which they visualized in terms of their own standards and achievements rather than in terms of the boy's capacities.

Dynamically he presented the picture of an inhibited boy who withdrew from tasks which he found too demanding and still tried to do well anything he undertook, who felt lonely, and still was afraid to make contacts with other children. He felt guilty about not living up to his parents' expectations and was convinced that he could not be loved by anybody who thought he was stupid. His feelings of loneliness had been increased by the arrival of his sister. He had hoped that a baby brother or a baby sister would be a play companion but when Louise was born she was so tiny and helpless that he could not play with her. Furthermore, his parents had had to give her so much care and attention that he was lonelier than ever. From that time on he had conceived a resentment of his sister which showed itself later in various forms. He disliked to watch her, beat her when left alone with her, and liked to torture her by telling her scary stories. On one occasion he expressed a wish for a brother of exactly his age and school achievement, but with a different face.

About Louise, relatively less was known because the parents, at least in the beginning of the contact, expressed no particular concern about her. She was an easier child to deal with than Peter, although she was a bed wetter and still preferred to drink from the bottle at the age of three and a half. She also had sleeping difficulties and was afraid that during the night lions and robbers would come to hurt her.

FAMILY DIAGNOSIS—MULTIPLE INTERACTION PATTERNS

After the individual diagnoses of Mr. S., Mrs. S., and Peter had become clarified, there then arose the task of formulating a family diagnosis which would be more than a summation. In an experimental fashion we started out to select as a key concept social interaction among the family members. Obviously, we had to deal with an interaction pattern between the parents, an interaction pattern between Peter and his father, and an interaction pattern between Peter and his mother. Mr. S. was affected by his interaction with Mrs. S. and by his interaction with Peter; Mrs. S. was affected by her interaction with Mr. S. and by her interaction with Peter; and Peter was affected by his interaction with his father and his interaction with his mother. Upon further analysis we came to appreciate that actually the father was also affected by the interaction between the mother and Peter, the mother by the interaction between the father and Peter, and Peter by the interaction between his parents. In essence, then, every family member appeared affected by all the three diadic interaction processes occurring in the triad. Ideally, of course, the presence of Louise in the family household would have required the consideration of still more interaction patterns. Unfortunately, we were not yet prepared to deal with such complexity and failed to collect the necessary information. In consequence, we did not have a sufficient diagnosis for Louise and had to limit ourselves to the interaction patterns within the triad of father and mother and Peter. Occasional sidelights with regard to the interactions between Louise and the other family members, however, were obtained. This framework of three interaction patterns, all of which affected every member in the triad, will gain dynamic significance as soon as their nature and consequences are discussed in terms of ego psychology.

Returning now to our diagnostic information about the parents and Peter, what was the nature of the interaction processes operating among them? We knew that the father defended himself against anxiety by a striving for dominance. Having been treated with respect and catered to in household arrangements in the home of his childhood, he expected and demanded similar attention in the home which he had created through his marriage. Being married to a woman who recognized herself that she was not a good housekeeper, this defensive striving was frustrated by his spouse on an almost day-by-day basis. Thus, his insecurity and anxiety were stimulated in the minutiae of daily living. For purposes of illustration it might be mentioned that in his childhood home no one had been permitted even to open the newspaper before he had returned and had had first fling at it. In his married life his wife did not even like to get up in the morning before he left.

Another defense which the father had built up in his own childhood family was his tendency to look down upon women as intellectually inferior. This mechanism apparently had come into existence through the fact that his mother who deprived him of love had been a mentally limited woman while he himself was intellectually brilliant and scholastically successful. His wife, however, was also a college graduate and successful in any job she had undertaken, as well as in community activities, and thus jeopardized also this mechanism of defense.

The mother was an inhibited person who needed to feel successful as a basis of feeling accepted and loved. She found release from her anxieties by throwing herself into outside activities and by a craving for sleep which freed her from the stimulation of anxiety which accompanied her waking hours. The husband, however, made derogatory remarks about her intellectual capacity and reproached her over and over again for not fulfilling her homemaking and child-rearing functions with the necessary care. He recurrently tore at her defenses and increased her anxiety.

Thus, the interaction pattern between the parents appeared to be one of mutual attack upon their respective defenses against the threat of deep anxieties from which both of them suffered.

The interaction pattern between the father and Peter was characterized foremost by identification and projection. The boy's identification with his father showed itself in a striking similarity of personality traits. The father was afraid of animals and so was the son. The father felt that he lacked aggressiveness and was insecure about his masculinity. The boy's overall response pattern was passivity. The father had deep anxieties with regard to self-destruction and the boy had nightmares that something would fall upon him and crush him. On the Rorschach his associations were various forms of destruction by outside forces. The father in turn not only noticed this similarity of traits but showed the projection of his discomforts upon the boy by his overconcern about anything which indicated their appearance in the boy. Furthermore, the father tried to make the child adopt the same defense patterns, such as scholastic success by demands for school achievement, low opinion of women by pointing out to the child the failings of the mother, and avoidance of dangers by trying to teach Peter prudent caution in contact with other boys. Significantly, he said early in the contact that Peter was his son, while Louise was his wife's daughter. However, Mr. S. was only partially right because Peter was not only his father's son, he was also the son of his mother and identified with her as well, as will be seen from the interaction pattern between him and Mrs. S.

Again there was a pattern of identification and projection as shown by the appearance of maternal personality traits in the boy, the mother's overconcern about them, and her unconscious attempts to make the child adopt her own defenses. It will be remembered that one of the reasons for the referral to the Clinic was the boy's difficulty to get ready for school in the morning. In that connection it became meaningful to learn not only from the point of view of its being a reason for marital friction that Mrs. S. also had difficulty getting up in the morning. Another point of similarity was the specific configuration of sibling rivalry which we found both in the history of the mother and the current situation of the child. Peter's sister was felt by the parents to be an easier child to have around. The sister of

Peter's mother was the preferred child of Peter's maternal grandparents. The mother found it difficult to make friends and the same handicap was one of Peter's major difficulties. On one occasion he told the worker that the only happy time in his life that he could recall was a few weeks in a summer camp where the children had been friendly with him.

There was also a striking similarity of defenses. Like his mother, Peter believed that he could not be loved unless he was successful. And, finally, there was also a distinct overconcern on the part of the mother with regard to those of Peter's difficulties which reminded her of her own. Thus, the boy seemed to have adopted a number of his mother's anxieties, symptoms, and defenses through identification. The mother seemed to have projected upon the boy her concern about her own discomforts, and Peter's difficulties interfered with the operation of one of his mother's most important defenses, namely, achievement which she felt she had not accomplished in this child. By demanding more and more success from him, on the other hand, the mother interfered with Peter's defense of avoiding tasks which he felt unable to perform.

We must now turn to the effect of interaction patterns upon the third person. Peter's identification with his mother expressed itself among other ways in a striving to overcome his passivity by occasional outbursts of aggressiveness. These outbursts stimulated the anxiety and the defenses of the father because they questioned his own concern over finding the middle road between courage and caution. When Peter, after having been hurt by boys in the park, wanted to return to the same group on another day, the father was against it, and thus interfered with a mechanism of defense which Peter had developed in interaction with his mother. On the other hand, when Peter's identification with the father expressed itself in calling the mother "stupid" or other derogatory names, interaction between father and son affected the mother and hurt her in a sensitive spot of her own defensive armour. Finally, when the interaction pattern between his parents, namely, the mutual attack upon their respective defenses, expressed itself in fights between them, each tried to make Peter an ally and thus imposed upon him not only a conflict of loyalties but also a conflict among the defenses which he had adopted from both of them.

Last, but not least, Peter, like every human being, was not only the result of parental influences but a person with his own individual endowment and his own individual limitations. His average intelligence made him ill equipped to adopt the defense mechanism of either of his parents, whose success compensations were based upon intellectual endowments greater than his own and thus put upon him a special burden.

FAMILY DIAGNOSIS—INSTITUTIONAL ANALYSIS

We now had to ask ourselves how we could apply the meaning of these interaction patterns in terms of a family diagnosis so as to provide a framework for further understanding and also for planning. Here our deliberations followed an approach to the family which in postproject conceptualization could be formulated as follows: Seen as a social institution the family appears as an integrated cluster of human activities designed to satisfy basic needs.[1] The conjugal family,[2] consisting of parents and children, serves for the parents as a satisfier of the need for intimacy, companionship, and complementary economic arrangements, and for the children as a satisfier of the need for care and socialization permitting them to grow up into independent human beings. Thus, the family is characterized by a tendency toward unity between the spouses and a tendency toward separation between parents and children. In consequence, the family shows within one group of relatively permanent relationships the continuous operation of the two basic sociological phenomena of association and dissociation[3] in terms of need-satisfying functions.

This frame of reference may seem obvious if considered on

[1] Pollak, Otto, *Social Adjustment in Old Age.* Social Science Research Council, New York, 1948, pp. 31–42.

[2] Parsons, Talcott, "Age and Sex in the Social Structure of the United States," *American Sociological Review,* vol. 7, October, 1942, pp. 615–616.

[3] von Wiese, Leopold, and Howard Becker, *Systematic Sociology.* John Wiley and Sons, New York, 1932, pp. 37–38.

purely theoretical grounds. In practice, however, it seems to have great usefulness for the formulation of family diagnoses. In Peter's case, for instance, it makes it easy to see that the parents in spite of their different symptomatologies had basically similar problems, and the child in spite of the similarity of his symptoms to those of his parents had problems basically different from theirs. The parents frustrated each other's needs for closeness by mutual attacks upon their respective defenses against neurotic anxiety and seemed to prevent the child from achieving gradual separation and accomplishment within the limits of his own capacities by their identifications and projections. Thus, the two members of the family who should have been drawing closer together in the course of marital adjustment seemed to stay apart in continued, if not increasing, conflict. The child, however, who should have gone through a process of gradual separation toward realization of an independent identity seemed imprisoned in inhibitions created by the parents. This could be conceptualized as *family dysfunction and relationship tendency reversal on a neurotic basis.* The value of such a conceptualization for a family diagnosis in the true sense of the word is its inherent liberation from an exclusive focus on individual clinical diagnoses. It recognizes the clinical basis but puts the diagnostic formulation upon a group level which is different from the level of the persons composing the group. Many more such diagnoses would have to be attempted on the basis of a variety of cases before a system of family diagnosis can be created, but building blocks for such a system might be provided by attempts of conceptualization such as the one presented above.

PLAN OF FAMILY THERAPY

In order to formulate a treatment plan it was necessary to contrast our diagnosis of family pathology with the ideal type of family health, both clinically and institutionally for goal direction, and to consider the ego strengths of the various family members as well as available treatment resources for goal limitation.

The ideal type of phenomenon, of course, has no empirical reality. It is a thought construct in which certain elements of reality are stressed in their logically pure form and others are intentionally neglected.[1] The concept is only an instrument for the analysis of concrete problems. Health may be viewed as such an ideal type of desirable physical and emotional functioning of the organism. Although physicians and caseworkers will be the first ones to believe that complete health is hardly ever encountered in reality, it is a guidepost for the direction of curative and preventive effort. An example of an ideal type of family health can be found in Slavson's statement that "equilibrium in the family requires that each member of it has a specific role which he discharges adequately and that the result is emotional harmony rather than the discord of contending interests and drives."[2]

Applied to the S. family, an ideal type of family health would have suggested on the clinical level, parents and children free from emotional disturbances and on the institutional level, sufficient mutual need satisfaction between the parents so that their marital relationship would grow stronger and sufficient satisfaction of the developmental needs of the children so that they could grow into independent personalities, fulfilling their own capacity potentials through gradual separation from the parents. From the angle of limitation, however, the following had to be considered. Although these parents seemed very well suited for psychoanalyses because of their intellectual endowment and their mutual interaction which was attacking rather than fortifying their defenses, neither of them could afford such treatment. On the other hand, both parents and the child had shown in the course of their contacts with the worker that they had sufficient ego strengths to mobilize themselves and to show positive movement in psychotherapy. Although our child welfare focus did not permit us to treat the

[1] Parsons, Talcott, "Max Weber's Sociological Analysis of Capitalism and Modern Institutions" in *An Introduction to the History of Sociology,* edited by Harry Elmer Barnes. University of Chicago Press, 1948, pp. 290–291.

[2] Slavson, S. R., *Child Psychotherapy.* Columbia University Press, New York, 1952, p. 69.

parents for their difficulties as such, the resulting limitation actually proved to be helpful at least with regard to the father who, as was later seen, might have been threatened by treatment for himself but found it possible to gain insight in working out the impact of his relationship with Peter upon the development of the latter.

It was decided, therefore, to engage in an attempt at family treatment through psychotherapy with father, mother, and child conducted by the same worker. Child welfare focus was maintained but not in the sense of excluding consideration of the individual difficulties. Rather, these difficulties were seen and treated as partly producing the difficulties of the child and partly as being influenced and increased by the latter. Our main goal was to help Peter achieve a measure of freedom from the impact of the intrapsychic difficulties of his parents and to help the parents come closer together in working on the fulfillment of the child's developmental needs in this respect. This was to be achieved by helping the parents gain an understanding of their own self-involvement in the handling of the child. They were to be helped to see how their own identifications with their parents, their projections of their own difficulties upon the child, and the child's identification with them had led Peter to adopt in some measure their own anxieties and their own defenses, although not to the degree which their projections made them feel and think. They were to be helped to see how these mechanisms had left the child without sufficient learning experiences with regard to more adequate methods of managing his own difficulties and to see that if he tried his own solutions to the problems of living this need not be wrong even if his solutions differed from theirs. Finally, the parents were to be encouraged to increase reality testing of such changes in their handling of the child which their increasing insight might lead them to consider.

The boy was to be helped to bring out his fears, realize their exaggeration, and see their connection with the past. He was to be aided in overcoming his inhibitions, in gaining a measure of self-confidence, and in handling some of his aggressive feelings by better methods than the ones he had adopted. The goal was to bring about enough development in Peter so that he could see himself as a person with a pattern of affect and behavior distinct from those of his parents and to accomplish what he could within the framework of his own capacities.

It also was visualized that eventually even Louise might have to be included in the family therapy in order to help her and the parents also in bringing about the separation necessary for that child's development. This was considered because of the fact that Louise as a girl had a different meaning for the parents and thus was likely to be the subject of different identifications and the object of different projections, as could be noticed already from the parental attitudes toward her and the appearance of some signs of symptomatology in the child. This was left in abeyance, however, because of the uncertainty of the effect of family therapy with the parents upon their future handling of and feeling toward Louise.

While originally Peter and his mother were seen weekly and the father only biweekly, later on it was decided that the father should be seen weekly as well because he had entered a period of particular stress occasioned by the loss of his employment. This decision was made because of the possibly unsettling effect on the family if the father did not find sufficient help at a time when his reality situation presented particularly pressing problems.

The plan that the same worker should continue seeing both parents and child had proved its soundness already in the study contacts leading to the formulation of the diagnosis and therapeutic planning presented above. It had enabled the worker to see more clearly the interaction patterns among the members of the triad, and thus to understand better what each person meant in the family configuration, as well as what each family member meant to the others. It was considered essential to continue this case undivided because of the interrelatedness of the various parts of the family treatment plan which did not permit letting treatment with one family member go into directions which might upset the treatment process with the others. Furthermore, it was also the wish of both parents, with whom the possibility of dividing the case was discussed, to be seen by the same worker. From the beginning the father had expressed the desire to have contact with the worker who treated his child. In the course of the treatment the worker and he kept their discussions geared to Peter's problems. The father had found that exploration of the child's difficulties with the child's worker had made it easier for him to gain insight into his own difficulties and his relationship with the worker was positive. The mother in turn had shown considerable movement in the first phases of her contacts with the worker and also had a positive relationship with her. An incident in which the mother had quoted the worker to the father had been discussed with her as a possible indication for a division of the case. The mother, however, pointed out that she could have done so also if she had had a worker of her own. Actually the father's own contact with the worker had helped him take this incident better, because he could view it in the security of his own knowledge of the worker. The comment of a worker unknown to him might have been much more damaging.

THE COURSE OF FAMILY THERAPY

Now to the course and success of therapy. Giving every detail of the various therapeutic processes pursued under this plan would fill a book by itself. The description here attempted is confined, therefore, to some illustrative episodes. One of these occurred in the discussion of Peter's psychological tests between worker and father. When the father inquired about the test results and wanted to know whether the tests had shown anything new, the worker asked him in what areas he had expected that new information might be forthcoming. Thus, she made it possible for the father to bring out his own specific concerns about the child and by comparing the strength of these concerns with their reality stimulus to recognize his self-involvement. Among the father's worries was whether Peter had a very high IQ or was closer to average intelligence. He spoke about the boy's ability to think logically and to follow the conversation of adults. On the other hand, he had noticed the boy's tendency to stick very much to one topic, which indicated a lack of flexibility in thinking. Using the father's own statement as a starting point, the worker mentioned that the boy's good verbal ability led sometimes to the impression of his being brighter than the tests at this point showed. She said that the tests did not show Peter to have superior intelligence —and not even high average intelligence as the father hoped —but that it was difficult to say whether this would be final or whether an improvement might occur in the future. She asked the father how he felt about this, and he said that he was satisfied as long as the boy was of normal intelligence. He expressed the hope, however, that after Peter's emotional difficulties were removed he might show that he was capable of functioning on a higher level. The worker neither denied nor confirmed the validity of the father's expectation in this respect but pointed out that whatever the intelligence level of the child might be, it was important to enable him to utilize his given abilities as constructively as possible and that help with his emotional difficulties might be of value in that respect. She also mentioned that the parents' handling of their demands upon the child was important here and spoke of the child's tendency to react to pressure with withdrawal. The father was very responsive to this line of thought and himself gave many examples of how Peter lost enthusiasm or willingness to go on with things if father or mother put too much pressure on him through their criticisms. Mr. S. thought that both he and his wife had improved somewhat in this respect but still might be making mistakes by constant encouragement which he realized now also to be a kind of pressure.

Thus, an opportunity in the discussion of one area of the child's personality makeup was utilized by the worker to help the father see the difference between himself and his child in intellectual endowment and to see also the unfavorable effects which the demands of the parents for achievement had upon the child. This was done by her with full awareness of the defensive nature which the father's feeling of intellectual superiority served in his own personality makeup because our family diagnosis had indicated the necessity of helping the parents differentiate between themselves and the child, and the clinical diagnosis of the parents had indicated that they had sufficient ego strength to respond positively to help in such differentiation. For this reason, the worker carried out a similar discussion of the boy's performance on the intelligence test with the mother.

In further discussion of the psychological tests with the worker the father also showed concern about Peter's feeling of insecurity and was able to recognize similar feelings in himself. When the worker mentioned the boy's tendency to stick to detail, the father compared himself with the boy in this respect. He brought out that he also frequently had to be very certain that things fitted in every detail before he could act and that he also had continuous feelings of insecurity in spite of the fact that he was better equipped intellectually than Peter. Mr. S. mentioned that at times he was afraid of not being able to support his family and traced these anxieties back to his own childhood when he, his mother, and his sisters had lived under severe economic deprivations. He expressed the thought that since Peter did not live under similar conditions it might be his own childhood-based feelings of insecurity which he somehow conveyed to Peter. Thus, he was stimulated to recognize differences between himself and the boy beneath the cover of similarity of symptoms and to gain insight into his own role in determining the problems of the child.

Since the father was greatly interested in the details of the test results, the worker continued to use his questions for a discussion of another aspect of the father's self-concern about certain personality traits as compared with his concern about them in Peter. In consequence, when the conversation turned to Peter's fears of animals, the father mentioned his own fears. He pointed out that he as well as Peter was particularly afraid of dogs, but while the father's way of handling this fear was to avoid situations in which he might have to encounter a dog, he wondered how Peter behaved in similar situations. He thought that Peter did not tend to avoid them so much but rather tried to meet them by overcoming his fears.

Finally Mr. S. was able to voice the question whether the tests had shown Peter to have self-destructive tendencies. He wanted to know whether there was a preoccupation with death and destruction, since the worker had mentioned the child's interest in supernatural things, which had come out quite clearly in the tests. In answer to the father's question, the worker said that the tests had shown some preoccupation with explosions and destruction from the outside, but not self-destruction. She mentioned her interest in knowing from the father how much these things were discussed at home, how much the boy might have heard about them in school, and added that she was interested also in the father's concern about these thought tendencies in the boy. Mr. S. replied that, as he had stated on another occasion, there was talk both in the home and at school about atomic energy and about the possibility of atomic war, so that the boy's thoughts about these dangers of destruction might have originated there. At the same time he realized that Peter's concern about these things had a preoccupied quality which distinguished it from the thoughts of other children regarding such matters. He then smiled and said that it was probably his own concern about these dangers which he had transmitted to the boy. On the other hand, it was probably because he had self-destructive tendencies himself that he was looking for them in the child. In response to the worker's expression of interest in what respect the father had self-destructive tendencies, Mr. S. spoke about certain severe depressions from which he had suffered in the past and was still suffering to a certain degree. At such times he was afraid that the world was coming to an end, he felt defeatist about everything, feared that he could not support his family, and sometimes was afraid that he would commit suicide like his father. He thought that the latter had done so because he was in financial difficulties and was afraid of not being able to support his wife and children, particularly in view of the fourth pregnancy of Mr. S.'s mother at that time. To the worker's question whether Mr. S. had actually made any attempt at suicide, he said that there had been times when he felt like killing himself but he had never seriously planned to do so. Thus, the father again was helped by the worker to differentiate between his own anxiety and that of Peter, to recognize his own influence on the child and his self-involvement and projections.

Similar attempts to help the father achieve some power of distinguishing his own problems from those of the boy and to see their interrelationship were frequently made. Mr. S. tried very hard to keep every single interview related only to Peter's problems but almost always managed to take the step from an appreciation of the child's difficulties to a recognition of his own. Once he summarized the nature of the process by saying that from his discussion with the worker he had gained more understanding of the child and somehow through the child about himself. Thus, he expressed as his actual experience what we had set out to achieve, namely, to help the parents differentiate their boy's identifications with them from their own identification with their parents, through a recognition of their own projections and the boy's individuality. Incidentally, this was facilitated for the father, because by talking to the worker who treated his child he did not have to come out with his anxiety directly but could find his way to insight from the intermediary and less threatening steps of gaining an understanding of his son.

In her contacts with the mother the worker followed essentially the same goals. She tried to help Mrs. S. see her identification with her own mother, the projection of her anxieties upon Peter, and the effect which this had upon her handling of the child. She was also helped to see how Peter's difficulties affected her in turn. The process of the mother's differentiation between herself and Peter can be illustrated as follows. Peter had taken up the accordion, and had been successful on a small instrument but experienced difficulties in playing on an instrument with more buttons, to which he had shifted after a period of practice. The mother expressed some disappointment about this, but also began to show insight that she might have been pushing the boy too much, which was similar to the insight which the father had shown in this respect.

In the interview following this discussion of Peter's accordion playing, Mrs. S. mentioned that the last time she had talked a good deal about Peter. Actually she had been quite anxious about other things. She thought she might have talked so much about Peter for two reasons: first of all, in order not to talk about herself; secondly, because sometimes she felt guilty about her behavior toward him. She had failed to give him a nice Christmas vacation. Only once did she really take him out with her. In order to help her see that such a compartmentalization of thought was not really possible and certainly did not correspond to her strong involvement in his difficulties, the worker asked her whether talking about Peter did not include talking about herself. Furthermore, she asked Mrs. S. what it was that she wanted to avoid talking about by keeping the discussion centered on Peter to the exclusion of herself. The mother agreed that talking about Peter actually was very much like talking about herself, because she sometimes thought that she had rejected him when he was younger and that he had developed his difficulties for that reason. Even now when he was noisy or teased Louise she got more angry with him than with the girl when the latter proved to be difficult. This might be so because it brought back to her mind fights she had with her sister in which she often had been rather cruel to her. Another reason might be that she had always felt Peter to be much more of an interference with her life than Louise was. When Peter was born she was overwhelmed not so much by the demands for care which the baby represented but by criticisms of her performance from her mother who had at that time lived with them and also by the criticisms of her husband. The worker helped her see her displacement in this connection—that apparently she had directed feelings that she had toward her mother and her husband toward Peter—and the mother responded with a burst of insight. She said that this was so. Peter actually had had to bear the brunt of all her anger because she was better able to let it out on him than on her mother or her husband against whom she did not dare to take a stand at that time. In those days she had felt that just being a mother was something everybody could be, while her idea of worth was to be successful in a job or to be a leader in community activities. However, since she had to be a mother, she wanted to be the best one there was and each little difficulty with Peter or something which might not even have been a difficulty but only impressed her as such was for her a sign that she was a failure. With Louise it was different. With regard to her she had more or less accepted her role as a mother. At this point she felt that her evaluation of motherhood had changed and if she had a choice now, she would choose to have children.

In that connection the mother mentioned that it was not easy for her to accept the test result which indicated that Peter did not have so high a level of intelligence as she would have liked him to have. In contrast to her first reaction at a previous interview when the tests had been discussed with her and she had denied that it made any difference to her, she stated that, of course, she tried to make the best of it, but she would have been happier if the results had shown Peter to be an intellectually outstanding child. She had always felt somehow that Peter did not have high intelligence, but had hoped that she might be wrong in her assessment of his ability. She considered Louise to be more intelligent and felt that this in itself might have influenced her attitude toward the girl if she was really honest with herself. That did not mean, however, that she did not want to do everything that might help Peter make the best possible adjustment within the range of his own capacity. The worker gave her recognition for her increasing ability to see Peter as the individual he was and for her desire to help him as such in spite of her own and her husband's stress on intelligence and achievement. Thus, the mother was helped to lessen her identification with the boy and so to free him from the impact of her own drives and defenses.

This process of differentiation and resulting separation of the boy from the impact of the parents' intrapsychic difficulties, of course, was not achieved through one or the other discussions of the type presented here. These discussions repeated themselves over the whole course of therapy. On one occasion the mother recognized with the help of the worker that it was the recollection of her own loneliness as a child which made her particularly concerned about Peter's difficulties in making friendships and led her into attempts to arrange contacts with children for him. At another time she mentioned that she had noticed in Peter a certain hesitancy in making decisions. She showed concern about this and remembered that when she was a child she had been frequently undecided herself. Her mother had made so many decisions for her and she had been always under the impression that her mother was right. Only when she was older, in fact after her marriage, did she realize that her mother sometimes was wrong. Now she began to notice that Peter had the same attitude toward her and her husband, saw them always as being right, and looked up to them almost too much. For the same reason, she came to think that he was unduly upset when she or her husband got angry and shouted at him. On the other hand, she became particularly impatient with him when he could not make up his mind whether he wanted to wear this or that, whether to play one game or another, and what to do with his time generally. She began to feel that she had told him too often what to draw, what to paint, what to wear, and what to play, as her mother had done with her. And now she, as well as her husband, resented it when Peter asked them: "What shall I do, how shall I spend the day?" In response to these expressions of beginning insight, the worker discussed with the mother rather freely some of Peter's difficulties. She pointed out as she had done with the father the boy's tendency to withdraw if too many demands were made upon him, his fearfulness and preoccupation with all kinds of fantasies around animals. She showed the mother understanding of her impatience with Peter's difficulties in making up his mind and pointed out how particularly trying this must be for her in view of the fact that she had had similar problems with her mother. She agreed with Mrs. S. that Peter should be helped to make his own decisions, but pointed out that this would have to be done gradually and that he could not be expected to become independent in his decisions all of a sudden.

It will be remembered that our treatment goal with regard to Peter was to help him bring out his fears, realize their exaggerated nature, come to understand their connection with past experiences, gain a measure of self-confidence and achieve sufficient deidentification from his parents so as to free himself from the impact of their intrapsychic difficulties. The therapeutic work with regard to his fears might be illustrated by the following account of a discussion between him and the worker. After he had received a bird for a pet which his parents had given him so that he might overcome his fear of animals, he began in one interview to tell the worker that he had a fear of birds and did not know what to do about it. Later on the worker learned that Peter's father on the way to the Clinic office had impressed upon the boy that he should talk about his fears there. The worker told Peter that maybe he could speak a little more about this fear and say more exactly what it was that he was afraid of. Peter said that he had a strange feeling when he touched the bird. It was a kind of funny sensation. To the worker's question whether he had similar feelings regarding other animals, Peter mentioned salamanders, frogs, worms, or any small animal. With larger animals it was different. For instance, he did not get the same feeling when he saw a monkey. There his fear was of a normal danger, the monkey might bite him. But when he saw worms or frogs, or bugs, he got a feeling of wanting to look away. The worker asked him whether it was a feeling of disgust and Peter said it could be. It was not so much a feeling that they might hurt him but rather that he might hurt them. He might step on them and squash them. The worker mentioned that many people sometimes had a wish to hurt animals or even little people. Peter agreed emphatically. Sometimes he had a feeling of wanting to step on them, but then did not do so. With regard to people, sometimes he felt like hurting his little sister, especially when she was a pest or when he was annoyed that she had taken away a good deal of his parents' time. Returning to his fear of birds, he said that he did not like having a bird on his arm. He got the feeling of something warm. He preferred to touch things not alive. Then he mentioned an incident when a bird apparently had defecated on his arm and he had not liked that. He was afraid the bird might do that again if he took it on his arm. Also the bird might snap at him.

The worker asked Peter whether the animals he was afraid of might do something while he was not on guard. In reply, Peter stated that when he went into the water he sometimes was afraid that fish or worms might touch him. The worker suggested that perhaps he had a feeling that they might even get into his body. Peter said yes this was the reason. That was also why he did not like to lie down on the grass. Later on he brought out the idea that these little animals might come into his body through his mouth. His mother had told him that when he was about three or four years old he had eaten worms or caterpillars. He vaguely remembered having done so. His face showed disgust while he spoke about it. To the worker's question what he thought would be the consequence if worms got into his mouth while he was lying on the grass, he expressed some fear of germs which might thus come into his body. But then he laughed, corrected himself, and said how could they get into this mouth. When he was little he probably ate them while taking dirt into his mouth without realizing that there was a worm in it. He no longer did that, so there was no danger. He therefore thought that his fear of eating animals had not too much justification any more. However, while swimming or lying on the grass and not watching, little animals could still come into his mouth. The worker wondered whether this actually had happened to him recently, or whether it still might be his feeling because he remembered what he was told about the incident which had happened when he was three or four years old. She mentioned that such a thing often left an impression, so that one is later scared even if it does not happen. Peter could not recall that it had happened recently to him and seemed to see a relationship between experiences which he had had previously and his present feelings. In this connection it might be mentioned that the worker learned later from the mother that there really had been such an incident when Peter was a toddler and that Mrs. S. had mentioned it to him on a later occasion. Thus, her contact with the mother and the child made it easier for the worker to assess the nature of the fear which might otherwise have been open to an interpretation as impregnation fantasy.

Picking up the thought of the relatedness of current feeling with past experiences, Peter expressed his disgust about an incident which had happened the previous summer at a day camp when a boy had squashed a wasp and Peter had seen the blood oozing out. He put emphasis on the word "blood." He told the worker that since that time he was a little afraid of squashing animals and connected this with his fear of touching his bird. He thought that the best thing would be for him to try and really touch the bird. If nothing happened, this might help him overcome his fears. The worker agreed that this was often how people recognized that things were not in reality as they frequently imagined them to be. Peter decided that he would try each day to touch his bird so that he might learn that nothing happens in such an instance. The worker said that this was a good idea, but mentioned that there was a possibility of its taking quite a while before Peter found this method effective and that the fear might not disappear completely.

In the next interview Peter mentioned his loneliness and his desire for a twin brother. However, he knew that he couldn't have this wish fulfilled. His parents did not want any more children. He did not mind that, since he would want only a brother exactly his own age. In connection with the fact that his parents didn't want any more children, the worker asked Peter whether he was interested in the birth of babies and Peter showed himself well informed, stating that his parents had explained to him how children were born. Reviewing this knowledge, he said that he must have been very stupid to think that his sister would be big enough from the start to be a playmate. Of course, when she was born he was only three or four years old and did not realize that a baby could not be big. He had been disappointed therefore when he saw how small his sister was. Now he knew that babies are born so very small, that he could hardly risk even touching one. The worker wondered whether he also sometimes felt uncomfortable about touching babies. When Peter agreed, the worker pointed out that this was similar to the feeling he sometimes had about touching little animals, and Peter said yes this was so.

The way in which the worker helped the boy gain some de-identification and separation from his parents may be gathered from her discussion with the boy regarding his giving up the accordion and also from a discussion about plans for Peter's going to camp in the summer. During the first year of treatment and previously, Peter had spent his summers in a day camp in which his mother was employed as the camp nurse. In the second year of treatment the possibility was considered by the worker and the parents of having Peter attend one of the agency's therapeutic camps. When the worker asked Peter about his plans for the summer and whether he wanted to go to camp, his first reaction was that he had to consult his parents. The worker agreed that these plans had to be discussed with the parents by him, as well as by her. At the same time she emphasized that she would like to hear what his feelings and thinking about camp were. At first he said that he was not sure what the family plans were. His mother might want to go to camp again and take a job as a camp nurse, taking Louise along. The worker discussed with Peter in several interviews what his reactions would be if Louise were with his mother and he all by himself in another camp. He was rather definite, however, that he would like to be away from his family, at least for one month. Last year the children had laughed a little about him because his mother was so close while the other children's parents had been further away. Therefore, he would rather go to a camp by himself. He still had some concern about going to the toilet. Though he now went to toilets in other people's homes, he preferred a camp where no one could come into the toilet while he was there. Last year he had had to time himself in going to the camp toilet while the other children were not there because the toilet was an outside one and the children stood in line and looked on while another child was on the toilet seat. The children had often tried to open the toilet while he was in it. The worker asked whether the children had done this only with Peter, but he said that they had done it with everybody, only the other children had not minded. He was not specific about the reasons for his dislike; he merely repeated that he just did not like it. With the help of some questions on the worker's part, Peter managed finally to say that he did not like it when the children looked at him. They sometimes teased him. When the worker asked him whether he felt that they watched him while he was having a bowel movement he was not certain that this was the case. He just liked privacy. The worker mentioned that sometimes children touch themselves while they are in the bathroom and was it this that he did not like the children to see him do. Peter said that sometimes he did. He felt, however, that he did not care so much any more whether somebody saw him in the toilet. He felt the lack of privacy on the toilet would not keep him from going to camp by himself as other children did.

As has been mentioned, Peter had been practicing on the accordion. Once he came into the office and told the worker that he had given up playing. He looked much relieved and explained that it had become difficult for him. He had started too early to shift from a smaller to a larger instrument and he was glad to have been able to give it up. Practicing had been too much of a strain and had been too time consuming. He was only embarrassed because a friend of his continued with the accordion while he did not. It had been partly this other boy's playing which had made Peter continue practicing as long as he did, and which had made him even take it up in the first place. To the worker's question what had made him stop in spite of the fact that his friend did not, he replied that he had done so partly because his parents had felt it difficult to pay for the lessons while his father was out of a job and partly because he just did not like it any more. The worker then said that the fact of his friend's liking something did not mean that

Peter had to like it and that he had to have the same interest. Peter agreed to this and began to speak about some interests which he had, although his friend did not share them. This was only one instance of many in which the worker tried to give Peter a feeling that to have separate thinking and feeling as an individual was permissible and in order to do so she emphasized that Peter could have his own interests and likes even if they differed from those of other boys and that he sometimes might want something that his parents did not want him to have or do and vice versa. Peter seemed to respond to these efforts of the worker, as will be seen from the report of the gains made in therapy.

What still remains to be done in describing how the treatment plan was pursued is to show how the worker aided the parents in coming closer together in their various tasks and especially in helping Peter to a healthier development. Basically there was first of all the advantage of a de facto child welfare focus in the various aspects of our experiment with family therapy in this case. This provided a common concern which pervaded the worker's sessions with both father and mother. This made itself felt as a prolonged experience of a vital undertaking in which both spouses shared. The fact that the case was not divided also prevented the two lines of therapy from going off in different directions and thus impeding the unifying character of the experience. Naturally the parents observed each other's handling of the child, discussed together Peter's problems and their handling of the child, and noticed their individual improvements in their behavior toward the boy. By giving the parents a chance to verbalize their observations about each other and the improvements they noticed in their various interrelationships in the home, the worker used the child welfare focus and the gradual success of therapy to give the parents an opportunity for a continued revision of the negative images which they had developed of each other.

In a discussion of the father's own feeling of depression the worker asked whether Mr. S. felt a desire for more intensive help with these discomforts. Mr. S. denied this and said that if he could not have a full analysis, which was financially out of the question, he would prefer to receive help on the present basis. To the worker's question in what ways the contact with her helped him, Mr. S. answered that he had gained increased self-understanding here and that he knew very well that in general the family relationships in his home had improved. Mrs. S., in his own estimate, had gained most of all. She was much more efficient in organizing the household routine than she had been previously. They both had gained more understanding not only of Peter but also of Louise. In consecutive interviews the worker helped the father elaborate on his evaluation of the improved home situation. Repeatedly Mr. S. mentioned his wife's greater ability in managing the household and her greater understanding of the children. He was especially positive in his description of how she now handled Louise. As an example he mentioned that when Louise had had to wear braces on her legs, the mother had handled it very nicely and playfully so that the child did not resent it. He also praised the way Mrs. S. had dealt with Louise's problems of adjusting to nursery school and had made it easy for the child to accept the separation.

When Mrs. S. similarly began to speak positively about her marital relationship, the worker helped her identify the nature of these improvements. To Mrs. S. an indication of improvement was the fact that she and her husband had begun to show much greater respect for each other. In spite of occasional relapses, she felt that they had become more of a family unit. It was no longer as though she and Louise were on one side and Peter and Mr. S. on the other. There was much more mutuality between her and her husband as well as between them and the children. This was what gave them a feeling of greater stability.

A related feeling was expressed by Mr. S. when having given up his job he had an opportunity to take a position in the Far West. He felt that his family was not ready to move and he would not want to go there first by himself even if it was only for a couple of months. He would resent such a separation from his family now that there had been so many improvements in their relationships. As Mr. S.'s search for another job continued and proved to be more difficult than he had anticipated, Mrs. S. showed understanding and patience with his irritability and occasional feelings of discouragement. She also took a part-time job to help out financially. In a discussion of his employment problems and their impact upon his home life, the worker gave Mr. S. an opportunity to appraise his wife's attitude, which he did in a very positive vein; on the other hand, since the worker felt that this particular aspect of improvement in the marital relationship could be due to the fact that Mrs. S. might have some secondary gain from her husband's difficulties, she tried to help Mrs. S. distinguish for herself whether her new appraisal of her husband was due to her own feeling of personal importance which she had derived from the situation or was due to a real change in Mr. S. Mrs. S. reacted to that question with quick insight and was able to clarify for herself that, although she might have gained a feeling of increased self-value from the situation, her husband's behavior toward her had already improved before the unemployment situation arose.

THERAPEUTIC GAINS

From the foregoing presentation of the worker's efforts to aid the parents in coming closer together as a couple as well as from the description of her efforts to help Peter and his parents individually to greater insight into their own personal problems of identification, projection, and separation, some of the therapeutic gains have become apparent. However, a few remarks about the improvement in the clinical and dynamic picture of these persons are in order. At the end of the project period, Peter's difficulty with toileting had practically disappeared. He had more friends and actually was elected class president after one year of therapy, while formerly his loneliness and unpopularity among his classmates had been a point of serious concern. He had become more self-assertive and his parents were able to accept his expressions of independence from their wishes. He showed an increasing tendency to overcome his fears by reality testing rather than by withdrawal. This was demonstrated not only in his attempts to overcome his fears of animals, which were still somewhat inspired by parental influence, but also in other areas where these attempts expressed themselves with spontaneity. Once he expressed apprehension over having to recite a poem in class. After he had talked about it to the worker, he used her Ediphone to rehearse the performance. When he listened to the cylinder's rendering of his recital, he did not like it. He repeated the rehearsal with improvements, listened again, and did this until he was satisfied with the results of his efforts.

However, Peter still dawdled in the morning, and still had occasional nightmares.

The mother had gained greater ability to manage her household, a greater feeling of self-value, more perspective in the appraisal of the personality of her husband; had practically overcome her insomnia; and had learned to see her self-involvement in the development of her children.

The father had become more aware of the nature of his own intrapsychic difficulties, of his need to work further on their solution, and had freed himself from his defense of having to look down upon women, particularly upon his wife.

Both parents had become able to permit Peter a measure of independence and of freedom from pressures for performance beyond his own abilities.

Thus, at the time of this writing there had been improvement both on the clinical and relationship levels. There had been a reduction and in some areas a disappearance of symptomatology, a gain of insight, new and satisfactory reality testing on the part of the three persons treated. In terms of family health there had been an increase in unity between the spouses and a measure of separation between parents and children. On the individual as well as on the family level, improvement had been concerted.

III. The Case of Steven M.

PRESENTING SYMPTOMS

STEVEN, AN ELEVEN-YEAR-OLD BOY, was referred to the Clinic by his mother on the suggestion of a family friend because of his stuttering. This difficulty was a concern of long standing to the parents. From the time the boy was four and a half years old they had taken him from one speech clinic to another, always without success.

Other problems mentioned by the mother were: lack of friends, a strong feeling of inferiority when Steven compared himself with other boys, a tendency to complain about everything, spending hours on the toilet, and using rolls of toilet paper after every bowel movement. There was strong jealousy toward his younger brother. Actually, the mother's main concern was none of these symptoms but the boy's general inability to relax. She pointed out that in that respect the boy was like her; she also was unable to relax under any circumstances.

FAMILY COMPOSITION AND THERAPEUTIC CONTACTS

The family consisted of Steven, his parents, his two-year younger brother Ralph, and eight-year younger sister Marilyn. An older girl, Nina, had died before Marilyn's birth. Pathology in the family seemed to be widespread. The father had many fears and phobias. He suffered from nightmares and in earlier years had been a stammerer in turn. He reported that he also had suffered from "an inferiority complex" like Steven. The mother was a tense woman who showed compulsive concern about cleanliness and was punitive in disciplining the children. Ralph, the nine-year-old boy, had a rocking symptom which troubled his mother greatly. He also had a noticeable twitch in his shoulders and his neck, and was accident prone. Marilyn was a demanding and stubborn child who was overconcerned about cleanliness like her mother and seemed to have marked separation anxiety.

The relationships within the family gave the impression of people locked in mutually troublesome interactions. The father was critical of Mrs. M. but afraid of her and submissive. A psychiatrist whom he had consulted a number of years before the Clinic contact had advised him to go away occasionally by himself for weekends in order to relax. The mother was very limiting in her demands upon the children, who reacted to these demands with provocation. Finally, there was considerable sibling rivalry among the children, which troubled both parents.

In this case all members of the family except Ralph had therapeutic contacts. In accordance with our point of view that a division of a case should take place only if and when concentration of all contacts in one therapist actually proved unfeasible after it had been tried, the same worker saw both parents and Steven as well as Marilyn in the course of the treatment process. Steven was first treated only through group therapy, while his mother received individual therapy. Later on Steven was also given individual therapy. The father was seen first in two diagnostic contacts and then more or less regularly once a month. Marilyn was seen occasionally as the course of therapy suggested.

FRAMEWORK OF DIAGNOSTIC STUDY

A diagnostic blocking out of the three families of orientation, which we have to consider in an attempt to understand the problems of the children in this case, gave, on the basis of information received from both parents, the following interesting picture:

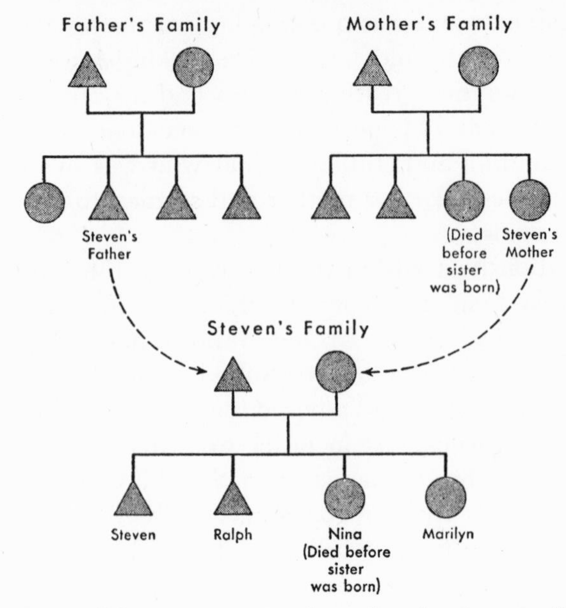

A number of features seemed strikingly repeated in these families. The mother's sister died before Mrs. M. was born, and similarly her own child Nina died before Marilyn was born. The mother was the youngest child and only girl among the three surviving siblings. The same was true of Marilyn. The mother was greatly outdistanced in age by the older of her two brothers and so was Marilyn. The father had a brother two years younger than himself and so had Steven. Certainly there were circumstances in the sibling situation of their children which were likely to remind the parents constantly of their own childhood situations. In consequence, these factors were likely to stimulate recall and reactivation of old patterns of emotions and behavior on the part of mother and father. In order to elucidate the meaning of these repetitive family patterns, however, we had to integrate again this mapping out of the three family situations with the psychodynamic information received.

DIAGNOSIS OF FATHER

The father was a severely neurotic person, who since childhood had suffered from symptomatic expressions of his emotional disturbances. Having overcome the stammering, he still had nervous twitches and on occasions woke up at night from frightening dreams crying "Mom." At the moment of waking from these nightmares he had feelings of breathlessness and a fear of choking. He was afraid of being left alone because he dreaded the thought of getting such an attack of breathlessness with no one around to give him assistance. He might die without anyone there to help him. He also had fears of riding on trains, in cars, or elevators. He fought with great intensity against being overcome by his fears but had to pay a heavy price of suffering for the victory of his will-power. When a train on which he was riding stopped, he had attacks of claustrophobia. The difficulties were of such long standing that he had become fairly hopeless with regard to freeing himself of their impact. On the other hand, he gave an impression of denying the severity of his suffering by a show of good humor.

The father recalled that he had a tic of the eye when he was a small child and had begun to stutter when he was about seven years old. That was when his second brother was born. The father recalled that he had been an extremely shy boy until he was fifteen or sixteen years of age. According to his own recollection his first fears had started when he was thirteen. He had been afraid that his father, who at that time had become chronically ill, would die. He had been unable to leave the house for fear his father might die in his absence. His thought had been that if he left the house there might be no one around to care for his father when the latter needed somebody. Actually, his father did die when Mr. M. was sixteen. Because of his father's illness and later death, Mr. M.'s mother had had to go out to work.

His relationship with his mother always had been lacking in warmth. As Mr. M. expressed it, she had never been home for him. Incidents after his marriage seemed to confirm this situation. When once asked, for instance, to stay with Steven while Mr. and Mrs. M. went out, Mr. M.'s mother had done so but had said that she was not a maid. There had been strong sibling rivalry between Mr. M. and his two-year younger brother and currently he was not on speaking terms with his other brother.

The information about Mr. M.'s family background certainly showed some reality factors for his fears, such as the father's illness and subsequent death and the mother's realistic need to go out to work. It must be remembered, however, that symptomatic expressions of Mr. M.'s difficulties had occurred relatively early in childhood and particularly that his stuttering had started when his second brother was born. Mr. M. had been the oldest boy, but was only two years of age when his first brother was born. These facts, together with his own recollection of the emotional aloofness of his mother and his shouting "Mom" when he awoke from nightmares as an adult, suggest that there had been an early disturbance of his relationship with his mother which had left its mark upon him. Whatever the nature of this disturbance might have been, it was reactivated by the fact that after his marriage to Mrs. M. the young couple lived with Mrs. M.'s parents. She felt that they had to do this because Mrs. M.'s mother had become very sick prior to their marriage and needed her daughter's care. Because of her sickness Mrs. M.'s mother moaned and screamed all night long. They never had a night undisturbed by these frightening noises, since the young couple and mother slept in adjacent rooms. Mr. M. said his nightmares had started at that time.

Dynamically the father's anxiety seemed to result from three experiences: an always unrewarded reaching out for an emotionally aloof mother, the guilt over death wishes against his father, and the fear that his brothers would outrank him in his quest for the mother. In order to lessen this anxiety he felt that he had to placate the mother figure in his wife in the manner of a frightened and submissive child. Against the anxiety resulting from his negative feelings toward his father he had defended himself with the reaction formation of intensive concern, feeling that if he left him the father would die unattended. And against anxiety resulting from his sibling rivalry he had striven to defend himself by an effort at establishing a particularly good relationship with his two-year younger brother with whom he always exchanged gifts and was in business partnership.

None of these mechanisms had been fully successful. His wife irritated and annoyed him. His reaction formation, expressing itself in the fear his father might die helpless and unattended, had developed into the recurrent fear that this might happen to him. And his relationship to the brother who was his business associate was by no means untroubled, although this expressed itself more in conflict between his wife and his sister-in-law than in direct conflict between him and the brother. With the other brother, however, the conflict was open. Mr. M.'s general tendency to reaction formation and denial expressed itself also in his general show of exuberant good humor, although he was aware of his many difficulties and had little hope that he ever would find relief from these emotional burdens.

DIAGNOSIS OF MOTHER

Like most mothers of stutterers, Mrs. M. suffered from a severe obsessional neurosis. She was fearful and tense, choosing her words carefully and deliberately. At the same time her speech had a rather explosive quality. It will be recalled she had stated herself that she could not relax. She suffered from excessive fears of high places, found it difficult to get away from home and particularly to sleep in strange beds. She was a meticulous housekeeper and became upset when either her husband or her children violated the extreme cleanliness and orderliness of the home. Toward Steven she expressed great impatience and punitiveness, asking support from the worker in her desire to punish the child severely. She was unable to have friends and lived in constant strife with her own relatives as well as with her husband's.

From the point of view of a genetic diagnosis it should be noted that her fears of high places and anxiety over being away from home had been with her since early childhood. Since her sister had died before she was born, she had been the only girl in the household of her parents. Her sibling rivalry with her two brothers was intense. Greatly outdistanced in age by the older one, she hated in him also the fact that he was the father's favorite. The younger brother had become a victim of infantile paralysis before she was born. He had never made a recovery and throughout her childhood Mrs. M.'s parents had taken him from doctor to doctor and from operation to operation. She felt that this had affected him very deeply and that he was nonrational even as an adult. He had never been able to get along with anybody and now lived the life of a recluse in a hotel.

Mrs. M.'s relationship with her own mother had been a disturbed one from early childhood on. She described her mother as a controlling and sadistic woman who had frequently hit her, had always accused her of misdeeds, and made negative comments.

As the only daughter, she had had to take over all household responsibilities, which became particularly burdensome when she wanted to get married. Her mother, because of gangrene resulting from diabetes, had to have her leg amputated. Following orthodox Jewish custom, the young couple had not wanted to postpone their marriage although the mother was in a hospital. Therefore they had dispensed with an elaborate ceremony, had been married in the house of a rabbi, and then immediately had gone to visit the mother in the hospital. The latter had been hostile and instead of wishing the newlyweds luck and happiness had simply said, "So what" when they had appeared in their new status. However, because of the mother's condition, Mrs. M. had felt that she must stay at home after her marriage in order to continue taking care of the mother's household, although she and Mr. M. had originally planned to set up their own. Also, she had continued working as she had done since graduation from high school. Thus, after her marriage Mrs. M. felt that she had to go straight home from work every day to take care of her mother's household. All her life she had hoped not to grow up to be a woman like her mother, who was overconcerned about cleanliness, went easily into rages, and screamed when things were not done exactly to her satisfaction. Her mother had never appreciated the sacrifice of an independent married life which she and her husband had made. Thus, the mother pictured her relationship to her mother as characterized by masochistic dependence similar to the description of the relationship of mothers of stutterers to their own mothers.[1]

In order to arrive at a diagnosis of Mrs. M., it seems indicated to draw attention first to the fact that she described in her mother striking similarities to her own behavior and situation. The mother was a meticulous housekeeper and so was she. The mother had been given to outbursts if her demands for cleanliness and orderliness had not been met, and she was given to similar outbursts under the same conditions. The mother had lost one daughter and had never been able to talk about it to her children. The same had happened to Mrs. M. and she likewise was unable to mention it to her children. The mother had been a frightening woman to her husband and to Mrs. M.; Mrs. M. was a frightening woman to Mr. M. and to her children. Thus, apparently, Mrs. M. had identified with the aggressor who had created in her tremendous anxiety. But Mrs. M. resorted also very strongly to the mechanism of repression. She liked to think of herself as a lenient mother who let her children get away with things. In order to justify her need to alleviate her anxiety with outbursts of aggression like those that she had experienced from her mother, she needed provocation and managed to convey this need to her children who satisfied it. Interestingly enough, Mrs. M. stated that Steven shouted at nobody except her. While her mother by her demands had made it impossible for Mrs. M. to have friends in her childhood, Mrs. M. herself tried to push Steven into having friends. Actually she did this, however, in such a way that it was not successful. Once having invited a number of boys for Steven into the house, she insisted that Ralph be present at the party, with the result that Steven had been embarrassed

[1] Glauber, I. Peter, "The Nature of Stuttering," *Social Casework,* vol. 34, March, 1953, p. 98.

and had had a temper tantrum after the boys left. Having always felt to be the disadvantaged child whose brothers received more than she did, Mrs. M. was preoccupied with equal allocation among the children. Although this was her conscious intent, she managed nonetheless with the support of one or the other rationalization to give more to Ralph than she gave to Steven. Being very punitive, she wanted the worker's permission and support for her disciplinary measures. Having ambivalent feelings toward her children, she was always worried that something might happen to them and was unable to let them separate themselves from her.

In essence, she used obsessional defenses, that is, reaction formations as manifested by perfectionism, aggressiveness, which she, however, could show only when provoked, and an overriding concern with equal allocation.

There was then in both Mr. and Mrs. M. severe conflict resulting at least in part from the disturbed relationships with their respective mothers and from pronounced sibling rivalry. Both parents resorted strongly to the defenses of denial and reaction formation which expressed themselves in separation anxieties. The differences, however, consisted in the generalized use which Mrs. M. made of aggressiveness both against her husband and her children while Mr. M., although sometimes aggressive toward the children, was submissive toward Mrs. M.

DIAGNOSIS OF STEVEN

From the clinical point of view Steven presented a mixture of paternal and maternal symptomatology. He seemed to repeat his father's childhood symptoms in his stuttering and shyness. He shared his father's and mother's fears of high places and resembled his father in his attempt to overcome these fears by conscious efforts. Like his mother, he was preoccupied with cleanliness and was meticulous about his clothes. It was difficult for him to sleep away from home, as it was for her. His mother could not relax and neither could he. Like both his parents, he exhibited intense sibling rivalry.

This sibling rivalry presented also a significant trend in his developmental history. His mother noted that from the birth of his brother Ralph, that is, from the age of two he had clenched his fists. The mother had sensed his anger and had asked him kiddingly whether he was ready to swing. Ralph had been a more appealing child and had stimulated everyone to comment what an adorable baby he was. She thought it likely that her handling of Steven had changed when Ralph was born. Before Ralph came she had been overconcerned about Steven, fearful that he might get some contagious disease. She had kept him clean with the greatest care for fear that germs might make him ill. At no time had she ever allowed him to do things for himself. She used to pick things up for him all day long, so that in the evening she was extremely tired. She had been afraid that he might topple out of the play pen if he dropped a toy outside and wanted to recover it by himself. In that way he had completely dominated her and only when Ralph was born had she felt it necessary to put her foot down and not to yield to his demands. Probably Steven had felt a tremendous loss when his brother was born and his sibling rivalry had its roots in this experience. Later on the admiration which the younger brother elicited from everybody and the mother's preference for this more lovable child increased his anger and feeling of being outrivaled. Having witnessed Nina's death and probably influenced by his father's fear of dying, he was always insistent that a doctor be called whenever he was ill and became very anxious when his mother did not accede instantaneously. He also shared his mother's concern that something might happen to Marilyn and was very protective of her.

Dynamically there can be no doubt that Steven was a very much frightened child. In the beginning of group therapy he showed this clearly by introducing every request to the therapist with a remark such as "You are going to kill me for this" or "Gee, I am always afraid to ask for this." He showed surprise when his requests were granted or his mistakes overlooked. He was also timid in his relations to the other boys in the group. That the basis of his fears were disturbed relationships with both his parents and not only with his mother, he showed in an outburst in which he yelled that he hated both of them. On an occasion when his mother had forbidden him to go out of the house he significantly turned against his father as if he resented that the latter did not protect him against the mother. In his later contacts in individual therapy he showed marked fear of rejection. When the worker discussed with him whether he wanted to go to one of the agency's camps he was reluctant to do so. A friend of his had been going to camp for four years and now that he was no longer coming to the Clinic the camp did not want him to return there any more. Steven was afraid that the same might happen to him. In view of his rejection by the mother after his brother Ralph was born, this fear seemed to be a persistent trait in his personality structure.

Against these fears he had built up various mechanisms of defense. In part, he tried to overcome them by ego strength in identification with his father; in part he covered them up by outbursts of aggressiveness which his mother unconsciously encouraged; in part he tried to assuage them by avoidance, as indicated in the camp incident.

DIAGNOSIS OF RALPH

Concerning Ralph much less information was gained than about his parents or siblings. He was the mother's favorite child and her perception of his difficulties was somewhat obscured by this preference. Still, some information was gained from both parents about this child. Clinically we knew that this nine-year-old boy had a rocking symptom and twitches in his neck and shoulders. Like all the siblings in this family, he clung to the mother. When he was separated from her in the daily routine of living, accidents seemed frequently to happen to him. In general behavior he appeared to be a smiling and joking sort of child, but from the parents' reports the worker gathered that he was provocative in a quiet and stubborn way. Genetically we learned almost nothing about him except that he had had a childhood more favored by approval than his brother but had presented a tremendous problem when he was sent to nursery school, where he refused to stay without his mother. From a diagnostic point of view it was clear that he had considerable separation anxiety and managed to defend himself against this by regression (rocking) and a stubborn attempt to show that when he was separated from his mother dangerous things would happen to him.

DIAGNOSIS OF MARILYN

The youngest child, Marilyn, showed symptoms of similarity to Mrs. M. in her overconcern with cleanliness. This was not reported by the mother but observed by the worker in the child's actions while finger painting. She had tried very hard not to smudge herself and became quite frightened when finally she spilled some paint, in spite of her carefulness, on the floor. Whenever she got paint on her dress she insisted upon being taken to the bathroom to be cleaned immediately. She also showed marked separation anxiety. The mother complained that the child was terribly tied to her and was afraid to go to the nursery school, as Ralph had been.

Direct contact with Marilyn, however, revealed that what had appeared to be separation anxiety created by the mother was actually oedipal in nature. Marilyn's resistance to going to nursery school was elucidated in one of the worker's interviews with her. Asked by her mother to try to help the child with her problems around nursery school, the worker learned from Marilyn that she was afraid that Jim, the bus driver, would forget her address and would not be able to bring her home, and that she would have to stay with him overnight at the school building. She revealed that she actually would very much like to do that because she was very fond of Jim, but still was afraid of it. An apparent displacement of her reaching out for her father and her fear of losing the mother as a consequence seemed to be in operation here. Without this direct contact of the worker with the child, the temptation would have been great to explain the child's reluctance to stay in nursery school also in terms of identification with the mother's own separation anxiety.

FAMILY DIAGNOSIS—MULTIPLE INTERACTION PATTERNS

Having arrived at our individual diagnoses of the various family members, incomplete as they may have been at least with regard to Ralph and Marilyn, we again were faced with the task of preparing a family diagnosis. Again we resorted to the concept of social interaction for doing so. The situation, however, was more difficult than it was in the case of Peter S. because more interaction patterns had to be considered. While in that instance we had limited our family diagnosis basically to the triad of Peter and his parents, our increasing acceptance of the concept of family of orientation led us here into a consideration of five family members. An understanding of interaction patterns in this case, therefore, according to Bossard's Law of Family Interaction, would have demanded a consideration of ten interpersonal relationships within the family group.[1]

These ten interpersonal relationships would have had to be considered, but also the impact upon each family member of all those interpersonal relationships of which he was not an immediate part. An examination of such complexity we were not yet ready to undertake. Actually, if we had faced the therapeutic proposition in so rigorous a fashion, the temptation to give up and to concentrate simply on the mother and Steven might have become overwhelming. What we did fell somewhere in between the two alternatives. First of all, we took account of individual pathologies and came to the conclusion that every family member was disturbed. Decidedly, we had to deal here with a phenomenon of group disturbance. We then looked for outstanding relationships which seemed to be accessible in terms of the understanding which we could gain from the individual diagnoses we had established and tried to utilize their understanding for a better comprehension of the group phenomena.

[1] Bossard, James H. S., *The Sociology of Child Development.* Harper and Bros., New York, 1948, p. 146.

This law states that with the addition of each person to a family or primary group, the number of persons increases in the simplest arithmetical progression in whole numbers, and the number of interpersonal relationships within the group increases in the order of triangular numbers. This can be seen in comparing the following two lines:

Number of persons in the family 2, 3, 4, 5, 6, 7, 8
Number of interpersonal relationships correspondingly ..1, 3, 6, 10, 15, 21, 28

In essence, these various interpersonal relationships gave the following picture. We knew that Mr. M. had not had a satisfying experience in the relationship to his mother who "had never been home for him." We had reason to assume that his unresolved oedipal strivings for her had led to negative feelings toward his father. During Mr. M.'s adolescence these negative feelings apparently had led to a reaction formation of fear that the father might die unaided. The father's serious illness at that time in all probability had been a factor in the reaction formation. We also knew that Mr. M. had later identified with the picture of the father dying without help. In Mrs. M. he had found a woman who because of her own identification with her mother had developed tremendous separation anxiety and encouraged this in the members of her own family. Mrs. M. was always home for everybody in the family. Thus, her behavior provided a source of reassurance and alleviation of the father's fear of being alone. At the same time Mr. M. had had his early marital experience under the shadow of motherhood, so to speak, having had to live in the household of his wife's parents and having to sleep in a room joining that of Mrs. M.'s mother, who had turned over to the young couple her own bedroom. Significantly enough, Mr. M. thought that his disturbance had increased at that time and that his nightmares had started then. It might be conjectured, therefore, that he saw in his wife and in his relationship with her a belated, and disturbed, satisfaction of his oedipal strivings. At the same time he got from Mrs. M. alleviation of the psychological discomfort which he had to pay for the identification with his father. Unconsciously his relationship to Mrs. M. had been, therefore, to a degree more that of a son than that of a husband. His closeness to and unity with her was from the point of view of a marital relationship, a pseudo-unity being on the unconscious level the unity of a child with his mother. The psychiatrist whom he had consulted over a period of time before the Clinic contact, might have sensed this and based his suggestion that Mr. M. occasionally should go away by himself, on the feeling that it would be damaging for the patient if this anxiety-alleviating and at the same time anxiety-creating pseudomarital closeness were permitted to grow uninterruptedly. In other words, he might have felt that Mr. M.'s marital relationship impeded the forces of repression in Mr. M. and thus contributed to the persistence of the latter's severe symptomatology.

On the other hand, Mrs. M. had identified with her harsh, demanding, and dominating mother and needed a husband who by his submission would make it possible for her to maintain the alleviation of anxiety which she derived from this identification. Thus, Mr. M.'s behaving like a frightened son rather than a husband provided her with the figure of a husband which her self-image derived from her identification with her mother demanded. However, her identification with the strong, forbidding, and punitive aspects of her mother's personality was not completely successful. After all, she had been the frightened child of this same mother during all her developmental years and had not forgotten this experience. To further confound her mechanism of defense against her anxiety by identifying with her strong mother, the mother had become an invalid for whom she had to care for a prolonged period of time. By identifying with her she had not only become strong and demanding, but also weak and handicapped. This part of the identification was therefore anxiety-creating and her husband failed to give her relief from this anxiety except the one of providing company in her misery.

Actually, this company in misery was one of the outstanding characteristics of the two marriage partners. Not only did their mechanisms of defense inadequately protect them from the impact of tremendous anxiety, not only did they mutually satisfy and at the same time frustrate their needs to get in adult life what they had missed in childhood, they also shared an experience of intense sibling rivalry. It might be surmised, therefore, that their closeness, although based on emotional immaturity and marred by mutually disturbing influences, was essentially so strong that it kept their marriage going. Perhaps its strongest foundation was the sympathy and the tolerance of the sick for the sick. This tolerance probably was facilitated by a similarity of symptoms sufficient to emphasize their bond.

Rather than get involved in the mass of relationships between the parents and the three children, we tried to focus upon similarities in these parent-child relationships. There was, first of all, a strong separation anxiety which the parents had managed to impart to all three children, particularly their clinging to the mother. Thus, the children shared with their parents one outstanding symptom, increasing the bond of disturbance in the family group through a common experience of emotions. The mother's preoccupation with equal allocation, one-third of her for Steven, one-third for Ralph, and one-third for Marilyn, probably increased further this feeling of sharing in a common fate which, though painful and disturbing, was their common lot and kept the parents geared to them as a group rather than as individuals. All the children seemed to have caught on to the fact that the mother needed their defiance for a release of her aggression and complied. The worker once noticed that when the mother tried to call the children from the office all of them made the telephone call frustrating by screaming into the telephone, thus making it impossible for the mother to get any but aggravating responses from them. All the children also accepted their mother's concern for cleanliness and all of them reacted to her demands and punitiveness with symptoms of discomfort. The children thus formed a group of siblings who shared compliance and shared rebellion against the parents and even their rebellion seemed to be an accommodation pattern designed to meet a need of the mother which they inarticulately and perhaps unconsciously felt.

The parents in turn found in their children, particularly in their sibling rivalry, stimuli for a reactivation of their own childhood experiences and thus stimuli for reactivation of their own defenses. The appearance of the symptoms in the children in turn strengthened the bond of sympathy and closeness in the total family group. The parents only had to look at any one of the children and were likely to find one or the other of their own symptomatic discomforts expressed in the child. Steven, Ralph, and Marilyn—they were truly their children. Father as well as mother was aware of this and could not help feel a unity with the children on this basis.

In a sense we had then in this family a condition which could be called a family neurosis, expressed in a family phobia against separation and in irritation over the price of discomfort which had to be paid for the alleviation of this phobic anxiety. The family phobia against separation, of course, had its roots in the two separate family experiences of the parents. Once established, however, it operated in the two spouses, keeping them tied together in mutual alleviation. Transmitted from them to the children it kept the children in turn tied to the parents and the parents to the children. Being afraid of separation, parents and children became prisoners of their mutual company.

Surrounding the common core of alleviated separation anxiety were the results of frustration which this alleviation imposed upon the members of the family in other repects. Dynamically the father would not only want a mother at any price but would prefer a mother less demanding, dominating, and punishing than the one which he had found in his wife. Being tied, however, to the partial satisfaction which he got from Mrs. M., he had to displace his hostility against her upon his children. Significantly enough, he permitted expression of these displaced feelings to himself only when Mrs. M. in turn had an outburst of rage against the children. Dynamically also, Mrs. M. sensed in her husband's fears and mother-centered nightmares unmanliness which frustrated her passivity strivings and need for protective support. The children, of course, were frustrated in their developmental strivings toward independence by their being tied to the mother and got support for their occasional needs of self-assertion in sensing their mother's need for provocation.

Finally, all members of this family suffered from their inability to meet the demands of individualization and independence which everyday life made upon them. Their own separation anxiety or the separation anxiety of other family members always seemed to interfere.

Thus, the father could not follow his doctor's advice to separate himself from his family for an occasional weekend. The fact that Steven had fallen sick while Mr. M. was away once over such a weekend had made the mother so anxious and desperate about his absence that they had a terrific argument upon his return and he decided he would never again leave Mrs. M. by herself. The mother could not tear herself away from the children, so that she could not have any social life for herself. The children in turn expressed their own anxiety by clinging to the mother. Steven sat around all day and did not want to make friends. As long as he did not reach out for friends his mother wanted to push him into friendships. When he gave signs of developing friendships, his mother objected because she felt that the new friends dominated the boy. Ralph, by developing the regressive symptom of rocking, managed to bring her into his room every night, thus protecting himself against separation, even in sleeping arrangements. However, he thereby irritated his mother, who had developed the habit of giving him a sharp slap on the buttocks every time his rocking forced her to leave her own room. Ralph had also refused to go to nursery school and thereby forced his mother to stay there with him, thus taking her away from her household duties which she felt very strongly. Marilyn, although she was the youngest child and probably had benefited some from the experiences of her parents with the two older boys, also showed tendencies to cling to the mother. When she showed signs, however, of overcoming that fear, for instance in the waiting room of the agency, the worker observed that the mother managed somehow to bring the child's mind back to the separation and to make Marilyn anxious about it.

FAMILY DIAGNOSIS—INSTITUTIONAL ANALYSIS

From the point of view of institutional analysis the parents seemed to fulfill the family functions of the spouse relationship. They satisfied their mutual needs of intimacy, companionship, and complementary economic arrangements. Actually they aided and abetted their mutual mechanisms of defense. The nature of these defenses being inadequate, however, the closeness so produced was overintensive and frustrating instead of being relaxed and satisfying. Thus, we had a situation which was significantly different from that between the parents of Peter S. The parents of Steven were locked in an exaggerated association pattern which forced upon them irritations which in turn stimulated their anxieties.

With regard to the children, the parents seemed to fulfill the task of child care better than the task of socialization. Their emphasis on child care was the logical outcome of their separation anxiety. With equal logic the parents could not permit the children to make significant advances on the developmental road to independence. The mother, with her need to be provoked before she could fight her anxiety with aggression, furthermore gave the children a wrong conception of the purpose and consequences of self-assertion. The father, on the other hand, through the displacement of his aggression against the mother upon the children, failed to furnish the children with a stabilizing influence and provided them with still another inadequate sibling figure rather than with the image of the father. From the relationship angle the dissociation tendencies of the children were discouraged and blocked. This had to be the case with two parents so bedeviled with separation anxiety as Mr. and Mrs. M. were. More than being discouraged, the dissociation tendencies of the children were internally counteracted by the separation anxieties which the parents had imparted to the children. Thus, the family functions in this case, although partially fulfilled, were actually abused by the membership for a bolstering of inadequate defenses against deeply rooted anxieties. On that basis the family disturbance could be conceptualized as *partial family dysfunction with relationship tendency exaggeration between the spouses and relationship tendency arrest between the parents and children based on a neurotic exploitation of both function and relationship.*

PLAN OF FAMILY THERAPY

This family diagnosis, although not yet conceptualized in the manner just presented, determined our goal-setting. The nature of the family disturbance suggested the need of helping the different members get a start in the modification of their relations to one another. We had to provide opportunities for individual growth and development within the family so that the various members would become able to free themselves of the familial prison which their mechanisms of defending themselves against their anxieties had so closely cemented. In the spouse relationship this effort was to be directed at a loosening of the excessive closeness and of the submission-dominance pattern between Mr. and Mrs. M. In the parent-child relationship, not only a loosening but also a reversal of the relationship tendencies had to be achieved. In planning therapeutic measures, however, we had to consider the following characteristics of the situation: the wide distribution of emotional disturbances among the family membership, the intensity of the individual disturbances, the overriding nature of separation anxiety in all members, the obsessional concern of the mother with equal allocation, and the anxiety-alleviating power which the pathological expressions of feeling and behavior on the part of any one family member provided for the others.

In view of this situation we concluded that psychotherapy with one or two family members alone, however intensive, was unlikely to bring about liberating changes in the interaction pattern of this family. No one, whatever his intrapsychic difficulties and their possible solution happened to be, could be counted upon to have sufficient strength for defending therapeutic gains against the impact of negative interaction on the part of other family members. Much less could he be counted upon to bring about positive changes in the others.

We decided, therefore, on a mobilization of all members of the family by giving everybody a chance to work on his problems as they became activated during our contact with the family. In this way, we expected that every family member could gain respect for the expression of the problems of the others and for attempts at their solution. We hoped that thereby various lines of positive social interaction might be set in motion within the family. In view of the fact that the parents as well as the children were so involved in a common pathology, it appeared more promising in the long run to give the entire family group a sense of participation in a common solution than to involve only selected family members in individualized therapy with individual therapists. We also had to consider that if we had started individual therapeutic involvement for every member at the same time we might have accepted and reinforced the parental pattern of equal allocation which in itself was an expression of pathology.

Thus, we provided group therapy for Steven, individual therapy for the mother, occasional contacts with the father, in a later phase of the relationship a series of therapeutic contacts with Marilyn, and finally individual therapy for Steven. In doing so we provided for the parents an opportunity of testing whether they could accept some differences, particularly in the experiences of their children. In order to stress the community of experience and also to keep track of interaction within the family membership, the same worker saw all members of the family. This also had the advantage of a heightened diagnostic perception throughout the course of family therapy.

THE COURSE OF FAMILY THERAPY

In the course of these various therapeutic contacts we initiated and supported a number of developments which in their cumulative influence had a loosening effect upon the neurotic ties which kept the parents and the children in their family prison. Several streams of therapeutic influences can be traced as having brought this about. Although we did not plan this in rigid detail but followed opportunities of therapeutic influence as the members of the family group presented them, we started what in retrospect appeared to have been four distinctive streams of liberation. These streams were distinctive in terms of the family members involved but otherwise interlocking in two ways. They were all directed at our therapeutic goals based on our family diagnosis and they were mutually supportive in preventing negative interaction of the family members with the changes which any one individual gained from his therapeutic experience.

There was, first of all, Steven's experience in group therapy. While Steven was very fearful in the beginning, would only listen to other group members and abide by their decision, after a while he began to come forth with ideas of his own and to defend them vigorously. Although his speech difficulty did not improve basically for quite a time, his voice changed from a whining to a more natural tone, and he became more self-assertive. The emotional root of his stammering revealed itself in the recurrent phenomenon that when he entered a group meeting he stuttered noticeably but when the meeting ended his stuttering was usually gone. As the meetings continued he stopped expressing concern over the fact that he might get his clothes dirty or his hands a little messy. He became more self-reliant in carrying out projects. While in the beginning he had asked the group therapist every few minutes for his opinion, later on he became able to finish a project before asking the group therapist whether he liked it. In the second year of group therapy the stammering had decreased to a point where at times it was not noticeable at all. He participated freely in group discussions, had developed competence in handling materials, and was able to relate well to the other boys. However, there remained a number of fears, particularly of high places, and it was felt that this neurotic residue required individual treatment which, as stated above, was provided for.

In the contacts with the parents and Marilyn the worker focused on the problems which were activated in the family group and handled them with the person who appeared specifically involved. With the mother the therapeutic process at first was slow in developing. In the beginning she presented over and over again material which indicated the great role she played in the discomforts of her husband and her children. She refused to see, however, any connection even on a purely intellectual level. She maintained stoutly that she was a lenient mother, not at all personally disturbed by any discomforts, and able to throw off quickly any impact which the difficulties with her family made upon her. Even when the worker pointed out to her statements to the contrary which she had made before making such a summation of her own role and feelings, Mrs. M. refused to see her own mechanism of denial.

The first help which the worker was able to give her in achieving better understanding developed when the mother once summarized the situation by saying that Steven was a stammerer, Ralph rocked, and her husband was nervous. When the worker pointed out to her that she was also nervous and asked why it was that she, her husband, and her two sons shared in these discomforts, Mrs. M. suddenly admitted her realization that she constantly drove herself relentlessly, as far as her household was concerned, in order to keep it immaculate. She guessed that this was due to not having had too easy a life. Maybe it was the result of some experiences that she had had as a child. From that time on she dwelt frequently on her own childhood and particularly on her relationship to her mother, her father, and her two brothers. She continued, however, for some time to deny that Steven's situation was similar to that which she had experienced as a child.

Mrs. M. was helped to overcome this rationalization by the involvement of the father in what could be called the third stream of emotional liberation which we started on its flow. When the mother, after two months' contact, mentioned as she had done before that her husband was a nervous type and became highly upset when anything happened to the children, the worker expressed her interest in seeing Mr. M. She did so as a means of reassuring the mother of our understanding that both parents were involved in the problems of their children and that we did not single out the mother as the only parent to carry the burden of either causation or cure of their developmental difficulties. Mrs. M. accepted this suggestion, although she denied any feeling over the fact that her husband had not been seen so far. When the worker indicated that she would telephone Mr. M. in order to arrange an appointment, Mrs. M. said that this was not necessary. She insisted upon informing her husband of the appointment and indicated that she knew his schedule well enough to make the necessary arrangements. Although Mrs. M. had an interview of her own on the day of her husband's first appointment, she returned with him to the Clinic and also accompanied him to the worker's office.

Mr. M. opened the interview with the remark that there were

no secrets between him and his wife, and that it was all right for Mrs. M. to sit in on the interview. Although he told the worker in a later contact how afraid he was of his wife, he started this first interview with the statement that most of the family's difficulties were the result of Mrs. M.'s rigidity and her insistence upon always having her own way with everybody. Apparently he took courage from the presence of the worker to express his grievance to his wife. He went on to say that he saw many of his own childhood difficulties repeated in Steven's development and mentioned that he also had been involved in strong sibling rivalry with his two-year younger brother. He also took this occasion to point out that Mrs. M. actually favored Ralph very much. He said that his wife had a tendency to hold in her feelings until they piled up; then she permitted herself to explode at Steven, with the result that Mr. M. exploded as well. Thus, in this first interview the involvement of the father gave the mother an opportunity to hear her husband's opinion about her own role in the difficulties of the family and particularly of Steven. It also gave her an opportunity to perceive that the father's own childhood difficulties in their similarity to Steven's might have been a contributing factor in the difficulties of the child and thus freed her from the lonely burden of guilt against which she had defended herself so strenuously. When the worker suggested another interview with the father and Mrs. M. wanted to participate in it again, the worker suggested that perhaps it would be possible for Mr. M. to come in by himself. Thus, she helped both Mr. and Mrs. M. to loosen for the first time the submission and dominance pattern under which they had been living in the pseudo-unity of their relationship.

Fairly soon after this interview with the father, the mother for the first time was able to express some self-blame for her handling of Steven. Mrs. M. reported that the boy had tried to pour chocolate syrup in his glass of milk and had flopped the syrup on the table. Ralph, on the other hand, had been able to add the syrup to his milk without spilling a drop. Mrs. M. had been so annoyed that she had hit Steven across the hands with a fork. Mr. M. had reproached her for her loss of control and had asked her why she could not keep herself better in hand after having come to the Clinic for several months. He had said that he was going to inform the worker of this incident. Mrs. M. reported to the worker that she had told her husband she was going to do so herself because she did not hide anything from her and did not try to protect herself. When the worker asked what she meant by this statement, Mrs. M. admitted that maybe she had been wrong in reacting so strongly to the child's clumsiness. She said that she definitely knew that as a child she herself had not been perfect and had no right to expect Steven to be perfect. To the worker's question why the spilling of syrup by Steven had upset her so, the mother expressed again her realization that now in adult life she was a perfectionist and became upset when anything was not just so. Apparently the father's encouragement from his Clinic contact to taking a stand against his wife's handling of Steven, as well as her experience of seeing Steven's difficulties tied up to a degree with her husband's difficulties, had made it possible for Mrs. M. to abandon somewhat her defense of denial and gain a measure of insight about her relationship to her son.

In one of the succeeding interviews she reported another incident of conflict which had occurred between her and the children. Steven had been ill and the doctor had ordered that he be given the white meat of chicken for a few days. Mrs. M. had done so for one day but on the second day had given him dark meat. Steven had blown his top and had said that if the doctor had made this recommendation for Ralph the mother would have followed it faithfully. Mrs. M. had become very angry over this reproach. She had told her husband that she hated the child. Mr. M. had spoken up again on that occasion and threatened again to tell the worker about this incident. The fact that two such incidents happened in quick succession showed how much Mr. M. utilized the Clinic contact as a crutch in his attempts to act like a father and husband rather than like a frightened son.

The worker took this up with the mother and asked her how

she felt about this threat of Mr. M.'s, particularly in view of the fact that he had made it for the second time in so short a period. Mrs. M. denied having any feelings about this and pointed out that she felt free to tell the worker about the incident herself and was not afraid of her. Although this was probably one of her usual defenses, the point must not be overlooked that the mother had experienced the permissive and accepting attitude of the worker and for this reason was better able to take the threat than she would have been if it had been made with reference to a worker whom she did not know. In such a case her apprehension that this other worker might be critical of her and might condemn her, as her mother had done, would have been unchecked by actual experience. We thus had a situation similar to the one reported in the case of Peter S., indicating that contact of the parents with the same worker provides a reassurance for both parents in situations where one tries to utilize the Clinic contact as a weapon against the other.

That Mr. M.'s attempts at self-assertion began to threaten his wife less than was the case before the contact with the Clinic, was also revealed in a change of her attitude toward his going away by himself over weekends. It will be remembered that at one time a psychiatrist had suggested this to Mr. M. as a means of finding some relaxation from his nervous tensions. At that time Mr. M. had been prevented by his wife from carrying out this recommendation. When he went away for the first time, Steven fell sick during his absence and Mrs. M. received her husband upon his return with such an outburst of anger and reproach that Mr. M. decided never to go away again by himself. In an interview following the one in which Mrs. M. had related her husband's second threat to talk about her handling of Steven to the worker, the mother mentioned that Mr. M. had been terribly upset at that particular time. She felt that for that reason it might be good for him to go away by himself again for a day or so. Apparently her seeing the father in the perspective of the Clinic contact helped Mrs. M. perceive him as an individual with his own needs and difficulties. Thus, she was helped to free herself from considering him only as a supplementary extension of herself and to see him as a person in his own right.

The child welfare focus, which, in fact, we maintained throughout, enabled the father to get help from us which he was unable to seek for himself independently. Fairly early in the contact he had raised the question with the worker whether he should not go into psychotherapy for himself. The worker explained that this was something which he certainly could do if he felt that he wanted it. The father pursued this idea for a while, to the point where we made a referral to a psychiatrist who was ready to treat Mr. M. as a private patient for a fee which Mr. M. could afford. Mr. M. did not follow through on this referral but he was able to maintain the contact with the Clinic and to gain help from the worker, to the point of verbalizing his great fear of Mrs. M.'s outbursts of anger and also his own fear of being outranked by Steven as the latter was growing stronger and physically more mature. In other words, he could face with our worker in her child welfare focused concern his submission and fear relationship with his wife and the displacement of his sibling rivalry upon Steven, although he did not find sufficient motivation in his personal suffering for a discussion of these problems with an outside therapist.

In the meantime Mrs. M. had become able to draw analogies between herself and her mother. Her mother also had worshipped her house, had to have it look exactly so, had worshipped her possessions, and heaven had to help anyone who placed something out of line. In that connection Mrs. M. acknowledged for the first time that in coming to the Clinic perhaps she had learned something. She had learned at least to control herself better, to be patient, not to get upset, and to understand Steven. She knew now that Steven was frightened and at times used anger and tantrums as a means of covering up his fears.

This gain in insight which the mother was able to make with the help of the worker, was very important because it made it possible for her to accept the increase in aggressiveness which resulted from Steven's experiences in group therapy. Thus, the help which she received made it possible for her to accept the expression of help which the Clinic was able to give to Steven. Otherwise, she might well have reacted negatively to the child's beginning emotional liberation and might have interpreted it as a deterioration resulting from his being in group therapy.

Her gain in insight and recognition of the help which she had received from the Clinic expressed itself also in an important connection between her own therapeutic experience and Steven's preparation for individual psychotherapy. When this type of therapy for Steven had to be initiated, his mother was able to tell him that she herself was receiving help from the Clinic in individual contacts with the worker, that it had helped her, and that she hoped that similar contacts would also help him. Previously she had been unable to let the boy know that he was not the only one who was needing and receiving help. At the same time she was also able to point out to the father mistakes which he made in the handling of the children without antagonizing or frightening him. Thus, the various streams of therapeutic influence touched and strengthened one another through therapeutically induced and therapeutically supported positive interaction among the members of the family.

As the mother gained insight into the nature of Steven's difficulties and recognized that his outbursts of aggression were not based on hostility against her, but rather on his own fears, she was able to turn more and more to her own problems of freeing herself from her neurotic ties to her children. This came into full effectiveness when the worker helped her see and accept the fact that parents very often do prefer one child to another, particularly when the former is easier to handle than the latter. When this was pointed out to her she spontaneously began to speak with greater insight about her own relationship to her older brother and about her resentment over his having been the preferred child. Shortly after this discussion she brought Ralph to the Clinic ostensibly to keep Marilyn company in the waiting room during her own interview. She used that interview mainly for a discussion of Ralph's tendencies to get into accidents and her terrific fears of leaving the children out of her sight. As she dwelt upon the difficulties which Ralph had experienced in going to nursery school, she revealed, however, that her concern was at the moment not so much with Ralph as with her fear that his separation difficulties would be repeated in Marilyn. Actually, it became apparent that she had brought Ralph as a demonstration object of the difficulties which she wanted to avoid in Marilyn. Thus, it appeared that her efforts to free herself from the impact of separation anxiety which she herself had created in the children now activated problems in the girl and we began to work with the mother and Marilyn on these problems. This then leads our presentation to a description of Marilyn's stream of liberation. That stream began to flow when Mrs. M., with our help, became increasingly interested in working out something for herself and therefore wanted Marilyn to go to nursery school.

The mother looked forward to the three hours during which the child would be away from home. These three hours she thought would make it possible for her to go out to do her shopping and also give her time to be with friends, something which she had missed since her marriage. However, there were difficulties due to Marilyn's reluctance to leave Mrs. M. The mother found it difficult to understand the reason for this and constantly asked the worker to see Marilyn.

Under routinized child guidance procedure such a request from the mother would have suggested that she should make a special application for this child and that another case would have been opened for Marilyn which in all likelihood another worker would have carried. In view of our general reorientation, however, as well as of our specific diagnosis and planning in this case, the worker agreed to see Marilyn herself. It was arranged that Marilyn should be seen in an interview together with Mrs. M. This was done for a number of reasons. First of all, the child preferred to be in the same office with her mother which, in view of her age, was something it seemed necessary to heed. Furthermore, the worker wanted to use this as an opportunity of helping Mrs. M. understand what it meant when a child was able to reveal the nature of her fears. Finally, the worker wanted to provide for the mother a special learning experience in reassuring a child, an area in which Mrs. M. had encountered so many difficulties.

In the interview Marilyn, who was a very verbal child, was helped by the worker to explain her unwillingness to go to the nursery school. It will be remembered from the presentation of the diagnostic material regarding this child that Marilyn at first said she was afraid that Jim, the bus driver, would forget where she lived, would not be able to bring her home from nursery school, and that she would have to stay with him overnight at the school. In the course of the interview, however, Marilyn was able to reveal that perhaps she would like to stay overnight at the nursery school with Jim because in a sense she actually liked him very much. Mrs. M. was able to get a great kick out of this, to laugh, and to comment "Out of the mouths of babes." The worker attempted to aid Mrs. M. in reassuring the child by verbalizing for her what Mommie would do and how Mommie would miss Marilyn if she were not at home. After this interview Marilyn created no further difficulty about going to nursery school and Mrs. M. was able to thank the worker for her help in solving this problem. In that connection she indicated how much meaning the worker had for her, her husband, and the total family. She frequently talked about the fact of how wonderful it was that one person could be interested in a total family and each of its members, as this worker was.

Significantly the worker's ability to help with Marilyn's problem and the mother's recognition of how much the worker was interested in the whole family activated in the mother the need to come to terms with the death of Nina. This was a fact which previously she had been able to report without, however, finding it possible to express her feelings. After having thanked the worker for her interest in all of them, she brought Nina's death into the conversation and for the first time in the whole Clinic contact she broke into convulsive sobbing. She described in vivid detail what had occurred and the tremendous feeling of guilt that she might have been to blame for the child's death because she and her husband had not called the family doctor sooner the first time, or another doctor when they were unable to reach the doctor in charge. The doctor came to see Nina at 7 o'clock in the evening. She died at midnight. It was Mrs. M.'s feeling that she should have immediately called a neighborhood doctor when, seeing that the child was growing worse, they were unable to reach the family physician again. She admitted, however, that when he had seen the child, her pulse was normal. Actually the child had died half an hour after the neighborhood doctor's arrival. At this point the mother made the remark that perhaps Steven's concern about his own health was connected with his having witnessed Nina's death. He also might have overheard his parents reproaching themselves for not having made greater effort in getting a doctor to the child.

The worker went back to Mrs. M.'s need to blame herself, raising the question as to whether it was actually true that she had not done everything that was possible. She pointed out that even the doctor a half-hour before death occurred had not been able to determine that the illness was possibly a fatal one. In reaction to this, Mrs. M. pointed out that it was her pattern constantly to blame herself in her heart for anything she did and that her mother always had reproached her for everything when she was a child. From here she went again into a description of her mother's overconcern about her possessions and her own likeness to her mother in that respect. Now for the first time she indicated an acceptance of her husband's point of view that she was too hard on the children in her demands for cleanliness and indicated a desire to move to a suburb for the children's sake. There they would have more freedom on the outside or would have an enclosed porch and would not have to play in the living-room. In essence, she showed considerable empathy for the children in terms of what her own concern about cleanliness might do to them and how they might develop resentment against the restrictions which she imposed upon them.

When, in subsequent interviews, the worker continued to

aid Mrs. M. in working through her feelings about Nina's death and her inability even to mention her name to the other children, the mother made an effort to break this pattern. She used a remark of Marilyn's that she would like to have a baby sister as an opportunity of mentioning Nina to the child. She told her that there had been a baby sister who had died. When Marilyn began to cry, however, Mrs. M. was unable to comfort her and called the worker to inform her how upset Marilyn had become. She told the worker that she herself had become completely helpless and unable to describe to Marilyn what had happened. She had had to tell Marilyn that the worker would explain it to her.

Here was another instance of how one family member's experience in therapy can affect other family members and how such problem activation requires therapeutic response. The worker saw the need for such response and asked the mother to come in and discuss this with a view of finding a way in which Mrs. M. herself could help the child. When the mother came in, she stated that in recent months Marilyn had bombarded her with requests to get another baby so that she could have a baby sister. A friend of Marilyn's had used the fact that she had a baby sister as a means of building herself up and Marilyn had reacted with a desire to have one also. In discussing her anxiety over this wish of Marilyn's, Mrs. M. revealed her own question as to why Nina really had died. She brought out her feeling, based on the Bible, that children were often punished for the sins of their parents and that Nina's death had been such a punishment. She was unable, however, to state what she thought had been her own sin for which Nina had been so punished. The worker gained the impression that Mrs. M.'s feelings of guilt were too great to make it possible for her to help Marilyn in this respect. The worker agreed, therefore, to see the child and talk to her about the death of her sister. In doing so she discovered that the mother's apprehension about the impact which the matter of Nina's death might have upon the child was unfounded. It also became clear that Mrs. M.'s statement that Marilyn wanted a baby sister because her friend had one was her own rationalization. Marilyn revealed that her request for a baby sister primarily was based on her wish to have a big bed of her own rather than having to sleep on a cot in the parental bedroom. Marilyn thought that if her parents had a baby she would graduate to a bed of her own. The worker had been aware of the sleeping arrangement for Marilyn and had been questioning it for some time. She now took the opportunity to suggest to Mrs. M. the advisability of changing this arrangement and utilized this incident to help the parents and child further in bringing about a separation which the growth process of the child demanded. Although the mother saw no way of providing a room of her own for Marilyn at the time, she placed the child in a room with the boys. She also took this problem as a stimulus for responding more and more positively to the idea of a larger house so that the girl could have a bedroom for herself.

In the meantime the worker's contacts with Mr. M. continued to give him strength in redefining his role as husband and father. Although this took, for some time, the form of expressing antagonism to his wife, the marital relationship did not seem to suffer. Mr. M. was able to notice improvements in his wife's handling of Steven; was able to help her admit to him that she preferred Ralph—something which she had never been able to do before. As to his own relationship with the children, he felt troubled about Ralph's insistence on being taken along whenever Mr. M. wanted to go out with Steven. He expressed uncertainty about the stand he should take in such a situation. The worker helped the father see that there were things which the boys would have to work out between themselves and that no matter what stand Mr. M. took he would place himself in jeopardy of being the bad parent to the child whom he deprived. In doing this the worker helped the father free himself from the concern for equal allocation among the children which he had adopted from the mother.

On the other hand, Mr. M., toward the end of the Clinic contact, became increasingly concerned over Steven's greater self-assertiveness and growing physical strength. He felt that

Steven became more provocative toward him than toward Mrs. M. He feared that before long Steven would be so strong that he would become unable to control him physically. Several incidents between father and son suggesting that Mr. M. needed to dominate his son were actually based on his displacement of sibling rivalry upon the boy. Seeing himself as the older brother who had been outranked by his younger one, he found it difficult to let Steven develop into an increasingly independent and physically mature youth. The worker tried to help the father understand the behavior of the boy as an expression of adolescent development and to see that his self-assertion should be looked upon as an improvement, since one of Steven's difficulties had been his timidity. Although the worker was doubtful whether she had been able to give the father effective help in this respect, she learned later that the father had gained such help. Although this problem activation in the father had happened toward the end of the second treatment year and shortly before the family moved from New York City, later reports from the mother, after treatment had been closed, indicated that the conflicts between Steven and his father had subsided.

With Steven himself the worker agreed first of all not to insist on weekly contact when the boy explained that with school, group therapy, and the study of Hebrew for his Bar Mitzvah there would not be any time left for him to be with friends if he had to come to the Clinic every week. She therefore arranged biweekly appointments. Since at the same time the mother felt that she had made sufficient gains to get along with biweekly interviews, the addition of Steven's individual therapy actually did not increase the workload of the therapist. In the interviews Steven was helped to face his anxiety about addressing an audience when he would be called upon to sing his prayers in the Bar Mitzvah ceremony. This seemed to have been helpful to a degree because he was able to go through the ceremony very well. In fact, he did not stumble once and he received considerable gratification from having done so well in spite of his previous speech difficulties.

With regard to the relationship between him and his father, Steven went through an interesting experience, shifting his discussion of his difficulties with Mr. M. to a discussion of his difficulties with a teacher. After having told the worker how aggravated he had been with his father one evening when as he was about to leave the house the latter had called him back into the living-room and told him to be home by 10 P.M., he did not elaborate on this incident. Instead, he launched into a discussion of his teacher, pointing out how this teacher always seemed to think that he was a big shot. He did not think that this teacher was basically a mean person but that he had to pick on the children because he needed to prove to himself that he was in control of the class. When the worker pointed out to Steven that in a sense he had the same feeling in regard to his father's calling him back, Steven sat quietly for a moment and then said that he thought that his parents yelled at him sometimes just for the sake of yelling. In a later interview, however, he showed that the worker had aided him considerably in gaining insight into the difficulties of his father, although he expressed this again in terms of his teacher. When the worker discussed with him whether he wanted to continue his own treatment, Steven said that he was not sure. He did not want to miss any benefit that he might derive from it but, on the other hand, he felt that he was "not such a terrible guy, only kind of mixed up." The worker laughed with Steven about this and commented that perhaps Steven felt that somebody else, perhaps the teacher, needed treatment. Steven agreed that this would not be such a bad idea and the worker at that point did not press the connection with Steven's father. The boy, however, made the connection himself by indicating that it was not only school and the teacher which troubled him, he also had difficulties with his father. He had fights with him which he did not understand himself. He guessed his father was right in hitting him recently when he was monkeying around with Ralph but he had not intended to hurt his brother. His father insisted that he had. He indicated, however, his own growing power of separation from the conflicts in the home by saying that at any rate he would be free of Ralph for two months when he went to camp, since Ralph would stay at home.

This was the situation after two years of treatment. The following summer the family bought a home rather far out in Connecticut, so that it was impossible for them to come in for regular contacts with the Clinic. However, Mrs. M. as well as Steven telephoned the worker several times and reported that things were going well and they managed much better for themselves than they had before.

THERAPEUTIC GAINS

In summary, the following improvements seem to have resulted from the child welfare focused family therapy which we employed. The mother had been able to free herself to a considerable degree from her separation anxiety and self-defeating mechanisms of her handling of the children. She had been able to overcome to a degree her neurotic concern with cleanliness and with the appearance of her household, and had gained a measure of free time for herself. She had become able increasingly to see in Steven positive characteristics as well as negative ones. She had begun to compare him favorably with other boys.

The father had been able to break the submission-dominance pattern which he had let grow up in relation to his wife, although his basic neurosis had not been touched. Steven had overcome his stammering, had been able to make friends, and had become generally more self-assertive. Marilyn had been freed to go to nursery school and to gain sleeping arrangements which were likely to be more conducive to a healthy development than sleeping in the parental bedroom. Nothing is known about Ralph's further development in any specific detail. However, the relationship between him and Steven had somewhat improved, with Steven assuming a rather protective role toward Ralph and taking him along when he went places.

In terms of relationships, the spouse relationship seemed to be launched upon a development of greater maturity and the relationship between the parents and the children freed from its arrested quality, thus giving the children a chance to grow away from the parents along the lines of individual development toward independence.

Neurotic residue seemed to exist at the time of closing in all members of the family except Marilyn, but the interlocking grip of the individual neuroses seemed to have been lifted.

PART TWO

THE THERAPEUTIC MANAGEMENT OF EXTRAFAMILIAL FACTORS

PART TWO: THE THERAPEUTIC MANAGEMENT OF EXTRAFAMILIAL FACTORS

IN THE SECOND PHASE of the liaison project between social science and child guidance practice our concern was mainly directed at phenomena of family pathology, family diagnosis, and family therapy. The very complexity of integrating social science and psychodynamic concepts in theory and practice made this relative limitation almost a necessity. The road from an emphasis on the mother-child relationship to a balanced consideration of the psychodynamic meaning of all essential human factors in a case is long and beset with difficulties. Extension of diagnostic and therapeutic thinking to the web of interpersonal relationships within the total family group is in itself a tremendous task. Its discussion in our seminar sessions and the burden of therapeutic work resulting from it absorbed, therefore, a great deal of staff energy. Still, our efforts and experiences were not confined to the family area.

Already in the first phase of our project attention had been paid to the influence of extrafamilial factors. Interest at that time had been directed at problems of pathogenesis.[1] In the second phase of our project, however, our increased perception of the importance of extrafamilial factors led us largely into problems of therapeutic management. This occurred essentially in two problem areas, the *preparation of cases for treatment* and the *orchestration of child psychotherapy with other lines of therapeutic effort*. The extrafamilial factors with which we had to deal in these two areas covered a range extending from schoolmates to school principals, from lay therapists in private practice to family physicians, and from defective mental en-

[1] Slavson, S. R., "Extrafamilial Influences in Pathogenesis" in *Social Science and Psychotherapy for Children* by Otto Pollak and Collaborators, pp. 78–100.

dowment to spinal meningitis. Our whole work in both these areas was guided, however, by an awareness of and attention to psychodynamics. Throughout our discussions in the seminar sessions and experimentations in practice, we managed to avoid the temptation of viewing only family members as loci of psychodynamic problems and to consider such factors as teachers and family physicians only as collateral sources of information. Furthermore, we managed to avoid such dichotomizations as constitutional disposition and intrapsychic problems, or somatic diseases and emotional disorders.

The case illustrations presented in this part of our report do not cover the whole range of extrafamilial factors which occupied our attention. Some of them occurred in cases which for special reasons, such as the severity of the pathology, resignation of a worker, or a worker's doubts about the approach of the research team, cannot be used for illustrations of the potential of our efforts. Cases free from such handicaps, however, fall within the range of constellations including extrafamilial factors to a degree sufficient for illustrative purposes. Two of them serve very well to demonstrate the importance of extrafamilial factors in preparing cases for treatment. A third one permits an illustration of the modification of psychotherapy necessitated by the child's limited mental endowment and the orchestration of such a mode of psychotherapy with a treatment effort particularly concerned with the psychodynamic meaning of planning a specific school program. It so happens that this case also demonstrates a family diagnosis geared to a conceptual level different from that of the two cases presented in the first part of this report.

The complexity of human experience and the comprehensive perception for which we struggled in our project did not permit us to single out extrafamilial factors and to deal with them independently from familial factors. As a matter of fact, it was just in their interrelationships that we found their meaning. Familial phenomena, therefore, will be referred to and sometimes given more emphasis than extrafamilial factors in this part of our report, although its purpose is a demonstration of our management of the latter. In the opinion of the writer, the achievement of this purpose is not impeded by such an integration of data. It rather reflects our approach of viewing extrafamilial factors meaningfully in a child guidance setting.

Before presenting material illustrating factors in the preparation of cases for treatment, it might be useful to indicate the essence of the theoretical clarification of this phase of clinical work, which we achieved in our seminar discussions. Psychoanalytically oriented therapy in a child guidance clinic, be it therapy utilizing play with an individual child, group therapy, or psychotherapy with an adult related to the child, is not yet so much part of our culture that everybody concerned with a child's welfare can be expected to be informed about the nature of the helping process involved. It can be assumed even less that everybody so concerned is in sympathy with this type of child guidance work and can be counted upon to cooperate with the Clinic. Parents, teachers, organically oriented physicians, and neighbors are likely to have various degrees of misconceptions regarding the nature of the Clinic's work. Occasionally, they may have considerable emotional involvement in their beliefs and considerable inclination to exert whatever influence they have in an individual case situation against the idea of therapy.

Not all misconceptions, however, need to be negative. Some parents and teachers expect magically quick and painless cures from the Clinic's efforts. When in such cases the results do not correspond to the expectations, disappointments and resentments may operate in causing withdrawals from treatment or at least a questioning and uncooperative attitude on the part of persons with power in the life of a child.

We found it important, therefore, to get the therapeutic situation structured within the framework of all realities of social power existing in a case constellation. The social matrix within which our helping efforts were to run their course had to be known and, if unfavorable, restructured so as to provide a favorable milieu for therapy.

It has been frequently stated and is generally recognized

that all therapeutic efforts have to be carried out in an atmosphere of resistance. The situational approach[1] in synthesis with our psychodynamic orientation helped to widen our perception of the loci of such resistance. We extended our concern in that respect from the internally caused resistance of the patient or patients to the internally caused resistance of nonpatients, who were also influential in the individual case constellation. In doing so, we found that an extension of therapeutic planning to a consideration of resistance in the latter group of persons may make the difference between getting a case into treatment or not getting it going at all. Of course, this does not mean that we tried to involve, for instance, a resistive family physician in therapy. It does mean, however, that the unconscious motivations of the physician, as far as they became apparent to the worker in direct contact, were considered in our efforts at a restructuring of the situation. Rather than leaving them out of our planning or simply regretting their impact as an obstacle to therapy, we made their recognition one of the decisive elements in our preparatory work with the parents. And this in turn became possible for us through our extension of the consideration of phenomena of social interaction beyond the persons composing the family group.

Another part of our efforts at restructuring the situation as a preparatory step toward treatment was concerned with the provision of a frame of reference for the parents, the children, and all other persons involved, within which they could come to terms with the phenomenon of therapy. It is a truism in child guidance work that much is to be gained if the parents can bring themselves to explain to the child why he is to go to the Clinic. It is also a truism that it is helpful, if not essential, that *both* parents and all other persons of importance in a case constellation can support the Clinic contacts of those who are involved in treatment. In order to enable them to do so, however, these persons need help in achieving at least intellectual clarity as to the nature and probable course of therapy.

[1] Pollak, Otto, and Collaborators, *Social Science and Psychotherapy for Children*, pp. 27–29.

Here we had to struggle with a phenomenon which seems to have grown up in the professional subculture of social work, namely, with the tendency of answering a question with a question. This is not the place to engage in a discourse about the appropriateness and the timing of interpreting irrational psychological mechanisms to clients or patients. The only point to be stressed here is that not all questions of clients or patients are determined by such mechanisms. They may be determined, particularly in the early stages of their contact with a worker, by a rational desire for information. Antagonism to the phenomenon of psychotherapy itself may be based on misconceptions which can be corrected by factual information. We encountered this more than once with fathers.

In consequence, we found it to be a desirable part of the preparation of a case for treatment to establish direct contact with as many persons of importance in the specific situation as possible and to provide them with a frame of reference within which to view the proposition of therapy either for themselves or for somebody in whom they had an interest. Fathers, sisters, teachers, and physicians fell into this group. In providing this frame of reference, we found it necessary to rely on specific statements rather than on generalities. We found it necessary to give answers rather than to elicit answers on the part of the persons involved. Even where our efforts to provide a frame of reference by such means were unsuccessful because of unconscious resistances, they did not prove useless. The fact that they had been made, proved to be helpful in our therapeutic planning. In such cases we were able to identify resistances rather than having to engage in conjectures about them. We also avoided the danger of remaining unaware of them because of an absence of testing their existence.

IV. Preparation of the Case of Peter S. for Treatment

THIS CASE HAS BEEN PRESENTED to the reader earlier from the viewpoint of family pathology, family diagnosis, and family therapy.[1] It is here utilized to demonstrate the interplay of familial and extrafamilial factors in preparing a case for treatment.

In accord with the demands of strict logic, an account of the preparation of this case for treatment should have preceded its presentation from the viewpoint of diagnosis and therapy. It was felt, however, in the arrangement of the material for this report, that our work on family diagnosis and family therapy constituted the main part of our efforts and, therefore, should take precedence in the order of presentation.

AMBIVALENCE OF THE MOTHER

It will be recalled that Peter was referred to the Clinic on suggestion of a Neighborhood Center because of difficulties in toileting, dawdling in the morning, inability to make friends, and unsatisfactory school work. Although the mother in her application for Peter's acceptance by the Clinic had added information regarding other difficulties, such as the boy's conflicts with herself, his temper tantrums, and feminine mannerisms, we were alerted from the beginning to the likelihood of her being ambivalent in evaluating the seriousness of Peter's difficulties and his need for clinical help. Already in the second intake interview, Mrs. S. showed this ambivalence by reporting that things had greatly changed for the better since she had seen the worker. Peter suddenly had more friends. For the first time she had found it possible to have a calm discussion with

[1] See pp. 35–67.

her husband about their marital difficulties. They had recognized how both of them contributed to their frictions through their internal conflicts and shortcomings. They had discussed Peter's difficulties, and Mr. S. had expressed the belief that Peter was a normal child who, if his parents could manage to get along, would probably fall in line with the spirit of the home and show improvement. When the intake worker, sensing the mother's ambivalence, asked her how she accounted for this sudden change, Mrs. S. replied that after her conversation with the worker she seemed to have found "an approach" to her husband. To the worker's question whether perhaps she would want to try for a while to work on this approach, Mrs. S. replied that she was thinking about this possibility. Remembering, however, that she herself had had childhood difficulties similar to those of Peter, she was inclined to think that it would have been good for her to have had treatment then. For this reason she thought that Peter needed treatment now. She "knew" that her husband would approve of it although he had some questions about it.

Further confirmation of the mother's ambivalence came to us from the staff of the Neighborhood Center. From their report, we learned that Mrs. S. had been seen twice by the worker at the Center and a third time by the worker together with the head of the Center. In these conferences the mother had stated that she was not interested in a referral for Peter. She had been receiving guidance from a professional person who also happened to be a personal friend. That person had been of the opinion that Peter would outgrow his difficulties. The Center's staff had gained the impression that although the mother had some awareness of Peter's difficulties, she was not ready to turn to a source of help other than the friend and counselor whose opinion she had stated. When we received this report, however, we knew that the mother had accepted the suggestion of the Neighborhood Center to the degree of making an application, of maintaining her interest through our waiting period, and of being able to involve herself in the intake process. This suggested another area of ambivalence. It suggested that the mother was not only ambivalent in her appraisal of Peter's difficulties, but also in her attitude toward the guidance which she had received from her counselor.

With regard to the latter, the intake worker learned that she was a nonmedical therapist in private practice and that both Mr. S. and Mrs. S. had received psychotherapy from her. Mrs. S. had been in treatment for one year and Mr. S. for two years. Mrs. S. felt that this therapeutic experience had helped somewhat in her handling of herself and of her children but that the therapist had not been successful with the husband. After the case was assigned to one of our seminar members for treatment, we learned further that while the mother's termination of contact with the therapist had been complete, her husband had retained some contact with her. He went to her or telephoned her on occasions when he felt a need for guidance, particularly with regard to his handling of Peter. We also learned that Mr. S. used this continued contact to bolster his position in conflicts with his wife. On such occasions he stated repeatedly to Mrs. S. that the therapist agreed with him.

The early contacts with Mrs. S. revealed still another area of ambivalence. In the first interview she had already shown a tendency to talk more about her marital difficulties than about Peter's developmental difficulties. As her contacts with the Clinic continued she showed that although this self-concern was undoubtedly related to her own emotional discomforts, it reflected also the position of her former therapist that the essential cause of Peter's difficulties was to be found in the intrapersonal and marital conflicts of his parents. Apparently that interpretation had considerable meaning for Mrs. S. She was worried that Peter needed help because he was "insane" or "abnormal." The private therapist's opinion that Peter did not need direct help if his parents could achieve a resolution of their own conflicts aided Mrs. S. in defending herself against this anxiety. It also permitted her to give priority to her own personal need and wish for further therapeutic help. On the other hand, this opinion of the therapist and the use which Mrs.

S. made of it did not block completely her recognition that Peter needed professional help.

Mrs. S.'s anxiety about the meaning of psychotherapy for Peter showed itself also in the difficulties which she encountered in preparing the boy for the Clinic contact. When the intake worker asked her whether Peter had been told about coming to the Clinic, Mrs. S. reported that this had been done. She had told him that he was to go to a place where he would be given a mental test to show what his special abilities were. Peter had been quite interested in having such a test. To the worker's question, why she had presented the Clinic contact in this way, Mrs. S. brought out her fear of confronting the boy with the "truth." She was afraid he might think that he was "insane" or "abnormal."

RESTRUCTURING THE SITUATION WITH THE MOTHER

From the first contacts with the mother we received, thus, the following impressions about the need for a restructuring of the situation. Persons of importance in the life sphere of the child apparently were the parents and their former therapist. The mother was much concerned about the implication of Peter's receiving psychotherapy. It implied to her that her own anxiety regarding the nature of the child's difficulties was well founded—that Peter was abnormal. In her defense against this anxiety she was tempted to be swayed by the opinion of her former therapist that Peter's difficulties were "only" reactions to the conflicts and difficulties of his parents. Furthermore, by accepting the position that this was so she stood to gain justification of her own desire to go into further treatment for herself. On the other hand, she felt that the therapist had sided with her husband when they both had been in therapy and still sided with him. If she accepted the opinion of the therapist and her husband that Peter did not need clinical help, she yielded, in her judgment, to that of two persons whom she had come to experience as antagonists. Worse than that, her attempt to score emotionally against her husband through a belief that she had received definite help from the therapist while her husband had not, was jeopardized. Accepting the view of the therapist that she as well as her husband would have to resolve their difficulties in order to help Peter and that this was all that was necessary, meant that she had been helped as little as her husband and that in this sense she had not made good and had not gained a competitive victory over her husband.

It appeared necessary, therefore, first of all, to aid the mother in freeing herself from the immobilizing impact of her ambivalence by helping her see that Peter's involvement in therapy was not to be visualized as an alternative to her own. An occasion for doing so arose in the first interview following the assignment of the case for treatment. After our worker had introduced herself the mother started the discussion by saying that she actually did not know whether she wanted more help for herself or for the boy. As she had mentioned to the intake worker, she felt that Peter had improved a lot. She herself, however, suffered from insomnia. On the other hand, she said she knew that the Clinic was concerned primarily with child guidance work and she would try to concentrate on Peter. The worker confirmed the mother's statement, but mentioned that often things might come up about which Mrs. S. herself was troubled and that she should feel free to talk about them. The worker then proceeded to support this intellectual communication by sympathetically listening to the mother's personal and marital complaints. Thus, she provided her with a chance of testing emotionally the intellectual reassurance which had been given to her. Toward the end of the interview the worker decided to give Mrs. S. another chance of gaining some clarity as to the nature of therapy for Peter. She raised the question of how the mother felt about having the boy come to the Clinic, since she had mentioned his improvement. Mrs. S. answered that she still questioned it somewhat and still felt that it was perhaps she who was more in need of help. The worker did not dispute this and expressed readiness to discuss further the mother's wish for personal help. She pointed out, however, her own professional thinking that Peter had shown some difficulties in his adjustment and reviewed them with the mother. She also drew her attention to the fact that according to the mother's own statement some of these difficulties still persisted. Mrs. S. agreed to this and thought that we should start therapy. To the worker's wish to see the father and get in touch with the therapist before seeing Peter, however, Mrs. S. was unresponsive. She said she herself wanted to discuss this with Mr. S. first to learn what his attitude was now. She did not have the address of the therapist and would give it to the worker at the next interview.

There ensued a number of contacts with Mrs. S. which showed that she was still caught between a feeling that she would admit failure as a mother, if Peter did not need therapy, and a feeling that his condition was very serious, if he did. The first-mentioned feeling seemed strengthened by the implication that she also had not been helped by the therapeutic experiences of the past any more than had her husband, if she still needed further help in order to improve the growth conditions for Peter. In order to help the mother further in her own struggle to free herself from the impact of contradictory thoughts and feelings, the worker repeated to her our clinical judgment regarding Peter's need for therapy but stressed the positive impact of therapy upon the future development of children. In other words, she emphasized the preventive aspects of therapy.

She also clarified with Mrs. S. the nature of the Clinic's work with mothers. She explained that we see mothers in relation to the therapy which their children receive and that often mothers are helped in some of their personal difficulties in this process. However, she and Mrs. S. could evaluate at a later time whether this was sufficient for her or whether she wanted to engage in independent therapy with somebody outside in addition to coming to the Clinic on behalf of the boy and herself.

Finally, the worker tried to aid the mother in liberating her concern for Peter's need for treatment from its implication of being a conflict issue between her on one side and her husband, as well as her former therapist on the other. In order to do this she repeated in her talks with the mother her interest in getting in touch with the father and the therapist. She made it clear, however, that this was done in order to achieve a pooling of judgments and a coordination of these judgments rather than to attempt to gather information for the decision of a conflict. She stressed particularly that she was interested in the opinion of *both* parents as an expression of a common concern rather than as an expression of a conflict. The mother responded to these efforts by giving her consent to the worker's getting in touch with the therapist and expressing the thought that the worker should consult with her husband, because she could not work against him.

RESTRUCTURING THE SITUATION WITH THE PARENTS' THERAPIST

An attempt to establish contact with Mr. S., however, seemed at first almost hopeless. A letter offering him an appointment for a day which his wife had indicated as the most appropriate one in the light of his office duties produced no result. Mrs. S. telephoned and told the worker that Mr. S. would not come in for the appointment because he had no time and also because he did not want to have anything to do "with the whole thing." Mrs. S. further reported that her husband had been more favorably inclined at first but then had changed his mind. She said that only their former therapist could sway her husband's opinion and asked whether the worker had been able to get in touch with her. Since apparently both parents used the therapist's opinion for an alleviation of their own anxieties rather than for a rational decision in the interest of the child, it seemed essential to clarify the difference between our approach and the approach of the therapist with the latter. The worker, therefore, when she got in touch with the therapist did not confine herself to receiving statements from her as collateral information given to us as a matter of professional courtesy but engaged her in a professional discussion.

The therapist talked at length about the influence of Peter's parents upon the boy. She dwelt, particularly, on the mother's difficulties and felt that Mrs. S. often overrated or underrated the child's behavior whenever he entered a new developmental phase. In her contacts with the mother, she had gained the impression that Peter in many instances which had given his mother concern had expressed completely normal growth. It was her opinion that the parents were in such conflict themselves that it would be impossible for them to permit the child to receive help from another person.

In the course of the ensuing discussion our worker helped the therapist review her position in the light of the information and clinical impressions of another professional person. She presented her with a new frame of reference for an evaluation of the concerns which Mrs. S. had expressed about Peter. Admitting that Mrs. S. might have on occasions exaggerated or underestimated the behavior of the boy, our worker pointed out that it was not only the mother who was concerned; that Peter had elicited similar concern in the Neighborhood Center. She also drew attention to the fact that Peter had fears and definite difficulties in social adjustment which in our judgment suggested pathology. Under the stimulus of this point of view expressed by the worker, the therapist clarified her own to the effect that she had never felt Peter was not in need of help and could not benefit by treatment. She felt, however, that the parents, because of their own involvement in the child's difficulties, could not permit Peter to get such help on a consistent basis. She stressed that on her part there was definitely no opposition to such help but only apprehension regarding the reactions of the parents to Peter's involvement in therapy. In that connection, she again referred to Mrs. S. and voiced her impression that Mrs. S. one day appeared willing to take over all responsibility and the next day to avoid it completely.

Since the therapist put so much weight on the personality of the mother in her assessment of the difficulties in the situation, the worker asked about the father, who at that time had not yet responded to our invitation. The therapist said that the father still sought her guidance and described him as an extremely brilliant man. Since she continued to describe him as more understanding and more mature than Mrs. S., our worker asked the therapist whether there were only positive elements in the relationship between Mr. S. and Peter. In reply to this the therapist again was able to clarify her position by saying that this relationship was affected by a great deal of anxiety on the part of Mr. S. and elaborated on this statement by giving examples drawn from her own contacts with the father. In the course of this elaboration, she furnished very meaningful information about Mr. S. She thought that he was aware of some of Peter's difficulties but was so threatened by them that he could not face the boy's need for help. She thought it possible that this was the reason Mr. S. had told his wife the therapist agreed with him that Peter did not need therapy. However, she had never said so. In the end, the therapist stated that she could see some positive aspects in our effort to help Peter through therapy now. She did not know whether Mr. S. would get in contact with her again. If he did, she would discuss with him the advisability of therapeutic help for Peter. She reaffirmed, however, her thinking that even if the parents should accept the idea of Peter's getting treatment now, there would be a great deal of inconsistency with regard to their support of the idea afterward.

Thus, we had prepared the mother for a new intellectual and emotional evaluation of Peter's as well as of her own need for therapy. We also felt that we had achieved some clarification of the situation with the therapist as well as some basis for expecting a measure of cooperation from her. Still, it seemed essential to restructure the situation with the father directly and a new effort was made in that respect.

The worker shifted, however, her original approach from addressing Mr. S. as such to an approach addressing both parents together. She wrote them a letter in which she referred to *their* questions about bringing Peter to the agency and offered *them* another appointment to discuss the situation once more. She mentioned also that she would appreciate *their* letting her know not later than within two weeks whether they were interested in the Clinic's services or not. By doing so the worker set up a situation in which the parents had to decide either to cooperate with the Clinic's plan for help or to take the problem elsewhere.

One day before the expiration of this two-week period the worker received a call from Mrs. S. In the morning her husband had mentioned that he still had our letter. He had expressed the thought that perhaps they should go ahead with treatment for Peter, since he realized we had a long waiting list. If they decided not to go on with the Clinic contact now, it might be a long time before they would be in line for help again, in case they should want it later. The worker expressed her willingness to discuss the situation again; Mrs. S. readily accepted an appointment for herself and told the worker that Mr. S. would also like one.

In the interview with Mrs. S. it became apparent that our emphasis on providing her with a new frame of reference had been helpful to her. In the discussion of her husband's coming in, she saw no objection to his being seen by the worker in spite of the fact that she previously expressed regret over the fact that they both had tried to receive help from the same therapist. She felt that it was different now since our concern was basically a concern for their child. Apparently, she had come to accept our definition of the situation that Peter's problems and help with them were not to be seen as a conflict issue, but as a problem concerning both parents and requiring their concerted efforts for a solution.

Apart from the contribution which this change in the mother's frame of reference made to the therapeutic milieu in our specific case, it might be worth noting here again how a child welfare definition of an agency's function may facilitate an approach also to personal problems of parents which in another frame of reference might prove less accessible. The implications for the greater ease with which on that basis an assignment of spouses to different therapists may be avoided also deserves emphasis.

With regard to the mother's paralyzing anxiety that Peter's need for treatment might mean that he was a very seriously disturbed child, Mrs. S. showed significant although only limited gain from our efforts to help her in a redefinition of this aspect of the situation. She once more expressed the thought that only very seriously disturbed children came to the Clinic. To the worker's remark that this apparently meant to her the great seriousness of Peter's difficulties, Mrs. S. smiled. She stated that she had discussed just this with her husband. She had suggested to him that if Peter was not seriously disturbed it might be well for him to come to the Clinic for help as a preventive step. If he was, why not face it rather than avoid the issue. She expressed, however, her own feeling that Peter was not seriously sick and said that her husband shared this feeling. Apparently, the worker's emphasis on the preventive effects of psychotherapy for children had not alleviated her anxieties completely but had made it more possible for her to consider treatment from that angle.

RESTRUCTURING THE SITUATION WITH THE FATHER

When Mr. S. finally came in, he said that he had taken time off from work in order to talk to the worker. The latter responded to this intimation of the importance which the father attached to the interview by saying that she was glad to have an opportunity of discussing with him the whole situation since she realized he had some questions. She thus established an open agreement with the father as to the purpose and weight of this discussion. Mr. S. then proceeded to raise a number of concerns which revealed to what degree a favorable restructuring of the situation required that he also be aided in gaining a new frame of reference.

The father mentioned that, of course, he was considerably influenced by his former therapist. He wondered whether she was not correct in thinking that only severely disturbed children needed individual therapy. He also was worried because of the therapist's impression that as a result of Clinic contacts children often became more anxious than they had been before. Finally, he wondered whether psychotherapy did not alienate children from their parents. He said that the therapist herself had said that this was frequently the case and therefore only adolescents should be given this type of help; it fitted into their separation needs.

From this elaboration it became apparent that also the father's own anxieties about the severity of Peter's difficulties and about his own relationship to the boy had been held in check by the therapist's opposition to psychotherapy for Peter. If Peter was not in need of therapy, he was not seriously sick. If he did not need a therapeutic relationship with a professional person, his closeness to his father was not endangered. Actually, the father's concern about the child's becoming more anxious in therapy than he had been before constituted a projection of the father's own difficulties on Peter. Since at that time, of course, we had not arrived at a diagnosis of the father's difficulties, the dynamic nature of this specific concern was not yet accessible to us. However, it was clear that this was another concern area which might have motivated the father in withholding his permission for psychotherapy for Peter.

Furthermore, the father corroborated an impression which we had gained already from statements of the mother. He used the therapist's position to indicate to his wife that she had failed and was still failing to function satisfactorily as a mother. Thus, it seemed that the parents had used their overt disagreement over the soundness of the therapist's opinion as a weapon in their marital battle.

In the discussion of the father's questions, it appeared that the worker's efforts to provide Mrs. S. with a new frame of reference actually had produced a long-distance effect. Mr. S. himself answered his own question whether treatment for Peter would not mean that he was severely disturbed by saying that he had discussed this with his wife and, like her, was inclined to see this proposition more from a preventive angle. He realized, however, that the boy currently had some difficulties which required attention.

When the father referred to his former therapist's feeling that psychotherapy made children more anxious than they had been before, the worker said she was not sufficiently familiar with the experiences on which this opinion was based. She made it clear, however, that the work of the Clinic was based on its belief of helping children through psychotherapy. A child in the beginning of contact sometimes might become a little frightened, but this depended on the individual situation. Mr. S. smiled and remarked that actually this was so not only with children but also with grownup persons. Apparently he used a recall of his personal experiences in therapy here in the attempt to reformulate for himself his original thinking about what therapy would mean for Peter.

With regard to Mr. S.'s apprehension that therapy might alienate a child from his parents, however, the worker had to be more specific. She clarified with Mr. S. that our aim was to improve the relations between a child and his parents and not, as he apparently seemed to feel, to take the child away from his parents or to take over. The worker continued, however, by explaining that in order to help a child improve his relationships with his parents it was often necessary to have the child develop a certain attachment for the worker. Such an attachment made it possible for the child to speak to the therapist with confidence. Also, a child might be better able to tell things that were on his mind to an outsider than to his parents who are too much involved. After having listened to this clarification Mr. S. claimed that this was the aspect of therapy which appealed to him most. He realized that he and his wife unfortunately involved Peter in their own fights and forced upon him a conflict of loyalties. In talking to an outsider, he would have, therefore, a much better chance to work out these conflicts.

After a pause he expressed a certain amount of bewilderment. As he had mentioned before, he believed in his former therapist who had always stressed that it was only he and his wife who needed help. And here he found himself listening to our point of view that the child as well as the parents needed treatment. It was hard to say who was right and who was wrong. At this point, the worker, sensing the danger of accepting the father's wish for a conflict decision rather than a conflict resolution, pointed out that this was not a question of right or wrong but a question of different approaches. Different workers, different psychiatrists, and different therapists came from different schools of thought. It was essential not to decide which approach was right but to clarify which approach had more appeal for him. Mr. S. felt this definition of the situation to be more helpful than the way it had been presented to him by his wife, who had taken the position that their therapist was wrong. He felt now that he wanted to go along with us. He, as well as his wife, was very willing to cooperate with us and he would like to be seen by the worker himself at least occasionally during our work with Peter.

RESTRUCTURING THE SITUATION WITH PETER

Our restructuring of the situation for the parents and their former therapist had made considerable progress, but there was still Peter himself. He also had to have an appropriate frame of reference. It will be recalled that during the intake period, his mother had not been ready to give him a truthful explanation. She had resorted to a pretext of representing our work as a kind of special capacities test. In the course of our efforts to help her gain a more appropriate frame of reference, she had, however, progressively worked on an improvement of the explanations which she gave the child in order to prepare him for his first visit. Once, after a night during which he had been disturbed by a nightmare, she had told him that our workers were people who helped children free themselves from such sleep disturbances. However, this compromise between her wish to conceal from Peter the nature of our work and her wish to prepare him meaningfully for it was not good enough. When Peter had had a few nights of restful sleep, he told Mrs. S. that after all he had nightmares so infrequently that he did not need help for them. Finally, the mother found a more meaningful connection between Peter's own awareness of his discomforts and the proposition of having him go to the Clinic. One day, shortly before the first interview of Mr. S. Peter complained, as he often had, that he had no friends. Mrs. S., obviously under the impact of her own increased clarification as to the meaning of our therapeutic work, took this opportunity to tell Peter that maybe he could get help for this discomfort just as people got help for physical discomforts when they were sick and that he could go to the Clinic for that reason. Although a little hesitant about it, Peter seemed able to accept this. Actually after the parents had reached their decision to have him come in, he offered no further objection. When in his first interview the worker asked him whether he knew about "this place," he said in a quite grownup fashion that he knew people came to the Clinic to talk about their troubles and worries. To the worker's affirmative nod, he responded by beginning to talk about his own.

CONCEPTUALIZATIONS

This account of the preparation of Peter's case has been presented to show that therapeutic work here required a restructuring of the situation for all persons involved in this constellation. Peter, his father, his mother, and the therapist all needed a frame of reference which would permit them to cooperate with the efforts of the Clinic, or at least permit them to abandon their opposition. This required an intellectual and emotional experience for these persons which could be conceptualized as an *alignment of perception.* The method by which we achieved this in turn could be conceptualized as an *orchestration of preparatory work* with the individuals concerned.

In these orchestrating efforts the worker was able to help all the persons involved to revise somewhat the viewpoints which they had formerly held and to revise them in such a way that they approximated one another's. This aid was provided step by step as the individual contacts were made and the specific thoughts and feelings of the persons involved became accessible to our understanding. The essential point on which all of them finally agreed was Peter's need for direct help.

Furthermore, the parents had been aided in seeing help with their own problems not as an alternative to direct help for Peter but as related to it. The scene was thus set for family therapy on the level of child welfare concern.

V. The Case of Edward N.

PRESENTING SYMPTOMS

EDWARD'S MOTHER WAS REFERRED to the Child Guidance Institute by a psychologist.[1] He was an only child, described as destructive at home and aggressive to other children. He pulled at their genitals, threw rocks at girls, and pulled boys off bicycles. At other times he showed completely withdrawn behavior. As a result of these difficulties in relating to other children, he had no friends. He was also aggressive to his mother who, the psychologist reported, was overprotective toward the boy. At the age of eight he had facial tics. There was an indefinite history of respiratory allergies, apparently accentuated at four years of age. He also complained frequently of abdominal distress. The family background showed a history of asthma in a maternal aunt. In the father's opinion, the boy was infantile, secretive, and had temper outbursts. The mother feared the boy's sexual interests. She worried lest he be "abnormal" like herself or a maternal aunt who had undergone psychiatric treatment.

Edward's health history revealed infantile colic, pneumonia at fifteen weeks, two and one-half years, and at three and one-half years, with frequent respiratory discomfort, eventually developing into known allergy at about the age of four. At six he had an ear infection with hearing difficulties, relieved by adenoidectomy. At nine, just before direct therapy, he devel-

[1] This case has been discussed by Dr. Maurice R. Friend and the author of this report in a paper entitled "Psychosocial Aspects in the Preparation for Treatment of an Allergic Child," *American Journal of Orthopsychiatry*, vol. 24, January, 1954, pp. 63–70. As far as the context of this report permits, the presentation here follows closely that publication. Appreciation is expressed to the Editor of the *Journal* for permission to reprint significant passages.

oped a fourth attack of pneumonia. A number of medical specialists had been involved by consultation, and a general practitioner occupied the foremost role in caring for the boy's allergies, as well as advising the mother on matters of child-rearing.

The mother suffered from recurrent depressions with obsessional thoughts and anxieties throughout her life history. An exacerbation of her depressions had occurred during and subsequent to her pregnancy, a further increase at the time of her menopause, which was prior to treatment at the Clinic. She had seen a psychiatrist twice during her postpartum depression, but had reacted with great apprehension and resisted psychiatric help for herself. She was the youngest of a large family, brought to the United States at the age of fifteen by an elder brother. She relied on the oldest sister in a very dependent way. As a child, she had been exposed to the rages of her father, and her pattern had been to withdraw from these scenes. The maternal grandmother was described as a frail, sweet-tempered woman who had tried to protect her daughters from the outbursts of their father by keeping them out of his way as much as possible.

Edward's father, an engineer, appeared to be more composed, and handled his wife's depressive moods with extreme patience. This served to increase guilt feelings and perpetuate her lack of effective effort. He recognized the difficulty of the mother-child relationship, was concerned about Edward's social adjustment and emotional attitudes, but had never taken any initiative in seeking professional help for the mother's difficulties. The contacts which the mother had attempted to make in this direction had been initiated by herself.

For many years it had been the stated policy of the Child Guidance Institute of the Jewish Board of Guardians not to accept children for psychotherapy whose psychosomatic conditions were so severe that ambulatory medical treatment had to go on apace with psychotherapy. It was felt that such cases would best be served in hospital clinics where total treatment, providing close cooperation between the departments of psychiatry and those representing other medical specialties could be given to the patients. However, the appearance of severe emotional disturbance in the mother-child relationship, which the social work therapist readily perceives as important, plus the pressure of the initial referral source, plus the wishes of the medical practitioner himself, lead frequently to a decision for exploration in our Clinic. In many instances, this leads to dramatic supportive help, despite questions as to the effectiveness of the use of our time and personnel. In the case of Edward, these pressures had also exerted themselves.

AMBIVALENCE OF MOTHER

The mother was offered an interview shortly after application, but she was already away on summer vacation with her son. Intake was completed in the fall, and there then ensued another wait considerably longer than the first one because an assignment to a therapist could not be made. Throughout this time the mother, while ambivalent and depressed, had telephoned the Clinic on occasions and indicated her wish to keep the application open. When we informed her that we could offer a therapist, she reported that Edward had facial twitching and had suffered another siege of pneumonia which curtailed his summer vacation. The boy had responded well to a brief separation in the hospital, but had suffered recurrent colds thereafter. The mother realized that there was definite correlation between her own symptomatology and the boy's demanding behavior with her. Medical treatment consisted of periodic hypodermic injection of nonspecific vaccine to clear up his infectious bronchitis. The family physician had advised her not to send the boy to school because of his debilitated condition and had expressed also the opinion that Edward would not be ready to receive psychotherapy for four more months. The mother did not want the Clinic to close the case, however, and asked the worker to give her a month to decide.

AMBIVALENCE OF THE INTAKE WORKER

The long delay from first application to a second intake reevaluation in this case was contrary to practice. It was in part related to the problems of the Clinic and in part to the disturbed mother-child relationship. The mother always left a tentative line of approach open, but at times used the physician-child relationship to sustain her own mixed feelings. This seems to be more characteristic of mothers whose children have allergic discomforts than of mothers whose children show other types of maladjustments. As far as the Clinic was concerned there also seemed to have existed ambivalence on the part of the intake worker as to whether this case should be accepted for treatment or not. Apparently the worker's conflict between our general policy not to accept psychosomatic cases in which ambulatory medical treatment has to go on simultaneously and the pressure to offer some help in this severely disturbed situation had remained unresolved. When the case came up for discussion in the project seminar, the uncertainty underlying the original decision to take on Edward's case for exploration had again to be solved. The seminar group expressed the idea that previous indecision of the intake staff regarding acceptability had itself now become a factor in the mother's own hostile reactions toward Edward.

After we had decided to take on the case for research purposes and contact with the mother was planfully established, Mrs. N. appeared depressed, anxious, and easily threatened. She gave much detail of Edward's illnesses, but was protective about his behavioral disturbances. Although she did not conceal the boy's destructiveness, she tried to see in it only a way of self-expression. Admitting that he also showed other difficulties in his behavior at home, she was inclined to present things as improving in that area. She stated her chief concern to be not Edward's behavior at home but his rejection by other children. She indicated a deep sense of brooding responsibility rather than love for Edward. She was deeply dependent upon her husband's patience and devotion to the family to prevent worsening of her depressive moods, serious obsessional thoughts, and her anxiety. She felt "heavy," slept excessively during the daytime, retiring into her bedroom from the family activities. At these times she ate excessively, and her brooding and irritability were more marked toward Edward.

AMBIVALENCE OF THE FAMILY PHYSICIAN

Initially, Mrs. N. saw the Child Guidance Institute as a place for help with Edward's behavioral problems, apart from the physical factors. This definition of the situation on her part appeared to be influenced by the family physician who apparently wanted Edward to come to the Clinic for treatment but thought that his coming for help would have to wait until his physical distress was considerably lessened. The general practitioner had previously resisted suggestions by specialists for testing gastrointestinal factors in the allergic condition. The mother's utilization of the family physician seemed to serve her own need to infantilize the child by excessive physical care, occasioning long school absences and curtailment of his social activities. In addition, she satisfied her own dependency needs by the authoritative, guiding figure of the physician. On the other hand, the worker gained the impression that the mother herself had some questions as to whether Edward's problems could be strictly divided into physical and behavioral problems and whether his physical difficulties were not in part the result of his emotional difficulties.

At any rate, the mother's dependency on the judgment of the family physician required that considerable attention be paid to him in any attempt to establish a common frame of reference among *all* persons involved in the situation. The next problem on which the seminar discussion focused, therefore, was that of consulting the family physician. The values of such a contact were seen in his ability to clarify fully the medical history of the child and to help the mother cooperate in providing psychotherapy for the boy. It was agreed that the physician seemed to be a person of power in the situation. On the negative side, it was mentioned that the schedule of the doctor as well as that of the worker might prevent their getting together for a conference. The thought was also expressed that the mother might regard this contact as a criticism of her, with the result that her feelings of inadequacy and self-reproach might increase. In the discussion which ensued, the psychiatrist pointed out that it was dangerous to develop set attitudes against approaching another professional person. Such an attitude would in and by itself preclude any possibility of exploring potentially available opportunities of arriving at a common frame of reference in many situations. Doctors often had the notion that a physical condition should be cleared up first and that only afterward should a child receive psychotherapy. His opinion was that only an attempt to interchange experiences could offset this and particularly in this type of case.

Following seminar discussion, several interesting developments occurred. Instead of a possible heightening of the mother's feelings of inadequacy, the therapist's request to see the family doctor occasioned surprise and pleasure—proof of the therapist's interest in Edward. The mother also felt that it would be good for the doctor to gain an idea of the Clinic's treatment procedure inasmuch as he might then feel that it would not endanger Edward's physical status. In other words, the mother herself felt that the physician needed a new frame of reference within which to view the feasibility and potential of psychotherapy for Edward.

The doctor, finally reached by telephone after several unsuccessful calls, refused a conference. He could only talk over the telephone because of his lack of time. He said Edward had just had a really old-fashioned lobar pneumonia, and that his allergies had acted as a hindrance to his recovery. Psychotherapy should be postponed until February. He thought that Edward needed the Clinic's help for "environmental and behavorial reasons," and did not allow the therapist to explain the aims and nature of the psychotherapy. In our seminar discussions, it was felt that the physician by his advice to postpone therapy until February, a time when the boy's medical history indicated frequent recurrence of increased respiratory difficulties, might have revealed unconscious hostile trends toward psychotherapy.

AMBIVALENCE OF THE FATHER

Quite apart from our position that an integration of the concept of the family of orientation with psychodynamic concepts required contact with the father in principle, such a contact seemed particularly indicated in this situation. In some cases which we carried in our seminar, the correctness of our belief in the necessity of seeing the father was substantiated only after the contact had been established. In Edward's case, however, the need to make such a contact seemed to be factually determined before the worker even met Mr. N. First of all, there were the mother's serious condition of depression and the boy's physical distress which was likely to restrict the parental power of seeing his problems in their totality. There was further the doctor's attitude which would not be supportive. Finally, there were some remarks by the mother that Edward showed traits which reminded her of Mr. N. All these factors suggested that the father was a key figure in this situation and that without his support it was unlikely that we would be permitted to render meaningful services in this case. From the angle of preparing the case for treatment, it seemed imperative that we should find out what the father thought of the mother's depression, what he thought of the condition of the boy, how he viewed the position taken by the family physician, and what his ideas were regarding the treatment of his wife and son in the Clinic.

When the worker mentioned her interest in seeing Edward's father to Mrs. N., the latter accepted this without any trace of resistance and made an appointment for her husband. On the next day she confirmed the appointment by telephone. Mr. N., on his arrival, stated at first that he was on his way to his office and hard pressed for time. He could not stay more than five minutes. He said that he had come in only to tell us about his agreement with his wife that Edward should come to our Clinic for treatment. He was willing to give it a chance. His original attitude thus seemed to be one of submission to a proposition which he questioned and in which he did not see a reason for becoming personally involved. The worker, however, was able to convey to him our interest in his personal thinking so effectively that Mr. N. quickly changed his mind and decided to stay for a discussion of the situation. In the course of this discussion, he was helped by the worker to reveal his true concerns and in doing so showed how justified we were in assuming that his cooperation would require an effort of the Clinic to give him an appropriate frame of reference within which to view the potential of our service.

First of all, Mr. N. gave expression to the idea that he might have been under a misapprehension as to the nature of our service. He had had the impression that the Clinic was intended to help only mentally dull children. He felt, however, that Edward was a bright boy and had wondered whether—if this was so—our Clinic was the right place for his son. After the worker cleared up with Mr. N. this misconception and had freed him from his concern in this respect, Mr. N. gave vent to another concern. He felt that his wife could use psychiatric treatment but he did not think that Edward needed it. In his understanding, Edward's troubles were essentially "health problems" and they were improving. He felt that if Edward's organic discomforts were removed, the boy would not need psychotherapy. As Mr. N. elaborated this theme he became increasingly aware of the fact that his boy's difficulties were not confined to the organic area. He began to mention the conflicts between Edward and his mother, his difficulties in getting along with other children, and particularly his physical aggressiveness. This development of his own train of thought apparently led Mr. N. to question his original position that Edward needed help only in the physical area, because he concluded his description of the boy's difficulties by asking how our Clinic operated. In reply to this question the worker used directness similar to the procedure followed in the preceding case. She explained to Mr. N. our efforts to build up a positive relationship between a child and his worker, our methods of gaining access to his ideas and problems by play and discussion, and of coming to agreement with the child about the purpose of his therapy in terms which the child can understand and use. Finally, she clarified with Mr. N. the nature of the emotional learning and un-learning which children experience in therapy.

After having established a common frame of reference with the father along these lines, the worker engaged him in a discussion of Edward's history of physical difficulties in the course of which the father himself broached the topic of the attitude of the family physician toward Edward's treatment. Mr. N. seemed to appreciate the physician's concern for Edward's physical condition but showed signs of an increasing readiness to separate himself from the doctor's judgment. He felt there might be some reality in the doctor's wish to see psychotherapy for Edward postponed until he had built up his physical condition after his last bout with pneumonia. Mr. N. thought, however, that the boy had been well now for six weeks and that probably he had recovered sufficiently to start coming without further delay. When the worker suggested that she would want to discuss this again with the mother and the doctor, the father remarked that the physician was too busy to pay much attention to Edward beyond that required for giving him his injections. He thought it unlikely that the doctor would be able to tell the worker much about the boy's problems for that reason. With regard to his wife, he felt definitely that treatment at the Clinic would be helpful to her. Maybe she could find here some release from the emotional tension which made her so irritable at home and in turn affected the boy.

Toward the end of the interview, Mr. N. summed up the experience of his discussion with the worker by saying that at first he had not been convinced of the soundness of the idea of therapy for Edward. Now, however, and particularly in view of what the worker had told him about the type of child who received help here, he was in favor of Edward's coming to the Clinic for psychotherapy.

PLANNING A RESTRUCTURING OF THE SITUATION

When we reviewed our attempts at preparing this case for treatment up to this point, it became clear in our seminar discussions that again we had encountered extrafamilial as well as familial factors. Our identification of interpersonal relationships within the family of orientation, our appraisal of the relationships between the family physician and the parents, and our consideration of the physical manifestations of Edward's problems had suggested that three main factors in the situation had been dealt with so far.

The dependency needs of the mother which we had come to recognize in her use of the authoritarian attitude of the physician, in her beginning contacts with the worker, and in her relationship with her husband suggested that Mrs. N.'s narcissistic demands on the worker's patience and acceptance would be extreme. We had come to the decision, however, that these demands would have to be met if a positive relationship between Mrs. N. and the worker was to be established, and the existing pressures in the mother-child relationship were to be eased.

The father's misconception of therapy for the boy had been clarified. Since he had thought that therapy was only for dull children and since Edward was obviously bright, it was apparent that it was chiefly his concern for his wife's depression that had led him even to consider psychotherapy for the boy. The clarification of a more appropriate frame of reference for Mr. N., therefore, was of great importance. Without it, he might easily have become a silent antagonist with a truly masochistic participation until his wife was helped. With clarification, however, the father had seemed to lend support to the idea of psychotherapy for Edward—for Edward's sake. Secondly, he had also shown a measure of independence from the judgment of the family physician with regard to the start of this type of help for the boy.

Establishing a contact with the family doctor, while not assuring cooperation, was of great value to the family attitude and to our planning. Interestingly enough, the negative character of the contact with the family physician proved to be one of the cornerstones of our plan. It is tempting in our cultural value system to expect that a contact between representatives of two different professional disciplines will produce teamwork. When this cultural expectation is not fulfilled, the contact is considered as having resulted in failure. In therapeutic situations such a failure is then considered as an obstacle to treatment. This tendency to view open conflict as essentially negative may well lead to a certain avoidance tendency on the part of psychotherapists with regard to organically oriented physicians. Our experience in this case suggested, however, that a negative outcome of an attempt to establish a common frame of reference with a family physician and failure to enlist his cooperation can also be turned into constructive channels. Only the actual contact and the worker's personal experience of the attitude of the doctor toward psychotherapy gave an opportunity for a full appraisal of the force with which we had to deal in this physician. The comprehension of this force made it clear to us that we were faced with an impossibility of psychotherapy for Edward as long as the doctor's opposition maintained its dynamic power within the field of social realities in which we had to operate.

It had been clarified that an alignment of perception among *all* the persons who composed this field of forces was impossible. In order to provide a therapeutic milieu, this field of forces, therefore, had to be restructured in terms of a different composition rather than in terms of a different frame of reference for the persons who composed it originally. A beginning in that direction had been made by helping the father to visualize psychotherapy for Edward without complete dependence on the approval of the general practitioner. The mother, however, was not yet ready to view the situation independent of the physician's judgment. We felt, however, that the authoritative and magical meaning with which Mrs. N. had vested his opinion could be discussed by her and the therapist with a chance of developing some independence of judgment also on the mother's part. This required, of course, that the relationship between the mother and the worker be given a chance to develop. In consequence, we decided to initiate treatment first with the mother, emphasizing, however, from the start that this was done on the basis of her child's difficulties and with a view of working toward an improvement also of the latter.

The mother's treatment initially continued to reveal more

and more her deep dependency needs and the relationship with the worker provided great satisfaction of the needs on the basis of a "good mother" transference. Mrs. N. became less depressed after confiding to the worker her severe emotional difficulties of rage, overeating, and oversleeping. She recognized her infantilization of the boy, her concerns about his sexual interests, and her fears of his sadistic nature. She related her own family relationships, appreciated her resentment against her sister who had occupied an ambivalent mother role with her, and she was able to secure work as a professional person. This had coincided with the oft-expressed reassuring wish of her husband that when Edward would become older she would be able to spend less time with him. After four months of interviews, she was able to bring the boy in for treatment.

VI. The Case of Margaret R.

PRESENTING SYMPTOMS AND FAMILY COMPOSITION

MARGARET, a twelve-and-a-half-year-old girl was referred to the Clinic by one of her sisters, Mrs. Sarah B., on the suggestion of the school. The referral had been suggested because Margaret did poorly in school, seemed shy and withdrawn in the classroom, and was very much overweight.

Information from the school revealed that Margaret's mother had been killed by a man who had attacked her on the street. This had occurred three and one-half years before the referral. The family had expressed concern over the fact that Margaret had shown no reaction of sorrow at the time of her mother's death. The home situation in which Margaret lived was complex. The household consisted of her father, Mr. R., her married sister, Sarah, Mrs. B., the husband of the latter, Mr. B., a grownup unmarried sister, Alice, the four-year-old son of the B.'s, Alfred, and Margaret herself. The three sisters were very much separated by age. Sarah was twenty years and Alice was ten years older than Margaret. Offhand there appeared a nuclear conjugal family consisting of Sarah, her husband, and her son, attached to the remnant group of Mr. R.'s family, which had been broken through the death of his wife. Between these two family groups, Mrs. B. formed the connecting link. In their combination in one household the two groups formed Margaret's family of orientation.

In contact with Margaret herself, her father, and her two sisters, the worker gained the following additional information. The family complained that Margaret was slow, lazy, and uninterested in her personal appearance. She was lax in doing chores around the household and had to be told to do them over and over again. She refused to bathe unless pressure was brought to bear upon her, although she was diurnally enuretic and had a strong body odor because of this condition. Frequently when asked to do something at home, she went into temper tantrums, yelling and using vile language. Most of these conflicts occurred between her and her sister, Sarah, who had assumed the mother role. Margaret was a voracious eater and frequently raided the icebox, much to the concern of her sisters, who felt that she was old enough to exert some self-control. She also used sweets in an attempt to buy the friendship of her schoolmates. According to Alice, with whom she shared a room, Margaret was a restless sleeper, turning and tossing all night long, and suffering from frequent nightmares.

Margaret herself told the worker that it was difficult for her to fall asleep because she had "scary thoughts." She was afraid a burglar might enter the house, or she might die in her sleep. These fears had beset her ever since her mother's death. She was afraid that she might have to undergo surgery because of pains in her feet. Although she had shown no reaction of distress when her mother had died, she confided to the worker the thought that when she came of age, she, Margaret, would have to decide the fate of her mother's killer, who had been given a prison sentence of twenty years. At the age of twenty-one, she would have to decide whether he was going to live or die. Margaret also had some fears about the consequences of her raids on the icebox and told a story about a man having been killed by his wife with an ice pick for raiding the icebox.

In this case it did not seem possible to follow the procedure of formulating clinical, genetic, and dynamic diagnoses of all, or even of a selected number of family members as building blocks for a family diagnosis. The complexity of the household membership itself militated against this. Furthermore, the attitudes of the various family members were equally inauspicious in this respect. Mr. R., a craftsman by trade, saw his father function basically in terms of providing economically for the support of Margaret. After his wife's death he had left the girl's upbringing to her sisters, especially Mrs. B. Although he, too, was concerned about the child's lack of overt sorrow over the death of her mother, he saw no great problem in the other difficulties and felt that she would outgrow them. He was willing, however, to have her treated by the Clinic because he felt that this was something which Margaret's sisters wanted for her. Any thought of self-involvement seemed so foreign to him that the worker did not feel that she should even make an attempt to help the father in that respect. The sisters, on the other hand, presented a substitute-mother group, which in itself made it difficult to focus upon one or the other as the "maternal figure" in Margaret's life. It was true that Mrs. B. had assumed the mother role and that she wanted to be regarded by Margaret as a mother person. However, Mrs. B. was not clear enough in her identification with this role to accept self-involvement in the Clinic contact from the start. Mr. B. could not be involved because his wife withheld from him even the fact that Margaret was treated at the Clinic for a considerable time. It was only toward the end of Margaret's treatment that contact with him was established. Although somewhat competitive with Sarah in regard to the performance of the mother function toward Margaret in the beginning of the contact, Alice did not feel close enough to see any need for becoming part of the diagnostic or therapeutic nexus.

FRAMEWORK OF DIAGNOSTIC STUDY

We decided, therefore, to concentrate on Margaret herself, to keep perceptual awareness of the potential importance of including other family members in our diagnostic and therapeutic planning, and to attempt a family diagnosis in a theoretical framework which would not require individual diagnoses of the other family members. We were able to achieve the latter by using the concept of social roles instead of the concept of social interaction. By doing so we experimented with an interesting shift in conceptual and practical emphasis. From the point of view of the clinician the sociological concept of social interaction is a very congenial bridge to an understanding of pluralities of people. Designating "the reciprocal interplay of personalities within a given environment,"[1] it deals directly with the material essential to diagnostic and therapeutic planning, namely, with phenomena of personality formation, personality maintenance, and personality deterioration. Through Sullivan's work it has perhaps found its most highly articulated use in psychiatric practice.[2] In complex cases, however, it is likely to overtax the clinician because it requires an extension of his diagnostic and therapeutic thinking from two individuals to a number which is too large to handle. It multiplies his task in terms of basic personality studies and then superimposes upon this additive work the burden of integrating the individual diagnoses with one another. On the other hand, the concept of social roles and the theory of role analysis to which we resorted in this case is more foreign to the traditional thinking of the clinician, but is likely to facilitate his task of providing the information necessary for the formulation of a family diagnosis in complex social situations. The concept of social role has been defined as a pattern, or type of behavior which a person builds up in terms of what others expect or demand of him.[3] It is implied in this concept that the performance of such a pattern of behavior calls forth in another person a specific pattern of behavior in turn, that is, another social role. Social roles have stimulus and response quality in interpersonal relations. It can further be observed that one person in the course of his life is called upon to perform a considerable number of social roles and that the performance of one may interfere with the performance of the other. From this empirical observation Cottrell has proposed a theorem which facilitates a connection between role analysis of social situations and a psychodynamic approach to personality study. "All personality systems are subject to internal stress due to the activity of contradictory roles. The greater

[1] Bloch, Herbert A., "A Synthetic View of the Social Individual as a Primary Datum in Sociology," *American Sociological Review,* vol. 8, October, 1943, p. 506.

[2] Sullivan, Harry Stack, *The Interpersonal Theory of Psychiatry,* edited by Helen Swick Perry and Mary Ladd Gawel. W. W. Norton and Co., New York, 1953.

[3] Young, Kimball, *Personality and Problems of Adjustment.* F. S. Crofts and Co., New York, 1940, p. 138.

the number of incompatible roles and the more overlapping the situations which evoke them, the greater the amount of conflict in the personality."[1] To anyone experienced in clinical work two conclusions will appear plausible: (1) that the theorem proposed by Cottrell has dynamic probability on its side, and (2) that information about role content and role incompatibility is more easily gathered regarding a number of persons interacting in a complex situation than data regarding their fantasies, their superego structures, their mechanisms of defense, and similar phenomena necessary for the formulation of individual diagnoses. The following account of our approach in Margaret's case will show the fruitfulness of a combination of the individual diagnosis of a patient with a family diagnosis based on role analysis. It is presented in the hope that it will prevent defeatism with regard to the possibility of formulating family diagnoses in complex situations.

DIAGNOSIS OF MARGARET

In our concentration on Margaret we gained the following genetic data. Margaret's mother had greatly infantilized the child. She had been an inveterate card player and had played usually with success, so that she had considerable money to spend on the child. Every day she had given her a freshly starched dress and had bathed her daily until the end. In other words, she had still done this for Margaret at the age of nine years. Sarah had continued this at first, but had stopped it suddenly deciding that a child did not need a fresh dress every day and that a nine-year-old girl should be able to bathe herself. Both sisters were of the opinion that the mother had spoiled Margaret, who had been her mother's preferred child. They reported that Margaret always had presented difficulties in school, had always tried to avoid going, and had pleaded illness in order to be permitted to stay at home. Margaret's Rorschach and the fantasies which she confided to the worker, however, revealed that the mother-child relationship had been

[1] Cottrell, Leonard S., Jr., "The Analysis of Situational Fields in Social Psychology," *American Sociological Review*, vol. 7, June, 1942, p. 377.

disturbed. According to the Rorschach Margaret considered the mother figure as the more punitive parent. Although this could have referred to Sarah, it became clear in later interviews that it did refer to her mother. She remembered outbursts of fury against her mother which threw light upon the meaning of her fantasies that at age twenty-one she would have to decide the ultimate punishment of her mother's killer. Apparently she had identified with the latter and carried a tremendous burden of guilt because of this identification.

Psychological examination indicated that Margaret's I.Q. was only 67. The psychologist considered this, however, minimal and thought that generalized anxiety lay at the root of the many inefficiencies in Margaret's total functioning. In conversation with the worker, he expressed the belief that Margaret's I.Q. actually was likely to be in the 80's rather than in the 60's.

Dynamically it appeared that Margaret was a borderline defective girl, who with the trauma of her mother's death had internalized her fears and feelings of defectiveness. Having been in conflict with her mother to the degree of having identified with the latter's killer and being in conflict with Sarah, who tried to perform the mother function after the mother's death, Margaret seemed to be in perpetual quest of a "good mother." She found this partly in Alice, who had a better relationship with her than Sarah, and partly in the worker, to whom Margaret related well from the start. She also had fantasies of her father marrying a friend of her mother's, who had taken care of her for a number of days immediately after her mother's death. She always wanted visible signs of affection, particularly money or food. She was inclined to take a poor view of her own performance. When she began to paint in the worker's office she tore up what she had done and said it was not good. To the question of the worker as to whether she frequently felt that way, she gave an affirmative answer. She also showed great signs of dependency and asked the worker to do things for her that she could have done herself, such as handing her the paper for painting and opening the paint bottle. When the worker once went out with Margaret to buy some paints, they entered a toy shop. Margaret seemed fascinated with the toys and blurted out the words, "How I wish I were a baby!"

As she entered adolescence her anxieties and feelings of defectiveness were intensified, as her limited ability to cope with the role demands of her age-sex category, to live up to her school aspirations, and particularly to deal with competitive forces became more pronounced. Her conflict about her aggressive and hostile urges, her feeling of helplessness in meeting demands, and her diffuse fears of retaliation seemed to foster what appeared to be a retreat into a phlegmatic shell, sometimes interrupted by a breakdown of even this marginal defense in terms of temper tantrums. It was the impression of the psychiatrist that Margaret had a neurosis, but was of such borderline intelligence that this produced manifestations different from those usually encountered in a neurotic child.

INTERPERSONAL RELATIONSHIPS IN THE FAMILY

We then directed our attention to the nature of the interpersonal relationships between this child and the various members of her family of orientation. As stated above, the father had pretty much assumed the position of an absentee landlord in regard to Margaret. He took care of her economic needs by providing for shelter, food, and clothing, but left all aspects of child rearing to her older sisters. It was they who got the report cards from the school, and he said that for this reason he could not know whether anything was wrong with Margaret's school performance or not. He came home late in the evening and, therefore, saw little of the girl. Margaret reached out for his attention, and at the same time was afraid of his authority and discipline. She wished he would take her out and go places with her. However, he took her along only to relatives for visits which bored her. His only concern was that she had not reacted to her mother's death with any sign of grief. On the other hand, he felt that later on it would not be good for the child to keep the mother's death alive in her. Basically his relationship to Margaret was that of a distant and authoritative figure whom she did not dare to annoy and from whom she received little gratification.

Sarah's relationship with Margaret had many more facets than we were able to discern in the father-child relationship. When Mrs. R. had become pregnant with Margaret, Sarah had been twenty years old and had felt much embarrassed by the thought of having a baby sister, or brother, at that age. She had wanted her mother to have an abortion, but the latter had refused for religious reasons. Having started as an embarrassment, Margaret had continued to be that for her in more ways than one. When her mother died, Sarah, who had been sick for a year and had undergone serious surgery, had felt obligated to join the father's household and to assume the mother role toward Margaret. This was at a time when her own son, Alfred, had been born and thus she had been suddenly faced with the obligation to assume the mother function toward her own infant son and toward her nine-year-old sister simultaneously. Although she wanted to be regarded by Margaret as a mother, the girl defied her orders, yelled at her, and by her messiness and overweight showed Sarah up as not doing a good job as a mother substitute. The neighbors commented about Margaret's overweight and suggested that she take the child somewhere for treatment, but Sarah was not able to tell them that this was exactly what she had done. On the other hand, Sarah felt that she had to protect Margaret against her father and to keep from him such behavior problems as were presented by the fact that Margaret stole money from her. Similarly, Sarah tried to protect Margaret from the disapproval of her husband, Mr. B. When Margaret had once hurt her little nephew, Alfred, Sarah had kept this from Mr. B. She felt that she could not tell him that Margaret was in treatment at the Clinic because she feared that he would use this information against the child. Since her husband thought that her assumption of the role of mother substitute toward Margaret prevented them from setting up a household of their own, Sarah wanted to step out of this role, but felt that she owed it to Margaret not to do so. On the other hand, she frequently yelled at Margaret and on occasion hit her, when Margaret did not obey her orders. The girl in turn disliked nobody in the family as much as she did Sarah and rejected her as a mother figure. This became apparent in the first interview. When the worker met Margaret in the waiting room, she found her sitting as far away from Sarah and Sarah's little boy as the place permitted. In the course of the interview and in future contacts, the worker found that Margaret's antagonism to Sarah expressed itself in many ways. She disobeyed her, yelled at her, and used abusive language to her. When Sarah gave her money, Margaret managed to lose it so frequently that it appeared as if she did not want to receive anything from her, although material things were to Margaret the equivalent of love.

Both Sarah and Margaret experienced each other as a burden and on occasion expressed wishes for a separation. At first both of them dared to visualize this only as something temporary. Margaret mentioned to the worker, for instance, a wish to spend the school vacation away from Sarah, while Sarah expressed a parallel wish of spending the summer in the country with Alfred only, and of having Margaret go to a camp. Similarly, Margaret once wanted to spend the Christmas holidays with a cousin in Pennsylvania. For a time all these separation wishes remained abortive. The people with whom Margaret wanted to spend her vacation proved to be products of her fantasy. Sarah, on the other hand, could not bring herself to sending Margaret off to camp and took her along for the summer. Both sisters, of course, were ambivalent toward each other. Sarah, although extremely angry and exasperated over the behavior of Margaret, wanted to understand why the girl behaved the way she did, and Margaret, although antagonistic toward Sarah, still wanted Sarah's protection from her father.

Margaret's relationship to Sarah's husband was equally confused. On the surface she disliked him and expressed this dislike freely. She complained that he was a great tease and kidded her all the time, and that she could not take it. She felt that he accused her of misdeeds which she had not committed and that he fought with her without cause. She called him derogatory names and felt that she could hit him back if he dared to hit her. The worker gained the impression, however, that underneath her protestations Margaret had a definite liking for her brother-in-law, which was of a quasi-oedipal character. When she asked whether Margaret liked her brother-in-law, the child reacted with a fleeting smile, but refused to go into a discussion of any positive feeling toward him.

Toward Alfred, Margaret had very warm feelings. She liked him best of all the family, but she expressed some jealousy to the worker and, seemingly unaware of the age difference of almost nine years between her and her nephew, complained that he got things which she could not get. Still, she took the little boy along to the movies when she went and he responded positively to her warmth.

The relationship to Alfred was not the only one which Margaret enjoyed within the family circle. There still was her sister Alice, who also had assumed certain mother-substitute functions toward Margaret. Being employed, Alice, in fact, had assumed the role of a night and holiday mother and had left Sarah with the more burdensome, and for the child, less rewarding role of a day and, particularly, a week-day mother. The strength of this night and holiday mother tie between Alice and Margaret could be gathered from a number of facts. Although Alice was self-supporting and would have been able to make other housing arrangements, she continued to share a bedroom with Margaret, and she did this although Margaret was anything but a desirable sleeping companion. Neither the child's offensive body odor, nor her restlessness and disturbed sleeping had brought Alice to consider a change. On holidays and Sundays she took the girl out and gave her companionship. In relation to the Clinic, Alice felt impelled to bring information to the worker and to seek her advice about special aspects of Margaret's behavior which she had observed and which caused her concern. Undoubtedly she did so in rivalry with Sarah, whom she did not want to know about her own contact with the Clinic. The fact remains, however, that she was concerned about Margaret's difficulties and tolerant of their expression, even at the price of personal discomfort. That Alice was the more successful mother substitute for Margaret seemed to be suggested by the fact that one of Margaret's outstanding symptoms, her enuresis, was diurnal only, as if stimulated by her disturbing contact with her "day mother," Sarah.

In gathering the data for an outline of the interpersonal relationships between Margaret and the other members of her family of orientation, we gained also incidental information about the relationships of these family members to one another. We learned, for instance, that there was disagreement between Sarah and her husband about their living arrangements. Mr. B. felt that Sarah's concern for Margaret made it impossible for them to set up an independent household, which he thought would be more satisfactory for him as well as for Alfred. We learned that Sarah and Alice were somewhat competitive in their relationships with Margaret. We learned that Sarah was strongly tied to her father whom she admired and felt unable to leave with Margaret on his hands. However, we found also that Sarah and Alice formed with Margaret a sibling group which protected itself against the father. It also protected Margaret against the father-substitute aspirations of Sarah's husband.

As indicated early in this presentation, we found that on this level of information an understanding of the family could be achieved by a concentration on the social roles which the various family members were called upon to play and by an understanding of the psychodynamic effects upon the individuals which resulted from these roles.

FAMILY DIAGNOSIS—CONFLICTING SOCIAL ROLES AND INTERNAL STRESSES

The death of Margaret's mother had produced a family situation in which almost every member found forced upon himself social roles which he was not able to perform without conflict and found himself excluded from social roles which he would have liked to perform.

Margaret's father had delegated mother authority to Sarah, but Sarah found it impossible to enter wholeheartedly upon the fulfillment of this role. She could never really free herself from seeing in Margaret a sibling and thus from acting occasionally as a sibling-ally of Margaret's toward the father, rather than as a true mother substitute. On the other hand, she acted toward Margaret more frequently as a punishing mother than as a helpful sibling. Alice also assumed a mother role toward Margaret and similarly was unable to forget or disregard the fact that Margaret was her sister. Both mother substitutes, therefore, were handicapped in the performance of their mother roles by a cropping up of sibling roles and further handicapped by their own sibling rivalry in the performance of either one of these role types. Sarah's husband, finding his wife in a mother-substitute role to his sister-in-law, wanted to assume the role of the father substitute toward this child. He, however, was prevented from doing so by the existence of the real father in the household and by his wife's reaction, which excluded him from that role and forced upon him the role of an older sibling of Margaret's rather than that of a father substitute. Margaret was finally forced into a sibling role toward her nephew by the fact that her sister Sarah acted as a mother substitute as well as a sister of hers. Finally, the child was confused by the fact that she did not have only one maternal figure in her life but two maternal figures, and maternal figures who were her sisters to boot and on occasion acted as such rather than as mother substitutes.

On the dynamic level the mother-substitute roles in which both Sarah and Alice engaged could be expected to reactivate oedipal feelings toward their father and feelings of sibling rivalry toward each other. Their tendencies to exclude Mr. B. where Margaret was concerned and to force upon him a sibling role where his position as husband of a mother substitute suggested to him the appropriateness of a father's role were likely to reactivate in him feelings of childhood inadequacy. These reactivated feelings of childhood inadequacy in turn seemed to interfere with the demands which his social role as Sarah's husband and Alfred's father made upon him. He found himself married to a woman who in one daily aspect of their existence had assumed a spouse role toward his father-in-law. It was probable that this also reactivated whatever insecurity might have been latent in him with regard to the performance of his adult roles in a conjugal family.

The experience of seeing his grownup daughter performing the mother role toward a child of his seemed to affect Margaret's father. It seemed to create in him conflict about marrying a woman in whom he had become interested after the death of his wife. Margaret, finally, handicapped by genetic endowment, infantilization, and the trauma of her mother's death found herself in the midst of a family situation which forced upon her the role of a daughter, of a sister to her mother substitutes, of a sister-in-law to a would-be but frustrated father substitute, and of a sibling toward a nephew.

The family situation had created for everybody in the household contradictory roles and thus internal stresses which interfered with the performance of these roles. The situation thus corroborated Cottrell's proposition that the greater the number of incompatible roles and the more overlapping the situations are which evoke them, the greater the amount of conflict in the personalities involved. Margaret's need for a mother substitute and the responses of her two sisters to this need had created in the members of the family an intensity of conflict which was bound to affect adversely this disadvantaged child, who already had to carry the burden of a dull mentality and of a severe guilt-creating trauma.

FAMILY DIAGNOSIS—INSTITUTIONAL ANALYSIS

In terms of family functions we could arrive on this basis at the following institutional analysis of the situation. Her role conflicts prevented Sarah from performing adequately her functions as a wife to Mr. B., as a mother to her son Alfred, and as a mother substitute toward her sister Margaret. Role conflicts prevented her husband from performing his functions as husband and father. Role conflicts prevented Mr. R. from really performing his function as father and prevented Alice from performing her function as mother substitute for Margaret.

In terms of relationship tendencies their mother-substitute roles tied Sarah and Alice to their father, from whom as adult daughters they should have become dissociated. Role conflicts prevented the development of association tendencies between Mr. B. and Sarah, such as their spouse relationship would have demanded. Finally, the existing role conflict prevented the association tendency between Margaret and Sarah which the various handicaps of this child would have required as a start for a positive if limited development.

Role analysis in this case, thus, did furnish us with an understanding of the pervading problem of this family. This problem appeared to be incompatibility of roles in every family member. A family diagnosis, thus, could be conceptualized here as *family dysfunction due to multiplicity of incompatible social roles resulting in relationship tendency reversal between the father and his two adult daughters, relationship tendency reversal between one of these daughters and her husband, and relationship tendency reversal between one of these daughters and her neurotic and defective sister.*

PLAN OF THERAPY

Child welfare focused family therapy, therefore, seemed to require a simplification of the complexity of the family situation in terms of role reduction for the membership, alleviation of the guilt feelings in Margaret, and a plan of schooling which would take account of the girl's handicaps in intellectual and emotional respects.

The achievement of a simplification of the family relationships in this case seemed to be theoretically possible in either one of two ways—placement of Margaret, or a separation of the conjugal family, consisting of Mr. B., Sarah, and Alfred, from the broken family of Mr. R., through establishment of two households. Both possibilities were kept under consideration as treatment proceeded. From a preventive point of view, the latter solution seemed to be more constructive, because Alfred in turn had begun to show disturbances which suggested that as long as his parents did not set up independent housekeeping, his own development was likely to suffer. Thus, placement for Margaret might have simplified the living setup for the girl, but would not have provided any solution for the growth problems of Alfred. Since the operation of a Child Guidance Clinic has to be concerned with the extended impact of possible consequences of differential treatment methods, it was a happy turn of events that in the end we were able to achieve a separation of the two family groups rather than the placement of Margaret.

With regard to Margaret's enuresis, psychotherapeutic procedure obviously had to be modified because of her limited level of intelligence. This limited intellectual functioning presented assets as well as liabilities. The psychodynamics of the girl were easy to perceive just because she was functioning on an I.Q. level of 65. She did not and could not verbalize her feelings and anxieties in terms of insight, but she showed them in terms of appropriate moods. It was decided, therefore, to give in to her infantile demands for gratification in order to gain access to her fantasies and an understanding of her reactions, which she was likely to express with a minimum of defenses. On the other hand, the worker's treatment had to be more direct than is usual in child guidance practice. At the same time it had to be less concerned with insight than with providing guilt-relieving and maturation-enhancing experiences for the child.

As far as Margaret's school situation was concerned, we had to consider that the family's culturally determined aspirations in scholastic achievement were higher than the child's intellectual capacities warranted. We also had to consider that it was the school itself which had suggested this referral, and that Margaret, personally, was very much aware of her school difficulties. As we came to understand more and more of Margaret's retarded emotional life, and the limitations of her intellectual capacities, it became apparent that a home-making course was probably the most promising school plan for this child. Such a curriculum seemed to provide appropriate sublimation for an adolescent girl who had been arrested to such a degree on an oral level and seemed not to tax Margaret beyond her intellectual capacities. Margaret's sisters felt, however, that she should take an academic course, and that a home-making course was a disgrace. The teacher who had spotted the child's difficulties had been frequently asking Margaret whether she had been taken into treatment at the Clinic. Margaret herself was very anxious over failing in several subjects; over being ridiculed by the other children; and over having to select a high school in which she would be accepted. She was afraid she would have to go to a high school where only the "dumb kids" went. We decided, therefore, relatively early in the course of treatment to establish contact with the school.[1] Our aim was to reassure the teaching staff that their interest in Margaret's problem was appreciated by the Clinic, and to help the family and the school to agree on an educational program which would be appropriate in the light of our assessment of the child's psychodynamic structure and limited intellectual capacity.

Our treatment plan thus foresaw an approach that could be conceptualized as an *orchestration of three lines of therapeutic impact.* The first line presented modified psychotherapy with Margaret, the second line consisted of consultative relationships with Margaret's family of orientation, and the third, inserted the Clinic's understanding of the situation as a dynamic and coordinating force into the planning of school and family with regard to Margaret's education.

PSYCHOTHERAPY WITH MARGARET

The worker's efforts to help Margaret through the form of psychotherapy outlined above followed a line which was indicated by the child's continuing requests for money. Very early in the contact, Margaret had told the worker that she wanted to ask her a question, but was afraid to do so. Encouraged by the worker, she stated that she wondered whether the worker

[1] In the advance from formal history-taking and a routine visit to schools regardless of appropriateness there has been a trend in some child guidance clinics not to visit the school or to postpone school visits unduly.

could give her ten cents, because she had lost her carfare. There followed a number of sessions in which Margaret spent most of the time in painting, but soon again she asked for money. In two consecutive interviews, she asked the worker for fifty cents. The first time she gave as her reason that the teacher had asked her to buy a song book and had given her fifty cents for it, but that she had lost the money and was afraid the teacher was going to "kill her" when she found out this had happened. The next time she asked for the same amount and gave a similar reason; this time she said that her sister had given her the money for the purchase of milk and butter. Her sister was also going to "kill her" because this was not the first time that Margaret had lost money. She always lost things, mostly money, but also books, scarves, and gloves. When the worker, in the course of conversation about this request, told the child it was not important that Margaret asked for the money but why she did it and why she lost things, Margaret stated that once she had stolen money from her sister. It had only been ten cents and she had never done it again. She then returned to her request for fifty cents from the worker and after having received the money, said she would never ask for money again.

When these requests for money were brought up in the seminar discussion, the psychiatrist suggested that Margaret be permitted to act out in this area and that further requests for money should be acceded to by the worker. By permitting this acting out we would gain access to the child's emotional life in terms of needs, fantasies, and anxieties. Actually, Margaret, in spite of her statement that she would never ask for more money again, made such requests in every one of the ensuing interviews. In the course of this treatment phase she raised her demands from the original ten cents to a dollar and a quarter per interview. We decided, however, to limit our giving to one dollar per session.

At first, Margaret continued to base her requests on stories of having lost money given to her by the teacher for purchases. When the worker told her, however, that all girls were interested in having money for themselves, and that it seemed as if

Margaret felt she had no right to ask for money for herself, Margaret began to support her requests with the statement that she wanted to save the money for clothes. On a later occasion she said she needed money for a friend. If she could not give it to her, the friend would "kill" her. The worker applied the direct kind of therapy suggested by Margaret's intelligence level and pointed out to her that she seemed to put the idea of money and getting killed together. Although Margaret did not respond to this remark at the time the worker made it, she stated in the next interview that there was one thing that was more important than money, and that was life. Our granting of Margaret's requests for money thus seemed to give us an avenue to a better understanding of this child's mental life, as the psychiatrist had predicted it would. Apparently Margaret's requests for money were connected with guilt feelings over having taken from, or misused the money, which belonged to others. Apparently the punishment visualized by her was that of "being killed." Considering that the attacker of her mother had snatched a purse from the latter, that Margaret had a fantasy over having to decide whether the man should live or die, and that she saw the mother figure as a basically hostile one, the assumption that this child identified with the killer of her mother and suffered from an anxiety neurosis in consequence, seemed to present an increasingly substantiated hypothesis on which to proceed. Actually, this hypothesis was confirmed by later developments. After the worker had discontinued giving her money for a couple of interviews, the child stopped asking for it. After having stopped for two weeks, however, she stole money from the worker's purse and on the evening of the same day provoked anger in her father to such a degree that he gave her a beating. When the worker asked why her father had had to punish her, the child stated that she had wanted him to shift the TV program which he had been watching to another one she wanted to see. After having made this statement, she was silent for a moment, and then changed it. She said that she was bad and that was the reason why her father had had to punish her. To the question of the worker as to why she was bad, Margaret admitted that she stole and ate too many sweets, although she was frequently reprimanded for both by her sister Sarah. That Margaret used her requests to the worker for money for an acting out of her identification with her mother's killer finally was corroborated by information received from Sarah. Margaret had asked the worker not to tell her sisters that she got money at the Clinic. Sarah, who had noticed that Margaret spent more money than her allowance permitted, told the worker that she was concerned about how much the child spent and that she had to assume that Margaret was stealing the money. Apparently Margaret preferred to let her sister think that she was stealing and to be punished for that rather than admit to Sarah that these were gifts which she received from the worker. How justified we had been in this interpretation of the child's acting out in the money area finally was revealed toward the end of the treatment. Margaret, having achieved a certain ability of verbalizing her feelings, recalled that when she was seven years old her mother on one occasion had refused to give her money. At that time Margaret had gone into a tantrum, had gone to her mother's purse, and had thrown all the money out of the window.

Besides giving us thus an understanding of her neurotic mechanics, our permitting of this acting out enabled the worker to provide positive emotional experiences for the child. By continuing to grant the money after Margaret had admitted her stealing, the worker began to free her from her feelings of guilt over taking money from the mother figure and thus began to counteract through emotional reeducation the child's identification with the mother's killer and her need for punishment.

Parallel with our efforts at freeing Margaret from her anxieties resulting from her identification with the killer of her mother, the worker tried to permit the child a measure of aggression in other areas. She permitted her in painting to soil her smock and encouraged her expression of competitive desires which the child had suppressed in the realization of her limitations, by putting up Margaret's paintings on the wall next to the paintings of other children.

With relief of her anxiety over her mother's death, Margaret had become able to bring out more open aggression against Sarah. As the worker listened to Margaret's outbursts and complaints about her sister without criticism and punishment, the child was able to express with increasing force her desire for living arrangements separated from Sarah and her husband. Thus, the release of her aggressiveness in that direction actually prepared the child for the simplification of the household and living arrangements which we had visualized as one of our goals in treatment. Margaret also began to deepen her basically positive relationship with Alice. This became apparent in the second treatment year and paralleled Margaret's increased emotional separation from Sarah. During that period Alice started to take Margaret out on dinner dates and to take her along on shopping trips. Significantly Margaret began to show that she trusted Alice in a way similar to the one in which she showed her trust in the worker. She began to ask Alice for money, expecting that this form of her reaching out for gratification would be rewarded instead of being punished. She insisted, however, that this was only "borrowing" and that she was going to "pay Alice back," because Alice was nice to her.

CONSULTATIVE CONTACTS WITH FAMILY MEMBERS

Our attempts to prepare the various members of Margaret's family for a simplification of the living conditions of the child by helping the two families set up separate housekeeping, or to accept at least, the placement of Margaret, ran parallel with the child's psychotherapy. Keeping our contact geared to the family of orientation, the worker had consultative sessions with the father, with Sarah, with Alice, and finally, also with Sarah's husband. Although Margaret's father recognized some improvement in the child as treatment progressed, he was inclined to attribute this to normal maturation rather than to the contact with the Clinic. He showed, however, some realism in the assessment of the child's capacities in the planning of the school program, as will be reported below in the description of the third line of our therapeutic efforts. Sarah herself found it difficult at first to accept that our work required regular contacts with a member of the child's family and began to keep regular appointments only toward the end of the first treatment year. Until then she frequently broke appointments with the worker. Even so, she was able to relate from the start her husband's objections to the combined housekeeping arrangements which the family had made after the death of Margaret's mother. Thus, the worker knew of a potential source within the family which at one point might be activitated toward a simplification of the household. At first, Sarah felt that she could not even think of going along with her husband's wishes to set up a separate household, in view of the difficulties which Margaret presented and which required her continuation in the household as the girl's mother substitute.

In the following interviews, Sarah expressed her lack of understanding as to what was wrong with the child and wondered whether she and her handling were to blame for it. She was also concerned over the fact that Margaret had begun to smoke furtively in the bathroom. She had noticed that a hole had been burned in the shower curtain and was afraid to leave Margaret and Alfred alone in the house for fear that Margaret as a result of her carelessness would start a fire. Sarah again brought up her husband's desire for a separation of the households, but discussed it now without any reference to her former statement that if she ever made such a move she would have to take Margaret along. She complained of the frequent clashes between Margaret and her husband and used them as an explanation for not letting her husband know that Margaret was receiving treatment at the Clinic. The worker pointed out to her that it was just because of the bad relationship between Margaret and her husband that a visit of the latter to the Clinic might prove useful. Such a visit would make it possible for us to see how this tension and friction could be removed. Sarah promised to arrange for her husband to visit the worker, without following through for some time on this suggestion. Toward the end of the first year, Sarah finally began to show some understanding of Margaret's problem. She recognized that the child was under the impact of great anxieties and recognized also that she, Sarah, was not carrying the only responsibility for the child's difficulties. At the same time she felt increasingly helpless as to how to handle the situation. This helplessness increased as Margaret began to assert herself more and more. On the other hand, Sarah began to acknowledge that the treatment had meaning for Margaret, as did her own discussions with the worker for herself. That Sarah's beginning emotional separation from Margaret's problem became stronger, was demonstrated by the fact that in discussing again her husband's wish for a separate household she stated now that "in that case Margaret would have to stay with her father."

In the course of the second treatment year, Alice inserted herself more and more into the Clinic's contact and began to take an increasing interest in the solution of Margaret's problems. It will be remembered that she shared a bedroom with Margaret. Owing to this arrangement she once observed in the morning that Alfred had come into the room, had climbed into Margaret's bed, and that the children had engaged in sex play. Shocked, and frightened, she decided to see the worker in order to inform her about this incident and to ask her advice about how to handle recurrences. She had kept this, however, from Sarah and wished to keep her call confidential. This gave the worker an opportunity to point out to Alice how all of the family kept piling up secrets from one another; how Alice did not want to have Sarah know about her interest in the children; how Sarah did not want to have her husband know about Margaret's treatment; how both she and Sarah kept Margaret's misbehavior from their father; and how difficult such a situation was likely to become for all concerned. In response to this, Alice told the worker that there was considerable friction between her and Sarah. Alice felt that they would have to move because the neighborhood had deteriorated and because in their present arrangement, Alfred had to sleep with his parents in the same bedroom. She knew this was undesirable for the child and should be changed. Sarah, however, did not see this in the same light, and always blocked any opportunity of their moving to a new place. Alice felt that Sarah did so because of her husband's desire to set up a separate household, which might assert itself if the status quo was changed in any way. Finally, Alice brought out her own awareness that Sarah felt "put upon" by having to take care of the whole family. She admitted that there was a basis for this complaint, but pointed out that she took over the household responsibilities on Sunday and prepared dinner for her father on Monday after she came back from work, because that was the evening on which Sarah went out to play cards.

During the second treatment year, the worker's discussions with Sarah shifted somewhat from Margaret's problem to Sarah's relationship with her father. The worker helped Sarah see how, in her admiration for her father, she had relegated her husband, more and more, to the status of a sibling in the home who brought in money, but had no further say in the household. In response to the stimulus of this discussion, Sarah began gradually to talk about solving the problem of an at least partial separation of her household from her father's. She started to think about their buying a house in which she, her husband, and Alfred could occupy one floor, while her father, Alice, and Margaret could occupy the other. She also found, finally, the strength to tell her husband of Margaret's treatment, and an appointment was made for him to see the worker.

In this interview with the worker, Sarah's husband confirmed the worker's impression that he felt left out of things, that his wife at no time discussed with him problems pertaining to the household, and never consulted with him on anything relating to Margaret. Sarah and Alice were a closed corporation as far as Margaret was concerned, and Sarah and her father a closed corporation as far as financial matters were concerned. He had wanted an individual household from the start, but had given up his wish because he felt that Sarah was closer to her family than to him. He was able to recognize that he and Alfred should be considered by Sarah more as her family than anybody else. He had given up hope, however, that anything but Margaret's growing up would change this situation. The worker suggested that it was doubtful whether Margaret's growing up, as such, would be sufficient to change Sarah's ties to her father and her sisters, and wondered what the existing conditions would do to Alfred, in the meantime, even if that expectation was justified. She suggested further that Sarah and her husband might want to work this problem through with the help of a family agency. Sarah's husband made a new appointment with the worker in order to discuss this further, but canceled it and expressed doubt whether he would find the time to arrange for another one.

A FAMILY CONFERENCE

Since the various members of the household thus seemed to be alert to the need for a change in their living arrangements, the worker called a family conference. Its purpose was to mobilize the family's potential for positive social interaction by facing with them together the problem of Margaret's future. Although this conference did not produce immediate results, it proved to be effective in the end.

At first, it was apparent that every family member wanted to delegate the responsibility for a decisive step to the other family members: Sarah and Alice looked to their father for deciding what should be done with regard to Margaret. He in turn tried to delegate responsibility to his two adult daughters, since he felt that women were responsible for the care of children. However, the situation gave Mr. R. an opportunity to see that the father role demanded more from him than furnishing food and shelter for his child. It provided him with a chance to take stock of Margaret's change during treatment. He noticed that improvement had occurred in the child, that she did dress more neatly, and paid more attention to cleanliness and her appearance in general, but he continued to ascribe these positive changes to maturation rather than to any help received from the Clinic. Still, he was forced to take notice of the fights and difficulties at home and although he tried to minimize them as something which was likely to occur between sisters, their evaluation by the worker as a problem helped Mr. R. see them in a different light and to make him aware of the desirability of different arrangements. Mr. R. recognized that Margaret needed help with regard to her difficulties in having friends. He was given an opportunity to state that he would not consider placement because Margaret did not want it. This facing up to the unfeasibility of placement, together with the difficulties between Margaret and Sarah, strengthened his acceptance of responsibility for providing living arrangements separated from Sarah, her husband, and Alfred.

When the worker pointed out to him that Sarah herself had been thinking of setting up a place of her own, but had been reluctant to do so until now because of Margaret, Mr. R. stated that he did not see how Margaret in any way was an obstacle to such a plan, if an independent household was what Sarah wanted. Most of all, Mr. R. expressed his realization that Margaret needed help with her school problems and that in this regard the Clinic's professional knowledge would be of greater assistance than the aspirations and ideas of her sisters.

Sarah and Alice, on the other hand, were given the opportunity to see in this conference their father taking on responsibilities for the solution of problems which they had tried to handle on their own.

Finally, Sarah's husband gained for himself, and in the eyes of the family members, support for his wish to set up an independent household. Although no definite decision was reached in that conference, it proved to have been a decisive step toward the achievement of our goal to provide simpler living arrangements for Margaret, because after termination of our treatment we learned that the two families had set up separate households.

Finally, the father's realization that school plans should be made for Margaret on a more realistic basis than her sisters had visualized enabled the worker to arrange with the school a curriculum for Margaret which took account of Margaret's capacities, as well as her dynamic needs, and this leads us to the third line of our orchestrated efforts.

PLANS FOR SCHOOLING

That attention to Margaret's school problems, in terms of their psychodynamic meaning, as well as in terms of their educational impact upon the child, would have to be an essential part of our helping, had been recognized fairly early in the contact and had presented itself repeatedly as a topic of discussion in our seminar sessions. The child herself had defined her school difficulties as one of her major problems from the start. In the first treatment session she mentioned that one of her teachers was constantly after her, asking whether she had heard from the Clinic and when she was going to go there. To the worker's questions, Margaret said that she had not told the teacher anything about having received an appointment because she felt that it was not her business. To a further question as to how things were going in school generally, Margaret sighed deeply and expressed fear that she would flunk at the end of the semester. Although she did her homework with the help of her sister Sarah and a schoolmate, and seemed to know the answers at home, she seemed always to forget them when called upon at school, and the other pupils immediately began to laugh. The other children in the class always called her "dumbbell" and told her that she was perhaps the dumbest kid in the class. She admitted that this made her very angry, but stated that she did not hit the kids unless they hit her first. Then, she "let them have it." She was careful, however, not to hurt them because she had heard of a girl in the neighborhood who had become crippled in a fight at school and she would not want to hurt any of them. Returning to her fear of flunking, she said that before an examination, no matter how well prepared she was, a voice was telling her, "Margaret, you are going to fail," and sure enough, she always failed. To the worker's statement that this seemed similar to Margaret's feeling when going to bed that she would die during the night, the child nodded in agreement.

Margaret then expressed concern over the question as to what high school she could go to after graduation. She was scheduled for a high school where the children had a bad reputation for smoking narcotics. She would have liked to go to another school where nicer kids went, but when she mentioned that to her schoolmates, they told her that she was much too dumb to be admitted there, she would have to go to the school where all the dumb kids went.

On another occasion Margaret complained about a schoolmate to whom she had been very nice and to whom she had given many things, such as ice cream and candy. Instead of being nice to her in return, this schoolmate did nothing but tell her that she was too dumb to be admitted to the high school to which she wanted to go. In that connection she mentioned that Sarah had told her, "Maybe the worker would be able to help you to be accepted by the school."

In the next interview, Margaret mentioned again her fear of getting failing grades in all her courses. She was sure when she brought her report card home this time Sarah would be upset and would yell at her. Thus, it appeared from the beginning that Margaret's feelings of inadequacy were dependent upon her school experiences. A well-meaning teacher, hostile schoolmates, and the ambitions of her sisters combined to sharpen Margaret's feelings of defectiveness in a competitive setting, the demands of which she was not able to meet. Over and above that, Margaret's desire to go to a high school that would permit her to get away from bad boys seemed to suggest that her school problems were also related to fears of heterosexual contacts which her approaching puberty made a problem likely to be stimulated by her own physiological maturation, as well as by the youth culture of our time.

We discussed, therefore, the desirability of a Clinic contact with the school at this stage. There was concern about visiting the school without Margaret's permission, and the psychiatrist pointed out that there was no rule requiring preparation of a child for such a school visit. The other questions raised were whether such a visit was likely to become general knowledge among Margaret's classmates and whether such knowledge would not stigmatize her. On the other hand, it was pointed out that Margaret's status in the school was so low that a visit by the worker from the Clinic might, if anything, raise her standing in the eyes of her associates, rather than lower it. In the end it was agreed that the school had been instrumental in the referral; that the teacher who had been interested in Margaret's receiving help from the Clinic had a right to a communication from the Clinic; and that most of all, family, Clinic, and school were involved in a triangular interest in the child which would have to be utilized for the child's benefit. As far as social interaction between the teacher and worker was concerned, it was not only up to the Clinic to express appreciation of the school's interest, but also to help the school in understanding the situation and thus to enable the school to participate in constructive planning which took account of the child's psychodynamic as well as her scholastic problems.

In the end, the worker decided to discuss with Margaret the possibility of a school visit and found the girl not only amenable to it, but quite eager that it should be made. She wanted the worker to meet her at the school so that she could take her around to the various teachers and introduce her to them. She wanted the worker to explain, particularly to her mathematics teacher, that it was not lack of preparation, but her "nervousness" which made her fail. In effect, rather than feeling that she might be stigmatized by the worker's visits, Margaret expected that her situation in school would improve as a consequence.

When the worker met with the school principal, she learned that Margaret in no way constituted a behavior problem and in a group test had scored an I.Q. of 82. The principal agreed with the Clinic psychologist that Margaret probably belonged in the dull-normal group and stressed that it was in the emotional problem area that the school was concerned about the child. Margaret suffered from a short attention span, which suggested preoccupation with her private thoughts. This, and the fact that she was overweight, had been the reason for the school's suggestion that Clinic help should be sought. With regard to an appropriate high school, the principal and the worker agreed that the low academic capacity of the child suggested a vocational school and that the nature of the curriculum, whether commercial or home-making, might be determined on the basis of our dynamic understanding of the child. It was also agreed between the worker and the principal, that the Clinic would attempt to help the child to a more realistic conception of what she could do in high school.

In the weeks which followed this school visit, Margaret told the worker that her report card had been better than she had expected, and better than it had been for the last term. The teachers had encouraged her on the basis that she was "trying." She had become reconciled to going to a high school other than the one she had "set her heart on" previously and to take a general, rather than an academic course. We then arranged for a vocational test which indicated that Margaret could not take a clerical course, but would do best in a general curriculum with a course in filing, or retail trades. These findings were discussed with the school principal and Margaret was placed in a slow class with a special course in English and filing.

In the ensuing contacts it became clear that Margaret's infantilization and her equation of food with love seemed to make a home-making curriculum a more promising schooling program than it had appeared to the psychologist who had given the vocational tests. At the end of the first year Margaret herself indicated such a curriculum as the type of training that she wanted. This came about in the following way. After graduation the worker had arranged a party for her, had taken her out to a drugstore, and then bought her a gift. After having had both, party and gift, Margaret asked, hesitantly, whether she could have her usual dollar. Saying that she realized how much money the worker had spent on her, when she received the dollar, she broke into tears, turned on her heel and left. A few days later she wrote the worker that she had decided to go to a home-making school, because she wanted to take a course in catering which she had decided to make her life work. The idea of giving, so unconditionally experienced from the worker, and so closely related to her level of understanding of food as an expression of positive feeling, seemed to have helped her in arriving at this decision. However, in the fall, Margaret, under pressure from her sisters, reversed her plan and enrolled in the general curriculum. Particularly, Alice had told her it would be possible for her to become a filing clerk if she went through a general curriculum. Later, during the second year Margaret came to realize that this was not a good plan and asked the worker for another school visit. She had failed in three subjects, and the worker helped her verbalize her concern that she would be "left back" if she continued to fail. When the worker asked her what this would mean, Margaret indicated that she thought she would have to take the same courses over and over again. The worker pointed out to Margaret that there was no need to do that, since there were areas in which Margaret did have capacities, such as a home-making course. Margaret, however, found it difficult even with this encouragement from the worker to accept the idea because of the objections of her sisters, who considered such a type of schooling a cultural disgrace. Actually, Sarah confirmed this in an interview with the worker, saying that she and Alice had very strong feelings against Margaret's taking a home-making course.

Thus, the task remained to help the family accept the plan of a home-making curriculum for Margaret and thereby to accept a plan of schooling which would represent an adaptation to the girl's capacities, as well as her emotional needs. The worker's efforts in this direction were helped by Margaret's constant failure to perform acceptably in the general curriculum. After some further discussions with the sisters and Margaret, an agreement was finally reached that Margaret would take a home-making course and that the worker should visit the school in order to discuss the necessary arrangements with the school authorities. After this was done, Margaret's difficulties in school subsided and Sarah became acceptant of Margaret's training to such a degree that she permitted her more and more to cook at home, to experiment with salads and to make fancy canapes. Margaret also became interested in the food programs on television, and finally showed an increasing interest in diets and calories which led her to make an earnest attempt at losing weight.

At this point Margaret's school experiences began to connect with her experiences in psychotherapy. The worker perceived from Margaret's efforts in gaining control over her weight through dieting that she was ready to give up her acting out with regard to requests for money. For this reason, she indicated to Margaret that the Clinic would stop, within a few weeks, giving her the weekly sum which she had been receiving. When the girl did not show any sign of outward reaction, the worker asked her whether she had any idea why this was done. Margaret indicated that this was probably done because she was getting sufficient money now at home. Her allowance had been increased by her father and she was even able to save a dollar weekly for clothes. The worker then pointed out to her that in a way Margaret was saying that she did not need the weekly dollar any more from the Clinic. Margaret denied this, but stated that she had known for sometime that one day the money from the worker would come to an end. The worker tied this up for her by telling Margaret that in another sense also she was ready for the allowance to stop: since she wanted to reduce, she had been able to make some gains in that respect by restraining herself with regard to sweets and sodas, and consequently she did not need to have so much money as before. The girl was able to laugh at this, and proved able, when the allowance was stopped, to restrain herself for some time from asking the worker for money.

When she had a relapse and did once again ask for money, the worker helped her see how in the past she had taken the giving of money as a sign of being loved and how she did not need this type of reassurance any more. Margaret agreed that she had wanted the money as a reassurance of being liked by the worker in the past, but tried to show that now she needed the money for other things, such as entrance fees for ice skating, and the like. The worker took this as an occasion to point out to Margaret that, realistically, people have only so much money to spend and that everybody has to decide for what the money in his pocket was to be used. She then engaged in some budgeting with Margaret, going over her expenses for carfare, movies, and other recreational activities, such as ice skating and an occasional meal out. She indicated to Margaret that it would be necessary for her to decide whether she wanted the movies and the meal out all in one day, which would mean no more funds for the rest of the week, or whether she would want to distribute these pleasures over the whole span of seven days. Margaret reacted to this by deciding that on Sunday she would take only half of her allowance in order to prevent herself from having all the money at hand for spending at one time.

THERAPEUTIC GAINS

At the end of the second treatment year we decided that our achievements had gone as far as could be expected with a child of such limitations and a family situation of such complexity. Specifically we terminated treatment in view of the following considerations. The child had been freed emotionally from her identification with her mother's killer. She had been enabled to make some promising experimentation with self-control and had been helped not to react negatively to limitations. Her appearance and personal hygiene had improved. The family had been alerted to the need of separating the two family units which composed the household. A school plan had been worked out, together with the family and the school authorities, which took account of the child's native endowment and psychodynamic makeup.

We realized that Margaret's emotional development had only partially been freed from its arrests. We were doubtful, however, whether the child's limited intellectual capacities would permit further gains through psychotherapy. For this reason, we decided to leave the child's further emotional development to positive forces of life experiences.

Information which we received from Margaret in two visits which she made after the contact had been terminated proved that our judgment of having laid positive foundations for the child's further development within her limitations had been correct.

We learned that the household had been separated. Mr. R., Alice, and Margaret were living in an apartment of their own.

Sarah, her husband, and Alfred had moved to the suburbs. Margaret had transferred to a vocational high school for home-making. She was not doing badly there at all and had made some friends. Although still overweight, she continued dieting. What impressed the worker most was a definite gain in emotional maturity which became apparent in Margaret when she discussed her father's intention of getting married. Margaret mentioned that her father wanted to do so, but had said that he would not take this step as long as she did not want him to do it. When the worker asked Margaret how she felt about this, and what it would mean if she stood in the way of her father's getting married, the girl said that she would not want to do that because one day she might want to get married herself and then she would not want her father to stand in the way of her doing so.

PART THREE

RESEARCH OUTLOOK

PART THREE: RESEARCH OUTLOOK

When Russell Sage Foundation and the Jewish Board of Guardians agreed that an experimental team should test in practice the propositions set forth in *Social Science and Psychotherapy for Children,* it was visualized that a possible third phase of the project should be concerned only with the question of whether the methods developed by the team and the results achieved would justify a follow-up study on a statistical basis. As the project developed, however, other needs for the continuation of study effort were encountered. The research results which followed from the effort to meet them will be discussed in succeeding chapters.

A survey of those research needs which suggested themselves to the writer but could not be met in the course of this project will be presented at the end of this report.

As may be recalled, the original agreement between Russell Sage Foundation and the Jewish Board of Guardians foresaw two general lines of inquiry. One was to ascertain whether there were in existence specific funds of social science knowledge that could be constructively adapted to use in child guidance practice. The other was to investigate needs for information experienced by child guidance practitioners that could be met by social science research. While the first line of inquiry was pursued with vigor from the start, efforts along the second line of exploration developed impetus only after the liaison project had been well established. As a matter of fact, it was not before the end of the project's second phase that they gained predominance. In some instances, problem areas became identified and research questions crystallized for the first time during the preparation of this report. In retrospect, it appears as if the emphasis of the project effort had shifted from a practice orientation to a research orientation. In this shift of emphasis, however, one essential theme seems to have remained unchanged. In both the application of social science knowledge to child guidance practice and in the identification of research needs existing in the child guidance field emphasis on theory has remained pronounced.

VII. Theory and Practice as Reflected in Casework and Psychiatric Literature

ONE OF THE MOST INTERESTING research stimulations we received concerned the phenomenon of divergence between a theory that stressed the importance of the whole family and a practice that concentrated attention upon the mother-child relationship. Since a considerable part of our project effort had been an attempt at a rapprochement between the two, it seemed necessary to devote study to the question of how widespread this phenomenon actually was. Was it a characteristic only of child guidance clinics, or could it be found also in family welfare agencies? Was it an expression only of the mistakes of learners or did it characterize the work also of experienced persons in the field? Finally, did it perhaps represent a forgetting of principles which an earlier generation of caseworkers had known and practiced?

A review of the literature furnished answers to all these questions. These answers are presented here as a baseline for the explanations and tentative research proposals which will be found in chapters that follow.

GENERAL NATURE OF CONCENTRATION UPON MOTHER AND CHILD

The practice observations at the Jewish Board of Guardians on which our first report was based took place in the period from 1949 to 1951. Reports from other agencies for the same period or later suggest that the concentration of practice upon the child patient and his mother was fairly general. Closest to the writing time of this book is a report of Dr. Maurice J. Rosenthal, psychiatric consultant for the Institute for Juvenile Research, Chicago, and for the Division of Child Welfare, State of Illinois, which was published in *Social Casework* for January,

1954. From Dr. Rosenthal comes the following statement: "The principles to be discussed in the text of this paper apply to all types of permanent guardians of a child, fathers as well as mothers, and adoptive as well as natural parents. Generally, however, the mother will be referred to specifically, because she is by far the most frequent adult in the family to be treated at a child guidance clinic."[1] Only a few months earlier, there appeared a symposium volume, *Psychoanalysis and Social Work*, in which Dr. Abraham A. Fabian, director of the Brooklyn Juvenile Guidance Center, telescoped the problem from the angle of history, current practice, and postulates for change as follows: "Child guidance treatment of the parent has always been largely treatment of the mother. In the case of some children, work with the father may be just as urgent. The child may even be brought by the mother in the hope that the clinic will exert pressure on or draw in the sick father for treatment. In order to round out the child guidance program, therefore, provisions must be made to work with fathers. Some clinics arrange evening sessions for fathers who cannot attend during the day. Group therapy with fathers is also a valuable adjunct in their treatment."[2] Inclusion of the father into individualized treatment, thus, is not reported as current practice as of 1953 by this observer.

From Canada came a pronouncement corroborating this state of affairs in a review of *Social Science and Psychotherapy for Children.* In that review Dr. Hyman Caplan of the Children's Memorial Hospital in Montreal had this to say: "The role of the father as an important part of the 'family of orientation' is highlighted. The point is well taken because despite the lip service given to him in clinical conferences, group discussions, and dynamic theory, he is often left out of actual therapeutic management in most child guidance clinics."[3]

[1] Rosenthal, Maurice J., "Collaborative Therapy with Parents at Child Guidance Clinics," *Social Casework*, vol. 35, January, 1954, p. 18, note 3.

[2] Fabian, Abraham A., "The Contribution of Psychoanalysis to the Child Guidance Unit" in *Psychoanalysis and Social Work*, edited by Marcel Heiman. International Universities Press, New York, 1953, p. 145.

[3] Caplan, Hyman, "Review of *Social Science and Psychotherapy for Children*," *Canadian Welfare*, vol. 28, February, 1953, p. 46.

Dr. Jules Henry, formerly of the Washington University Child Guidance Clinic in St. Louis, Missouri, found practice in 1948 a reason for making the following statement: "We have the description of the father in many cases only from the mother, or from the child."[1]

The next question concerned the possibility of a difference between psychotherapy for children and casework with children, or—differently put—between child guidance clinics and work in family service agencies. The very designation of these two types of agencies involved in helping children with emotional difficulties suggests that in family welfare agencies, indeed, one might expect to find more attention paid to all family members than in child guidance clinics. There is some evidence in the literature, however, which indicates that this is so more on the level of exceptions than on the level of a rule. Word to this effect, for instance, has come from Elsa Leichter in a paper which was published in the symposium volume, *Diagnosis and Process in Family Counseling,* edited by M. Robert Gomberg and Frances T. Levinson in 1951. In that paper, work with both parents is presented as a pioneering effort. In introducing illustrative material, the author found it necessary to put her efforts into a relationship to general practice in casework agencies: "The S case illustrates a departure from the traditional approach to parent-child relationship problems in family agencies. In line with the deeply ingrained social concept that the mother is chiefly responsible for the rearing of the children, and therefore that it is her failure and responsibility if things go wrong, treatment services have in the past concentrated on the mother-child relationship as the core of child problems in working with such situations. When Mrs. S. expressed question about our wanting to see her husband, she was not merely expressing her own problem in letting her husband be the man in the family, but in part was stating her knowledge that what we asked of her was not customary in treating problems of children."[2]

[1] Henry, Jules, "Common Problems of Research in Anthropology and Psychiatry," *American Journal of Orthopsychiatry,* vol. 18, October, 1948, p. 699.
[2] Leichter, Elsa, "Participation in Treatment by Both Parents" in *Diagnosis and Process in Family Counseling,* edited by M. Robert Gomberg and Frances T. Levinson. Family Service Association of America. New York, 1951, p. 80.

The impression gained from this statement is strengthened by a document circulated by the American Association of Schools of Social Work about the same time the observations of practice described in our first report were made. At the 1951 annual meeting of the Association, a workshop was devoted to the teaching of advanced casework with emphasis on the treatment of children. In it Madeleine Lay presented for review and discussion the syllabus of a course on "Casework with Emotionally Disturbed Children," given for the first time in the fall of 1950. This syllabus presented seven cases as teaching material. Of these seven cases only two made specific reference to the fact that the father was seen. In both cases the problem was a placement request of the parents, and in one of these the child was not yet born. Of the other five cases used in the course, four represent situations where the father was not part of the primary group of the home for reasons such as death, divorce, or working in another town. In the fifth case it was not clear from the presentation of the syllabus whether the father was seen or not and whether the students had been given any instruction in this respect.[1] If fathers were involved routinely in the practice of casework with children, it might be assumed that teaching material of the type referred to probably would have presented a different selection of cases. Pedagogical considerations very likely would have suggested the advisability of presenting cases of intact families rather than of cases broken by the absence of the father from the home. The very fact that these cases could be used and that they were considered effective teaching material leaves no alternative to the assumption that they were considered to be representative of casework with children in general. Such representativeness, however, could have been the case only if concentration on the mother-child relationship was as much part of casework practice as it was part of psychotherapy practiced in child guidance clinics.

Interestingly enough, a volume entitled *Child Therapy:* A

[1] American Association of Schools of Social Work, *Workshop Report:* The Teaching of Advanced Casework with Emphasis on the Treatment of Children, Annual Meeting, January 24–27, 1951, Toronto, Ontario. (Mimeographed)

Casework Symposium, published by the Family Service Association of America, shows the same tendency to have prevailed also a few years earlier. This symposium presents in great detail four cases treated during the period between 1942 and 1946. These cases show considerable attention to collateral sources of information, such as schools and hospitals, but are relatively lacking in father contacts. Similar to the material presented by Madeleine Lay, three of these four cases preclude involvement of the father because the latter is physically absent from the home. In two cases he is serving in the armed forces and in one he is hospitalized. In one of the three cases contact was made with the father during a furlough. In the fourth case presented, however, the father was at home and although intensive treatment with mother and child went on for more than four years, the father was seen only twice. The first contact with him was made two and a half years after intensive treatment had started and the second one, six months later.[1] Certainly this case suggests that even if the fathers in the other cases had been at home and accessible to involvement in the diagnostic and therapeutic process, their chances of having been drawn into the nexus of casework concern would have been small.

It seems, therefore, that noninvolvement of fathers in the diagnostic and therapeutic considerations of children's cases during the forties and early fifties of this century could be found in family welfare agencies as well as in child guidance clinics.

A tendency to pay insufficient attention to fathers has been noted not only for the clinical field of child guidance but also for the field of parent education. Two authoritative statements have appeared to this effect. In 1952 Dr. Gunnar Dybwad, director of the Child Study Association of America, commented upon the general disregard of fathers in circles concerned with child welfare as follows: "Actually, considering the tremendous interest in parent education in this country for the past several

[1] Clifton, Eleanor, and Florence Hollis, editors, *Child Therapy:* A Casework Symposium. Family Service Association of America, New York, 1948.

decades and the amount of specific material available concerning the mother's role, astonishingly little has been written on behalf of the father."[1] One year earlier there appeared a book by Dr. O. Spurgeon English and Constance J. Foster entitled *Fathers Are Parents, Too.* The choice of the title indicates the existing situation. And the first page of the book's introduction reaffirms it. "In recent years many words have been written about '*mom,*' and penetrating analyses made of her attitudes and influence. But what about '*pop*'? Somehow he has managed to remain in the background. No one has put the spotlight on him."[2] Thus, concentration of interest upon the mother-child relationship seems to be a characteristic phenomenon of the whole professional subculture of child welfare work.

The third step in the writer's search for indications of actual practice as reflected in the literature concerned itself with the question whether involvement of fathers and siblings in child therapy was attributable only to the mistakes of learners. Actually, the quotations from the literature furnished so far are sufficient to suggest that this explanation does not hit its mark. However, further evidence is available which shows that this explanation is unlikely to be correct.

In recent years the *American Journal of Orthopsychiatry* has published a number of papers which reflect mature professional experience and judgment rather than the mistakes of caseworkers still in the learning stage. The authors of these papers have recognized standing in their field, and their reports are presented as gains in the development of practice and research in the clinical field.

Again there seems to exist a wide distribution of the same phenomenon. Let us look for instance at the city of Boston. There we have two such outstanding agencies as the Judge Baker Guidance Center and the James Jackson Putnam Children's Center. From the former have come interesting studies of the etiology of learning difficulties in children. Two papers

[1] Dybwad, Gunnar, "Fathers Today: Neglected or Neglectful?" *Child Study,* vol. 29, Spring, 1952, p. 3.

[2] English, O. Spurgeon, and Constance J. Foster, *Fathers Are Parents, Too.* G. P. Putnam's Sons, New York, 1951, p. vii.

have been published reporting on this research project. One was presented at the annual meeting of the American Orthopsychiatric Association in 1951, the other at the annual meeting of the same association in 1952. The first of these was coauthored and the second was written by a psychiatric social worker, Nancy Staver.[1] In the description of this project there are references to practice regarding parent contacts along these lines: "The children and one or both parents, most often the mother, have been seen weekly, for from eight to thirty-six months, in psychoanalytically oriented psychotherapeutic interviews."[2] "The seventeen families included in this study are chiefly intact families. . . . All the cases have been in treatment for over one year, with usually weekly interviews for mother and child and an occasional interview with many of the fathers."[3]

The question could be rightly raised whether this was only dictated by the nature of the project and whether the procedure with its relative neglect of studying the father was not unrepresentative of the general practice of the agency. The answer to this question, however, can be found in a statement from another social caseworker on the agency's staff, which has to be considered authoritative. In preparation for the annual meeting of the American Orthopsychiatric Association of 1952, the Judge Baker Guidance Center was requested by Dr. H. Whitman Newell, president of the Association, to present a child guidance clinic case which illustrated "the concomitant treatment of parent and child by two people." In response to this request the paper "Artie: A Victim of an Inconsistent Parental Relationship" was presented. In the discussion of the paper its coauthor Miss Holmes, the chief of the agency's social service department, made the following statement: "It is our general practice in the first interview to explain to the mother the pro-

[1] Sperry, Bessie M., Nancy Staver, and Harold E. Mann, "Destructive Fantasies in Certain Learning Difficulties," *American Journal of Orthopsychiatry*, vol. 22, April, 1952, pp. 356–365; and Staver, Nancy, "The Child's Learning Difficulty as Related to the Emotional Problem of the Mother," *Ibid.*, vol. 23, January, 1953, pp. 131–140.

[2] Sperry, Bessie M., and others, *op. cit.*, p. 356.

[3] Staver, Nancy, *op. cit.*, p. 131.

cedure of the clinic, and subsequently to keep her in touch with what is going on."[1]

That the same characteristics of practice prevail also at the James Jackson Putnam Children's Center can be gathered from two papers, one published in 1948 and the other in 1952. In 1948 Dr. Marian C. Putnam had this to say: "From the worker's description of her work with Mrs. M., it will be clear that in this, as in other cases at the Center, she does not attempt to effect a total reintegration of the personality and life of the parent. She focuses primarily on those elements which affect the parent's—usually the mother's—relationship with her child, and his treatment at the Center."[2] To those who might be inclined to point out that this practice description is taken from the case study of a two-and-a-half-year-old child, it will be of interest to note that the same concentration upon mother and child is maintained also for children who are likely to have reached the oedipal stage of development. This can be seen from the practice description made in a report on the treatment of a child who was brought to the same agency at four and a half years of age. "Eva . . . was included in our study of children with atypical development. . . . Our particular interest focused on the treatment possibilities and on what these children under minute observation during their years of treatment would reveal to us about early ego development and the mother-child unit. . . . Eva was unwanted by her mother. Her father hardly sounds like the kind of person who would pay much attention to a baby. . . . In the next (second) interview mother was remarkably friendly and reported that she and father had come to the conclusion that they had found a place that would help Eva. . . ."[3]

Certain important inferences can be drawn from this ac-

[1] Holmes, Elizabeth H., and Joseph P. Lord, "Artie: A Victim of Inconsistent Parental Relationship, Symposium, 1951," *American Journal of Orthopsychiatry*, vol. 22, January, 1952, pp. 1, 45–46.

[2] Putnam, Marian C., "Case Study of an Atypical Two-and-a-Half-Year-Old," *American Journal of Orthopsychiatry*, vol. 18, January, 1948, p. 30.

[3] Pavenstedt, Eleanor, and Irene N. Andersen, "Complementary Treatment of Mother and Child with Atypical Development: Workshop, 1951," *American Journal of Orthopsychiatry*, vol. 22, July, 1952, pp. 607–641. Quotations from pp. 607, 610, 614.

count. The clinic is primarily interested in the mother-child relationship. The father "sounds" like a certain kind of person. Jules Henry's observation of practice in St. Louis finds corroboration in Boston. Apparently the therapists knew the father only from the description by the mother. They received information about the father's attitude toward the clinic from the mother, and he in turn received a description of the clinic from the mother. The professional caliber of the persons who presented these descriptions for publication, and the fact that these descriptions fit into the pattern of practice generally described by such authorities as Dr. Fabian and Dr. English, make it clear that the concentration upon the mother and the child cannot be explained as a manifestation of the mistakes of learners.

THE PROBLEM IN HISTORICAL PERSPECTIVE

What remains to be done, then, is to inquire into the question of whether the concentration of practice upon the child and his mother which had provided the major stimulus for the work done in the liaison project represented a general forgetting of principles established and followed by an earlier generation of caseworkers. In that respect a review of the literature reveals exceedingly important and partially substantiating evidence. Since any search into the theory of social casework has to begin with Mary Richmond's classic, *Social Diagnosis,* it is fortunate that the work makes specific reference to this problem. The tendency of social workers to concentrate their interest upon the child and his mother is noticed and deplored. Specifically, the reader finds the following statement: "Husband and wife are not of the same blood, be it remembered. They have a past in common, but each has had an earlier past apart, and, since, in many forms of social work we see much of the wife and children and little or nothing of the husband and father, it is necessary deliberately to keep him in mind. Faulty methods of social work may have led him to think that his wife should do all the applying and explaining, but an understanding of the plans and purposes of the man of the family—his ambitions for his children and for himself—cannot be had without early personal contact with him. It is safer and it is fairer so, and our later planning and conferring should include him. . . . As plans for various forms of child welfare multiply it is more easy than ever to overlook the man of the family."[1]

Since nobody will contest the knowledge of Mary Richmond regarding prevailing practices, one must conclude that noninvolvement of the father is something which has been characteristic of social casework practically from the beginning. It was a point of concern to Miss Richmond as it was to the people involved in the liaison project between social science and child guidance practice thirty-five years later. The only question still to be answered is whether Mary Richmond's warning was heeded at least for a certain period and if so at what point it fell victim to a forgetting. Looking again for case descriptions which might reveal actual practice, the writer gained the impression that such a period existed.

One of the first case reports indicating that Miss Richmond's warning had made an impact upon practice appeared in 1924. In that year Dorothy Wallace, psychiatric social worker at "Child Guidance Clinic No. 2," wrote a paper in which she described a number of cases where the clinic had furnished only diagnostic services and cases where treatment measures had also been taken. Of the latter, she described five cases. Of these five, only two were families in which the father was present, but in both cases the father was included in diagnostic and therapeutic concern.[2] In the year 1930 Marion McBee, psychiatric social worker at the Illinois Society for Mental Hygiene, reported on a number of cases in a paper discussing the effects of family attitudes on the behavior of children at school. Altogether she presented eight cases; in two of these the father was absent from the home, but in the remaining six the fathers were involved in the helping process.[3] A case presentation in the

[1] Richmond, Mary E., *Social Diagnosis*. Russell Sage Foundation, New York, 1917, p. 143.

[2] Wallace, Dorothy, "Problem of the Quasi-Delinquent in the School," *Mental Hygiene*, vol. 8, January, 1924, pp. 160–163.

[3] McBee, Marion, "Family Attitudes Affecting School Behavior," *The Family*, vol. 11, March, 1930, pp. 13–16.

following year by Julia Mathews, psychologist at the Child Guidance Clinic of Pasadena and Los Angeles, confirms this impression. Again the father was intensively considered in the study of the child's problems and involved in the service contacts.[1] Similar impressions can be gained from a collection of child guidance cases which was published by the Commonwealth Fund in 1932. This volume contains eight cases. In five of these, there was some contact with the father, although clinic contacts with the mother were preponderant. In two cases clinic concern was equally directed at a father and a father substitute respectively. In only one case, no contact with the father was made.[2] However, at about the same time there appear in the literature expressions from social caseworkers which suggest that Mary Richmond's warning against noninvolvement of the father had not been fully effective and was on the verge of being forgotten in practice if not in theory.

Thus, in the twenties and early thirties, Miss Richmond's position that fathers should be involved in casework processes concerned with the problems of children seems to have found some reflection in practice. However, notice should be taken of the nature of this involvement and of its extent. Without these two considerations, it would not be possible to state clearly the nature of the forgetting for which present-day caseworkers seem to show a propensity to blame themselves. Actually, it appears possible to show that this self-blame is unjustified. The type of father involvement that was forgotten is not the father involvement that is seen as indicated today. And there is even considerable doubt that the type of father involvement which appeared in case reports following Mary Richmond's advice presented a generally accepted pattern of practice.

As to the nature of involving the father in the helping process, it should be remembered that in the period under consideration all parental involvement occurred only in two forms, in utiliz-

[1] Mathews, Julia, "Personality and the Parent-Child Relationship," *The Family*, vol. 12, November, 1931, pp. 208–213.

[2] Sayles, Mary B., editor, *Child Guidance Cases*. Commonwealth Fund, New York, 1932.

ing the parents as sources of information and in giving them advice. The contact between parents and the agency occurred on an essentially intellectual plane. Elements of relationship between worker and parents must have occurred, of course, but they were not part of the theoretical orientation underlying the contact, that is, not intentionally and planfully therapeutic. Furthermore, there is evidence from reliable resources that quantitatively contact with fathers even at that period was overshadowed by contacts with the mother. It appears now that when as a result of the integration of dynamic psychiatry into child guidance practice, advice-giving to parents shifted to involvement in treatment, the father became the forgotten man in child guidance. At first, there was still concern about this oversight as expressed, for instance, by Charlotte Towle in 1930. In her paper describing the treatment of behavior and personality problems in children as practiced at the Child Guidance Institute of New York City, which for some time operated under the directorship of Dr. David M. Levy, she had this to say: "It is generally agreed that fathers have been left too much out of the picture. This has occurred largely through the inconvenience in reaching them and the scarcity of their time. They are now generally interviewed at least once during the social examination and occasionally during the treatment process. The fine point of seeing the father first and making him the focus of treatment if the case indicates this need, is not a very general practice due to the inconvenience, in spite of a realization of his significance in the situation. . . . Since most of our treatment of parents has been with mothers, we probably have more of a beginning philosophy about handling the mother-child relationship than of any other in the family."[1]

At this point the scales seem to be in balance. On the basis of this recognition of the state of affairs, will the father be taken

[1] Towle, Charlotte, "The Social Worker" in "Symposium: The Treatment of Behavior and Personality Problems in Children," *American Journal of Orthopsychiatry,* vol. 1, October, 1930, pp. 26–27, reprinted in *Orthopsychiatry,* 1923–1948: Retrospect and Prospect, edited by Lawson G. Lowrey. American Orthopsychiatric Association, New York, 1948, pp. 589–590.

into the developing practice of child therapy in guidance work or will he be left out of the stream and increasingly lost sight of? Will caseworkers take him along into the new venture or will they lose him? It should be stressed that while as a person the father seems to be in danger of being forgotten, as a family member to be involved in therapy it is not really a question of forgetting but a question of discovery, because such involvement had not existed in the past.

To make a long story short, in practice he was forgotten or not discovered, however one wants to express it. In theory he continued to be mentioned by some and not by others. This development can be traced with considerable clarity through the literature of the thirties and the forties. As of 1934 the literature contains an indication of the things to come. "It has been recognized from the early days of child guidance that the close involvement of the child with its parents and especially with its mother, made treatment of the mother an almost inevitable concomitant of treatment of the child. But the first approaches to the mother were on the level of advice and enlightenment—the social worker or psychiatrist tried to clear away parental barriers to the child's development by explaining them and trusting to the mother's intelligence to act on the explanation, or by making specific suggestions and expecting the mother to follow them. Too often this failed. The mother accepted the advice intellectually, but was estopped from putting it into effect by emotional needs or conflicts of her own of which she might or might not be conscious. To free the child from deleterious pressures it became necessary to help the mother solve the problems in herself which led to them."[1] There still is a reference to "parents," but the equalization of the parental phenomenon in therapy with the phenomenon of the mother for the future is distinctly under way and significantly retrojected into the past.

From here on it becomes possible and necessary to trace three

[1] Stevenson, George S., and Geddes Smith, *Child Guidance Clinics:* A Quarter Century of Development. Commonwealth Fund, New York, and Harvard University Press, Cambridge, Mass., 1934, p. 91.

lines of development in child guidance work which, although differing from one another in emphasis and orientation, combine to bear testimony to the reality that in practice the father—and other persons in the environment of the child—were not involved in therapeutic planning while the mother dominated the scene. There were, first of all, those who stressed the importance of both parents in theory but presented cases and made generally descriptive statements which indicated concentration on the mother-child relationship in practice. Into this group belongs, for instance, Phyllis Blanchard who, in her contribution to the Commonwealth Fund publication *Psychiatric Interviews with Children,* felt it necessary to make the following statement which, however, confirms rather than refutes the general picture of the situation: "Since in the two cases illustrating therapy that I have contributed to this volume (the present case and Case 9) the clinic worked with the mother and child, this might lead to some misconception unless it is stated that this is not invariably what happens. There are other cases in which the therapy with the child is supported by social work with both parents, and some in which the focus of social work is the father's relationship rather than the mother's."[1] Into the same group seem to have belonged for a period also Drs. Stanislaus Szurek, Adelaide Johnson, and Eugene I. Falstein, who in a paper published in 1942 permit us to appraise the situation as it seems to have existed in Chicago about 1940. This paper showing awareness of the dynamic importance of the father reveals again divergence between theory and actual practice with regard to father contacts. "There is an increasing awareness on the part of clinicians dealing with children that the behavior of a child is to be understood fundamentally only in the context of the intrafamilial interpersonal relations. Pathological relationships between mother and father and child play a great role in helping to maintain the distorted and unintegrated tendencies in the child. It is unnecessary here to refer to the many years of excellent and successful collaborative work

[1] Witmer, Helen Leland, editor, *Psychiatric Interviews with Children.* Commonwealth Fund, New York, and Harvard University Press, Cambridge, Mass., 1946, p. 66, note 12.

that has been done with the psychiatric social worker seeing the mother and the psychiatrist seeing the child in treatment disorders that are not too firmly crystallized."[1] The same development also seems to be presented in a paper written by Katharine M. Wickman and Dr. William S. Langford, referring to work at the Columbia Medical Center. The time span covered by the practice description contained in that paper was apparently the period between 1937 and 1944, as can be inferred from the following passages: "In collaboration with Dr. William S. Langford, psychiatrist in charge of the psychiatric clinic of the Babies Hospital [children's service of the Columbia Presbyterian Medical Center] there has been experimentation with cases over a period of seven years in an effort to see how knowledge gained from experience in psychiatric social treatment in which a specialized therapeutic method is used could be applied in other work. . . . The bulk of experience has been with mothers. While less knowledge has been gained about feelings of fathers, the particular treatment considerations to be presented are believed in general to be applicable to interviews with fathers as well as with mothers."[2]

A second line of development shows a solidification of the practical concern with the mother-child relationship into a theory suggesting a belief in its exclusive importance. While that development was apparently shaping up in the early thirties, it had nearly reached completion in 1937. In that year Dr. David M. Levy gave a description of attitude therapy in child guidance, which shows that the father's noninvolvement was about to be distinctly established. "In child guidance work the original plan was to utilize the social worker as a means of ensuring the child's appointments with the psychiatrist, of following out the program of social treatment, and of imparting to the mother such information as was considered essential in solving the difficulty. Out of her rich experience in interviewing

[1] Szurek, Stanislaus, Adelaide Johnson, Eugene Falstein, "Collaborative Psychiatric Therapy of Parent-Child Problems," *American Journal of Orthopsychiatry*, vol. 12, July, 1942, p. 511.

[2] Wickman, Katharine M., and William S. Langford, "The Parent in the Children's Psychiatric Clinic," *American Journal of Orthopsychiatry*, vol. 14, April, 1944, p. 219.

mothers, the worker gained skill in verbalizing difficulties and in giving insight by demonstrating the influence of the parent-child relationship. The treatment was centered on the child, who was treated directly by the psychiatrist, all other aids being furnished by the psychologist and social worker. What happened in many cases, probably in most, was a curious shift in function. The psychiatrist had often very little to do with the child when the problem was activated primarily by intra-familial relationships."[1]

While this still was a description of practice, a statement made in 1949 shows that this practice had become supported by a succinctly expressed theoretical position. Carrying on Dr. Levy's description of what happened in the development of clinical work in child guidance, Annette Garrett brought the account to the following climax. "The main task of the treatment often devolved upon a social worker who was forced to develop a method of treatment with the mother with the purpose essentially of modifying her attitudes in order to insure a better adjustment for the child. This method was developed because treatment of the child failed, due to problems in the mother."[2] And 1949, significantly enough, was the year in which the liaison project between social science and child guidance work with its concern of securing consideration of other factors besides the mother was initiated by Russell Sage Foundation and the Jewish Board of Guardians. In attempting to make this particular contribution the project ordered itself into a third line of development in child guidance work, which already had started to voice objection to a concentration of therapeutic concern upon the mother-child relationship and thereby had testified to its existence.

This third line of development represents a beginning reorientation in the field of child guidance which was paralleled by similar trends in social casework and marriage counseling and requires attention. The character and promise of this re-

[1] Levy, David M., "Attitude Therapy," *American Journal of Orthopsychiatry*, vol. 7, January, 1937, p. 104.

[2] Garrett, Annette, "Historical Survey of the Evolution of Casework," *Journal of Social Casework*, vol. 30, June, 1949, p. 223.

orientation, however, can best be described and evaluated after the reasons for the divergences between theory and practice described in this chapter have been studied. Thus, it is the causation of this phenomenon to which attention will be paid in the next chapter.

VIII. Principles Operating in the Divergence Between Theory and Practice

OUR REVIEW OF THEORY AND PRACTICE has revealed that concentration of concern upon the mother-child relationship is widespread in the field of child guidance. It has indicated that a tendency toward concentration existed in casework practice related to child welfare long before the impact of psychoanalytic thinking upon social casework had typed the thinking of the profession. It seems to be true, however, that under the influence of Mary Richmond's teaching a start was made in the child guidance clinics of the twenties to include the consideration of the father in their work. Because of the period in which this occurred, the inclusion was on the level of the social study and of advice giving only.

Apparently the practice of including the father was discontinued when child guidance work became permeated with the thinking of dynamic psychiatry, which in turn led to the involvement of the child and his mother in psychotherapy. In essence, an involvement of the father in *psychotherapy* practiced in child guidance clinics was not forgotten, because it never got under way. A tendency to forget the father as a phenomenon in the child's life, however, had existed before Mary Richmond, had been counteracted by her, and had reasserted itself when psychotherapy became established as a method in child guidance work. Whereas consideration of the father in child guidance work thus appears to have fallen under the spell of a forgetting, involvement of other family members and particularly of siblings as essential parts of the helping concern in the same case seems never to have come to the fore at any stage of development in child guidance work.

ABSENCE OF APPROPRIATE FORMULATIONS

These developments of practice occurred in spite of the fact that dynamic psychiatry and social casework represented from the beginning theoretical positions which by their very nature might have suggested that such a concentration upon the child and his mother was counterindicated. In this respect reference might be made to the concepts of oedipal involvement and sibling rivalry as developed in psychoanalysis and to the concern with total families as expressed in the orientation and aims of social casework. It is puzzling how professionally trained persons operating with the theory of the oedipus complex could come to disregard the father in practice, if not in theory, and how such persons assuming the dynamic forces of sibling rivalry could come to treat one child suffering from this psychological discomfort without the inclusion of his sibling in the orbit of direct therapeutic concern. It is equally puzzling that the same thing could happen to members of a profession so oriented to a consideration of the family that it designated its specific service organizations as family welfare agencies. When these phenomena were pointed out in the first report, it was not foreseen that representatives of the professions concerned would be inclined to explain this divergence between theory and practice as mistakes of learners, of people working in child guidance, or of a new generation of caseworkers. It was the purpose and content of the first report to relate these phenomena to the absence of an appropriate conceptual underpinning of practice and to propose social science concepts as aids in a situation which, according to leaders of both child psychiatry and social casework, required remedial attention. The reaction of self-blame which the pinpointing of these phenomena produced required further study of this situation and led to the growing conviction of this writer that the divergence between theory and practice regarding the importance of environmental factors in a child's life beyond his mother was due not only to the absence of appropriate theoretical formulations but also to the presence of inappropriate ones. In other words, the writer was led to the belief which he presents here as a hypothesis that the noninvolvement of the father, for instance, was not a disregard of theory in practice but forced upon practice by the very formulations of the theory. It increasingly appeared to the writer that therapists who concentrated their concern upon the child and his mother did not violate "laws of nature" as the critics of the first report were willing to admit, but acted according to "laws of nature" which the very formulation of their theory brought into operation.

It so happened that the first report on the liaison project came to terms only with one of these principles and thus did not do justice to the full force of psychological laws which enforced the divergence between theory and practice with which it was concerned. It based its propositions only on the principle that "obvious" facts "cannot be grasped until we possess adequate descriptive concepts enabling us to perform this task."[1] It still is the belief of the writer that this phenomenon exists and accounts, in part, for the noninvolvement of significant family members in the therapeutic nexus of child guidance practice. In this respect also, he finds endorsement in Mary Richmond's writing. It drew the attention of caseworkers to the need for "funded thought," that is, concepts, as a basis for perception.[2] Unfortunately, her own formulations of theory frequently remained on the level of descriptions rather than reaching the level of conceptualizations and thus robbed her wisdom of lasting communicative power. This becomes apparent, if one studies her references to the phenomena conceptualized in sociology as "family of orientation," "social interaction," and "culture conflict." To the first of these, for instance, she made reference in the following passage: "The term Family Group . . . includes all who share a common table, though the parents and children . . . will receive most attention here."[3] Here no distinctive concept is really presented because the term "family group" in common language usage includes also relatives who

[1] Ichheiser, Gustav, *Misunderstandings in Human Relations:* A Study in False Social Perception. Supplement to *American Journal of Sociology*, vol. 55, September, 1949, part 2, p. 2.

[2] Richmond, Mary E., *Social Diagnosis*. Russell Sage Foundation, New York, 1917, pp. 66–68.

[3] *Ibid.*, p. 134, note 1.

do not share a common table. Furthermore, no functionally descriptive term is coined which would guide the worker to use it when concerned with family functions. In child-rearing matters the term "family of orientation" designating the group of people that Mary Richmond had in mind appears to be stronger, because it indicates the social phenomenon which justifies the specific designation, i.e., the orientation, which the group of those who share a table, i.e., a home, essentially provides for the growing child.

A similar absence of conceptualization can be found in the social casework literature with regard to the phenomenon of "social interaction." Reference to it is frequently made but always in descriptive terms. Mary Richmond again gave a description rather than a concept. "It is a sobering thought that the social worker's power of influence may extend, through his daily acts, to many whom he has never seen and never, even for a moment, had in mind. This is peculiarly true of all the members who are unknown to him in the Family Groups of his clients. For better or worse he influences them and they, in turn, help or hinder the achievement of the ends that he has in view."[1] The same type of discussion can be found thirteen years later in a statement from the pen of Charlotte Towle. "Treatment cannot be given to any member of a family without affecting the group."[2] And as late as 1951 we find the same form of reference to the phenomenon made by one of the outstanding authorities on family centered casework, Frances Scherz. "It is essential always to keep in mind the effect of casework treatment on family balance."[3] In the same descriptive vein, Mary Richmond took cognizance of the phenomenon of culture conflict. "One of the social worker's difficulties with foreigners is that he does not understand their conventions any more than they do his."[4]

[1] *Ibid.*, p. 134.

[2] Towle, Charlotte, "The Social Worker" in "Symposium: The Treatment of Behavior and Personality Problems in Children" in *Orthopsychiatry, 1923–1948*, edited by Lawson G. Lowrey, p. 596.

[3] Scherz, Frances H., "Criteria for Defining Program and Emphasis in the Family Agency," *Social Casework*, vol. 32, March, 1951, p. 111.

[4] Richmond, Mary E., *Social Diagnosis*, p. 73.

There are three qualities to be noted in these references to the phenomena involved. There is always a lack of one noun clearly and unequivocally designating the phenomenon and at the same time summarizing its description; there is an implication that the phenomenon referred to is overlooked in practice; and there is an admonition, implied or clearly expressed, that such overlooking should be discontinued. Apparently there is no recognition that the perceptual tool which would prevent the overlooking is not provided. It seems to the writer that this failure to conceptualize the wisdom of the profession has made for the necessity to give social workers instruction about the same phenomena over and over again and that this experience of repeated admonition has made the profession inclined to think of its practice as mistake prone rather than as insufficiently conceptualized and therefore difficult to teach. The thought might be expressed in this connection whether the extended need for supervision of workers who hold professional degrees has not one of its roots here.

INAPPROPRIATE COMBINATIONS OF CONCEPTS

Next to the lack of concepts which makes omissions in perception "natural," there seems to exist also a characteristic of both psychiatric and social casework theory which enforces distortions of perception, namely, the combination of concepts of different degrees of abstraction, of concepts of different quality, and the presentation of these combinations in the form of misleading dichotomies. That the formations of such combinations are theoretically unsatisfactory has been pointed out by Dr. John P. Spiegel in his incisive evaluation of the symposium *Mid-century Psychiatry*. It might well be the case that in times to come Spiegel's postulate of "a conceptual scheme, pitched at a level of abstraction from human behavior appropriate to the unification of the various points of views"[1] will be considered the outstanding contribution of that symposium to a science of human behavior. What is attempted here should

[1] Spiegel, John P., "Critique of Symposium" in *Mid-century Psychiatry:* An Overview, edited by Roy R. Grinker. Charles C. Thomas, Springfield, Ill., 1953, p. 181.

be considered only as an elaboration of this postulate and an attempt to suggest its justification through the adaptation of theorems of Gestalt psychology to perceptual problems encountered in social casework, in child guidance, and in child psychiatry.

THE PRINCIPLE OF SIMILARITY

As is well known, Gestalt psychology is a branch of the behavior sciences which has identified a number of significant principles in the area of sensory perception. One of them claims "that the equal and the similar tend to form units separated from what is dissimilar to them."[1] This is frequently referred to as the Law of Similarity. Thus, when only a number of similar phenomena such as dots are arranged in a field as presented below:

• • • • • •

the observer is likely to state that he perceives a line. In other words, his thought process becomes directed to the plurality of these phenomena with equal strength and he deals with them in their totality. However, if the observer is confronted with combinations of phenomena that are different from one another, as would be the case for instance in the arrangement below:

x x x
• • • o o o

he will be tempted to group the similar ones into unities for his attention. The sum total of these phenomena will not impress him as a unity and he will find it difficult to deal with them in their totality.

[1] Kohler, Wolfgang, *Gestalt Psychology*. Horace Liveright, Inc., New York, 1929, p. 157.

An attempt to adapt this Law of Similarity to the consideration of concepts which are used in clinical work, would suggest that therapists are more likely to consider together concepts of the same quality than concepts of different quality. In consequence, such concepts as "the child and his mother" would be perceived and utilized together with greater ease than such concepts as "the child and his family." And such concepts as the "child and his family," although less accessible to perception in totality than "the child and his mother," still would be more manageable in efforts at integrated perception than the combination presented by the formulation of "the child and his environment." The concept combination "child and his mother" represents two units which are both of the same quality of abstraction, because both units remain on the level of the individual. The concept combination "the child and his family," however, is an attempt to represent as a totality one concept which is coined in terms of singularity and one concept which is coined in terms of a plurality, one which compared with the other is more concrete and one which in comparison with the preceding one is more abstract. The differential quality of the concepts combined, of course, is even more striking in the so frequently used dichotomy of *child and environment* because "the environmental influences to which he [a child] is being subjected . . . fall into three categories:

"(1) The real physical world.

"(2) The influence of other people—most notably that of parents, teachers, and older siblings.

"(3) The influence of the social mores. . . ."[1]

In other words, the concept "environment" encompasses human and nonhuman organisms, organic and inorganic objects, material and nonmaterial things.

If we utilize sensory perceptions in an effort to illustrate the perceptual difficulties which the current concept combinations create for the clinician, whether he is a psychiatrist or social

[1] Pearson, Gerald H. J., *Emotional Disorders of Children.* W. W. Norton and Co., New York, 1949, p. 307.

worker, it would appear that we ask him to perceive as totalities with equal ease phenomena somewhat comparable to the following combinations:

Even if this view should be granted only suggestive merit, it might become difficult to blame clinicians for mistakes, if they confine their attention to the child and his mother. One would have to consider at least the possibility that the mistake lies with the current concept combinations, that is, with the theory itself.

SINGULARIZATION OF PLURALITIES

It is proposed here that the dichotomies of "child and his family" and "child and his environment," as well as the corresponding dichotomies of "client and his family" and "client and his environment," enhance perceptual difficulties rather than diminishing them. What is worse, they conceal them, because they present combinations of singularities and pluralities as combinations of two singularities. The "environment" after all is grammatically a singular noun, and so is "the family." The impression is thus given that the concept referring to greater complexity is of the same order as the concept of lesser complexity. Plurality is equipped with the grammatical appearance of singularity. This language usage of theory and practice could be called a *tendency toward a singularization of pluralities.*

Perhaps the best expression of this tendency can be found in the utilization by authors of the singular "parent" in place of the plural "parents." Although there is usually in the text also a reference to "parents," it becomes easily apparent that the use of the substitute term "parent" leads to treatment suggestions which really consider only one parent and to theoretical discussions which do the same. That this singularization of the parental couple into "the parent" was common usage already in the early thirties can be gathered from the following statement made by Dr. Gregory Zilboorg. "It has become a truism to say that you must frequently treat the parent, if you want to help the child who has psychological difficulties."[1]

A similar implication for therapy can also be found in the following statement by Dr. Frederick H. Allen in his work *Psychotherapy with Children.* "While my major emphasis in this book is on the participation of the child in the therapeutic process, it must be kept in mind that the value of what the child and therapist accomplish together is enhanced when the parent is an integral participant in the therapeutic procedure."[2]

Not any more an implication but a clear-cut statement of singularization in practice is expressed in the paper "The Parent in the Children's Psychiatric Clinic" by Katharine M. Wickman and William S. Langford. It begins, as is frequently the case, with a reference to parents in the plural and then engages in singularization. "Psychiatric social workers, in their therapeutic services to parents, have included treatment which has been carried on in accordance with specialized therapeutic methods. . . . Significant therapeutic results may be achieved without dependence upon the conditions in treatment which obtain when a specialized therapeutic method is used. . . . The social worker may offer the parent planned therapeutic service and in the same interview use the parent in behalf of the patient as the responsible relative in the clinic." In this passage, singu-

[1] Zilboorg, Gregory, "Sidelights on Parent-Child Antagonism," *American Journal of Orthopsychiatry*, vol. 2, January, 1931, p. 35.

[2] Allen, Frederick Harold, *Psychotherapy with Children.* W. W. Norton and Co., New York, 1942, p. 10.

larization does not only occur, but its process actually is referred to. The worker may "use the parent" as "the responsible relative."[1] It is the worker's doing which produces the result. Although the law, as well as social reality, places responsibility on both parents, the worker transfers this phenomenon of plurality into one of singularity. It is the opinion of the writer that the worker almost must do so as long as theory asks him to consider the singularity of the child and the plurality of the parents together. Again, the temptation may arise to call such singularizations "mistakes." The point here made, however, is that this "mistake" is not individual deviation from a performance level generally attained but a perceptual distortion which is imposed upon the clinicians by a dichotomization of unequal and therefore in their combination unmanageable concepts. How far the effects of this necessity of singularization under existing theory go, can be seen from the fact that they have found expression also in statements regarding the division of labor between psychiatrists and social caseworkers. "The psychiatrist may work with the child while the social case-worker sees the parent; or, again, the psychiatrist may see the parent and the case-worker have interviews with the child."[2]

These examples which illustrate the consequences of a singularization of pluralities for practice can be paralleled by quotations from the literature which indicate the consequences of this same tendency for theory as such. A statement of Dr. Lawson G. Lowrey may start us off. "The affectional relationships between parents and children are, however, not especially simple. For the most part, the attitude of a parent towards a child is a blend of acceptance and rejection, liking and disliking, dominating and submitting, and sympathy and envy, etc. That is to say, the parent does not ordinarily accept everything that the child does. . . . Similarly, the parent does not approve or

[1] Wickman, Katharine M., and William S. Langford, "The Parent in the Children's Psychiatric Clinic," *American Journal of Orthopsychiatry*, vol. 14, April, 1944, p. 219.

[2] Robinson, J. Franklin, "Current Trends in Child Guidance Clinics," *Mental Hygiene*, vol. 34, January, 1950, p. 110.

like all of the things which the child does. . . . There is a tendency on the part of the parent to become identified with the child and at the same time a tendency to reject the child."[1]

The same shift in the grammar used can be found also in the published writings of caseworkers. "The emotional growth of the child is a continuing process and at each level problems may arise. The child's developing urge for increased freedom may often be blocked by his need to retain the protective love of his parents. Coincidentally, the problem of the parent may manifest itself in his difficulty in relating to his child's growing need for being treated on a more mature level. . . . In coming to the agency, the parent and child involved may or may not see the problem as one in which both have a part."[2]

While in the preceding examples it is still possible to discount the singularization as a figure of speech, the next quotation shows that it leads to theoretical justifications of the assumption of singularity in parental influence. The opening sentence of the paper on "Collaborative Psychiatric Therapy of Parent-Child Problems" by Drs. Stanislaus Szurek, Adelaide Johnson, and Eugene Falstein indicates this consequence. "This paper describes a technique for psychiatric treatment and research in the behavior problems and psychoneurotic disorders of children in which concomitant therapeutic efforts are made by two psychiatrists, one of whom deals with the significant parent and the other directly with the child."[3] Since the singularization in practice and theory come into conflict with the realities of parental couples, the resulting fractionalization of the environment under consideration must be justified in assumptions of differential importance.

Thus, we have seen what unfortunate dichotomization of the type deplored by Dr. John P. Spiegel can do. We know from reality that families as a rule contain two parents and fre-

[1] Lowrey, Lawson G., "The Family as a Builder of Personality," *American Journal of Orthopsychiatry*, vol. 6, January, 1936, pp. 119–120.

[2] Baumann, Caryl, and Ethel Hurvitz, "Treatment of a Parent Adult-Child Relationship," *Journal of Social Casework*, vol. 28, June, 1947, p. 217.

[3] Szurek, Stanislaus, Adelaide Johnson, and Eugene Falstein, "Collaborative Psychiatric Therapy of Parent-Child Problems," *American Journal of Orthopsychiatry*, vol. 12, July, 1942, p. 511.

quently more than one child. The theory and practice of casework, child guidance and child psychiatry, however, know the parent and the child. The environment is fractionalized as it must be when pluralities are singularized. And the Law of Similarity requires singularization when perception is forced to deal with dichotomies which baste together concepts referring to one individual and concepts referring to a group.

THE PRINCIPLE OF FIGURE GROUND ARTICULATION

Perhaps even more important than the difficulties for perception which the dichotomy of "individual and environment" creates because of its running counter to the principle of similarity are the difficulties which it creates because it conforms to another principle of Gestalt psychology, namely, the principle of figure ground articulation. Taken like most principles of Gestalt psychology from the visual field, this principle suggests that when the perception of a figure and the perception of its background or framework are compared, we always find the ground parts "to be simpler, in the sense of greater uniformity, less articulation" than the figure.[1] Although discovered in the visual field the distinction seems to be valid for all types of sensory perception. "For audition, it is clear; we can hear speech on the background of the patter of the rain, or the roaring of a mountain stream."[2]

Adapted to the manipulation of concepts in thought and clinical activity, this principle would suggest a fascinating and perfectly "lawful" though regrettable consequence for the actual perception of phenomena under the impact of the dichotomy of individual and environment. As early as 1928, Edith N. Burleigh, chief of Social Service, Child Guidance Clinic, Los Angeles, took the occasion of social work's concern with the environment to point out that according to Webster's dictionary, environment is "(1) Act of environing. (2) That which environs; the *surrounding conditions, influences, or forces.*"[3]

[1] Koffka, K., *Principles of Gestalt Psychology.* Harcourt, Brace and Co., New York, 1935, p. 186.
[2] *Ibid.*, p. 200.
[3] Burleigh, Edith N., "What Is Environment?" *The Family,* vol. 8, January, 1928, p. 317.

While she went on to stress the dynamic nature of the environment, the family membership composing it, and pointed out that there was more to it than "purely economic and social factors," by implication she described a theoretical position which apparently has always been accepted by clinicians—as it has by many others—namely, that the environment surrounds the individual; in other words, that the individual is seen as the figure and the environment as the ground. That this occasionally has been done as a conscious teaching device comes out quite clearly in a paper devoted to an elucidation of the nature of field work instruction. "In the first conference with the student the field instructor went over the family situation with her, emphasizing Paul as the central figure and presenting Mr. and Mrs. Szabo and the home setting as background."[1] By dichotomizing phenomena of equal importance into a relationship of figure and ground, theory forced practice into an unequal treatment of these phenomena. It brought into operation the perceptual tendency to differential articulation. Now it becomes understandable why social caseworkers whose definition of function and special competence was primarily seen in the knowledge of the environment became actually specialists in individual psychology. That this psychology was psychoanalytically oriented, undoubtedly was due to the intellectual and emotional power of that particular discipline, but that it was psychological as such follows with necessity from the dichotomization of a figure and ground relationship. It was not a mistake, it was almost absence of a perceptual choice. It was not complete absence, however, because the principle of differential articulation permits the counter experience, if a special effort is made to overcome the general tendency. "In changing from ground to figure a field part becomes more solid, and in the reverse change more loose."[2] Such a counter effort was made in our seminar discussion through the presence of the sociologist on the team, which provided stimulation to look at the persons forming the environment of the child in terms of

[1] Byars, Doris, "Learning by Doing," *The Family,* vol. 12, June, 1931, p. 118.
[2] Koffka, K., *op. cit.,* p. 186.

the "family of orientation." And as the psychiatrist commented, our cases became "richer." But the laws of perception are harsh. As one seminar member observed, our clinical and dynamic diagnoses were slower in coming than in routinized practice. Apparently the perception of the "child patient," the figure, was impeded though not prevented by the shift. And thus the task arose to find a framework of concepts which created a new and wider focus, which we found in the concepts of *family diagnosis, family therapy,* and *orchestration.* Through this wider framework we achieved a measure of liberation from the need to shift perception. Rather than seeing one *or* the other phenomenon well, we began to see them together. Such seeing together, however, required an overall concern as an organizing principle of wider perception. This concern we found in the purpose of our service, that is, in *child welfare.* In our experience, it so happened that this proved to be more than just an organizing principle. It appeared to be also a principle facilitating access to the emotional difficulties of parents in actual therapeutic effort. Furthermore, it helped in the restatement of the function of a child guidance clinic as a concern with families in questions of child welfare. To state this as child focus, as we still did in our seminar discussions, now appears dangerous, because of the restraining impact on perception which such a formulation is likely to have. The focus is the family. Tendencies of pathology producing interaction and association which are found in the family, however, are studied and treated with regard to its child-rearing function.

CONSEQUENCES FOR THERAPEUTIC PRACTICE

Having made an attempt to show the probable consequences of the traditional concept combinations and their dichotomizations for clinical perception, it might be useful to investigate at least tentatively what their apparent consequences have been for the development of specific therapeutic methods. Logical thinking alone would have suggested the conclusion that a dichotomization of therapeutic methods derived from a perceptually misleading dichotomy of phenomena would be likely to produce similar consequences regarding the perception of the nature of the two types of therapy. Actually perusal of the clinical literature supports this logical conclusion. There we find the dichotomy of individual and environmental treatment sometimes reformulated as direct and indirect therapy. Both formulations imply the consequences of the principle of similarity and of the principle of figure ground articulation. We have shown already through references to the literature how the principle of similarity caused singularization of the environment in terms of one of its parts which can be perceived as similar to the individual who is treated in individual or direct therapy. In other words, we have shown how treatment was likely to become dual rather than multiple, that is, how the child and one parental figure were likely to be treated in synchronized therapy, with the consequence that other important figures remained uninvolved.

The conformity to the principle of figure ground articulation, on the other hand, seems to have blurred the nature of the environment and led clinicians to assume simplicity where complexity is likely to exist. This has expressed itself in a tendency to think that the environment can be "manipulated" in order to produce better growth conditions for a child.

Both these consequences, the singularization of the environment as well as the blurring out of its complexity, are well illustrated in a statement of Dr. Lawson G. Lowrey. "*Indirect treatment.* This involves environmental manipulation, from utilization of community resources and modifications of educational and other programs, to direct therapy with a parent."[1] It might be difficult to find in the literature of the clinical field another statement which in a single sentence shows so clearly the consequences of the dichotomization of the two types of treatment. Both a tendency to deal mechanistically with the environment and a tendency to singularize it where mechanistic impact is abandoned are expressed succinctly in a few words.

The differential intensity of therapeutic effort which results

[1] Lowrey, Lawson G., "Orthopsychiatric Treatment," *Orthopsychiatry, 1923–1948*, p. 540.

from this dichotomization was expressed also by Margaret W. Gerard. "In recent years many clinics have developed programs for 'collaborative therapy' of mother and child in which they are treated by different therapists, but synchronously. . . . Other members of the family who play a role in the development of a child's illness must be considered in the treatment plan. I shall not elaborate details of the relationship to these persons. . . . In some instances, occasional interviews with the father, with the parents together, or with the nurse if she is important in the child's life, are most useful in maintaining a consistency of approach and continuity of the overall plan."[1] Here the concentration upon the mother-child relationship is put in particularly clear perspective because other possible human factors in the etiology of a child's illness are mentioned. The mother, however, is treated and for the others "occasional" interviews are considered sufficient. The human environment of a child with the exception of his mother is "not elaborated in detail" and thus by implication is denied its share in the exposure to an operation of psychodynamics, which would make treatment necessary. To quote just one more authority in the clinical field, attention may be drawn to the following statement by Maurice Levine. "Indirect psychotherapy consists of procedures which influence the patient indirectly through having a direct effect on his surroundings. One example is environmental manipulation, i.e., a modification of the external living conditions to lessen noxious pressures or to provide a more beneficial type of influence. A simple example of this is the placement of a child in a well-chosen foster-home. Another type of indirect psychotherapy is the treatment of a parent to produce changes in his attitudes toward the child who was the original patient."[2] Again we have "environmental manipulation" and treatment of "a" parent.

In this dichotomization of types of therapy which follows

[1] Gerard, Margaret W., "Trends in Orthopsychiatric Therapy: V, Treatment of the Young Child," *American Journal of Orthopsychiatry,* vol. 18, July, 1948, pp. 418, 420.

[2] Levine, Maurice, "Principles of Psychiatric Treatment" in *Dynamic Psychiatry,* edited by Franz Alexander and Helen Ross. Copyright (1952) by the University of Chicago Press, Chicago, p. 348.

from the dichotomization of individual and environment, the existence of psychodynamic factors in *all* persons who populate this environment is apparently denied. The blurred perception of the environment as background permits the suggestion that some persons in the environment can be manipulated or influenced in a few interviews. Since reality is likely to refute this underlying assumption, actual practice had to withdraw from those parts of the environment which were suggested for manipulation. The relative noninvolvement of siblings, of teachers, of doctors, of nurses, and other nonparental figures, as well as that of fathers, may well have one of its reasons in this phenomenon.

From the articulation of the patient as the figure and the environment as the ground or framework, with its resulting mechanistic implications for environmental treatment, seems to follow also an underevaluation of the task which under customary divisions of labor in many child guidance clinics is assigned to social caseworkers. The psychiatrist works with the child and the social worker with the environment. Or the psychiatrist contributes to the clinical team "psychiatric" knowledge and the social worker "environmental" knowledge. Once it is fully perceived that the environment of a child with intrapsychic difficulties is likely to be composed of the intrapsychic difficulties of others, it will be also perceived that under such divisions of labor the task of greater complexity is assigned to the social worker. As long, however, as the dichotomy between direct and environmental treatment is maintained, that situation will be blurred. Since social caseworkers, of course, are also under the influence of the laws of perception, they are likely to fall in with this underevaluation of "environmental" therapy, which results from the implication of mechanistic manipulation. Status assurance and professional satisfaction, then, are almost thrown upon the mercy of singularization which permits psychodynamically oriented therapy of "the environment" by extolling one part of it as its essence.

This situation has been pinpointed by Irene Josselyn in her paper "The Caseworker as Therapist." "Historically, environmental therapy was the first area in which the caseworker assumed the role of therapist. With the recognition of the effect of the impact of the environment upon the individual, it became apparent that if the environment were modified, the individual's pattern of behavior might also be modified. Children were removed from undesirable homes and schools, adults were helped to find congenial jobs and adequate recreation, and disturbed individuals were protected from excessive pressure from reality as they struggled with their internal conflicts. The results in many cases were, and continue to be, excellent. In spite of the success, caseworkers are sometimes embarrassed about these humble endeavors. It is unfortunate that treatment of this character is being relegated to a stepchild position in casework, since it is the unique contribution made by casework in the area of therapy. It deserves to be defended, since when applicable, it is one of the most constructive types of therapy."[1] This observation, however, begs the question. Why are social caseworkers inclined to consider "environmental" therapy as "humble" endeavors? It might be worth investigating whether this feeling does not relate to their awareness that if such environmental changes can be achieved without the consideration of psychodynamics, this is due to fortunate coincidences in case constellations rather than to efforts requiring professional skills. If environmental therapy was relieved from the perceptual trap of figure ground articulation, the psychodynamics operating in teachers, doctors, and other important persons would be recognized and arrangements now left to "manipulation" by the caseworker would be recognized to involve sometimes, if not frequently, tasks of greater complexity than direct psychotherapy.

POSSIBLE REASONS FOR SINGLING OUT MOTHERS

Our search for factors which may be identified as determining the divergences between theory and practice pointed out in the preceding chapter, so far has thrown some light on the reasons why consideration of the dynamic nature of the environ-

[1] Josselyn, Irene M., "The Caseworker as Therapist," *Journal of Social Casework*, vol. 29, November, 1948, p. 351.

ment is restricted in child guidance practice. Since we have seen, however, and—as a matter of fact—have started out with the observation that this restriction expresses itself as a concentration upon the mother-child relationship, the question has to be asked why it was just the mother who was singled out in the perceptual distortions which the traditional formulations of theory seem to have imposed upon the practitioners. Here we must go back to Mary Richmond's observation that social caseworkers showed a tendency to do that from early times on. Undoubtedly they had social convention supporting them, because in our society the task of child care and child rearing, particularly in the early years of individual development, is assigned to the mother. This reality factor always has been recognized also by those who, like Mary Richmond, Charlotte Towle, Gordon Hamilton, Nathan W. Ackerman, and Peter B. Neubauer, took exception to the exclusive concentration of diagnostic and therapeutic concern upon the mother-child relationship. However, the support of this practice by the conventions of child care and early child rearing in our society, somehow, does not seem to tell the full story. First of all, neither the folklore of the late nineteenth century nor the scientific gains of the twentieth have discounted the father's influence upon the personality development of children to a degree even remotely resembling the picture suggested by routinized practice in our child guidance clinics. "Maternal child care" and "determination of personality" have nowhere been considered synonymous as they apparently have been in child guidance practice. Actually, we have had occasion to note that particularly classical psychoanalytic thinking, which in some ways gained such dominance in the thinking of social caseworkers, would have suggested the opposite. But in this area, psychoanalysis apparently failed to exert an influence. More than that, it fell into line.

In this respect a sociological observation may open an avenue to understanding. Among other things sociology is particularly concerned with the study of group characteristics, such as the sex composition of group memberships. No sociologist engaged, for instance, in the study of the professions can fail to perceive the implications of the predominantly female composition of some service professions, such as nursing, grade-school teaching, and social work. The number of women among child analysts also is significant. From that point of view a correlation between the sex composition of child guidance workers and their interest in the mothers of emotionally disturbed children immediately suggests itself. But a statistical correlation is only a starting point in any search for causation. "Taken in themselves statistics are nothing more than symptoms of unknown causal processes."[1] That similar people show a tendency to associate with one another is an old observation reported in essence and made part of his speculations in social philosophy by Bishop George Berkely in the eighteenth century. More recently but still sufficiently long ago to appear somewhat obsolete in our present and future-directed culture, the same thought was expressed by the sociologist Franklyn H. Giddings who coined the term "consciousness of kind" and offered this phenomenon as an explanation of association.[2] Although little reference is made currently to Giddings' works in the sociological literature, it might prove fruitful to give some attention to the possibility that women social workers, women clinicians, and women psychiatrists may prefer to associate with women clients or women patients because they recognize them as of like kind with themselves and thus determine "the parent" with whom they prefer to associate in clinical contacts.

The inconvenience imposed upon fathers by interviews during office hours may have played a role. Very likely feministic tendencies of the social workers of earlier generations were also influential in starting this concentration of helping efforts upon the mother, because in a way this denied the importance of the father as the head of the household.

A phenomenon of cultural lag may also have come into play. The *cultural lag* concept has been formulated by several soci-

[1] Thomas, William I., *The Unadjusted Girl*. Little, Brown and Co., Boston, 1923, p. 244.

[2] Giddings, Franklyn Henry, *The Principles of Sociology*. Macmillan Co., New York, 1916 printing, pp. 17–18, 147, 190.

ologists outstanding among whom is William F. Ogburn.[1] This concept designates the phenomenon that various aspects of a culture change at different rates of speed. In its original formulation the concept referred particularly to the differential between the speed of change in the material aspects of our culture and the tempo of change in its nonmaterial aspects. Actually in some areas nonmaterial aspects of our culture may change faster than its material aspects. This could well be said for instance about our ideas of child rearing and child guidance in the 1930's. In *Social Science and Psychotherapy for Children,* it has been pointed out that the discoveries of psychoanalysis and the professional experiences of child guidance workers have produced a therapeutic culture which in social values and patterns of communications differs from and at times conflicts with the social values and communication patterns of the parents whose children are treated in child guidance clinics. This therapeutic culture requires, for instance, consideration and discussion of sexual material which is not yet and certainly was not in the early thirties approved in the wider community. It may well be that child guidance workers were aware of this culture conflict and more confident of overcoming it with members of their own sex group than with members of the other sex, that is, fathers. In that respect they simply may have acted in accordance with the conventional behavior pattern of our society, which permits greater freedom in the discussion of sexual material in one sex group than in groups composed of two sexes. Thus, their concentration upon the mother and child in clinical contact may have been an expression of the theorem that differential speed in social change creates social problems.

Similarly unconscious mechanisms may have played a role. From that angle, the concentration upon the mother-child relationship while consciously denying the importance of the father may unconsciously have been an attempt to express antagonism to mothers.

[1] Ogburn, William F., *Social Change:* With Respect to Culture and Original Nature. B. W. Huebsch, Inc., New York, 1922.

The phenomenon which here may have been and still may be exploited by the unconscious of the therapist has been pointed out by Berta Bornstein. "We know that in the analysis of the child-patient the parents play a unique role and are uniquely affected. To stress only one aspect: the narcissistic injury which the child's analysis entails for most parents. Feelings of guilt arise when their child's development takes a deviating course. Not only does the neurosis of their child awaken their own childhood conflicts, but it threatens their hopes, their trust in the future, and their self-esteem as parents. Alarmed by this threat, the parents call in the assistance of the analyst. Yet if the child's neurosis is taken as a danger, calling in the analyst symbolizes a definite defeat."[1] This is true also in child guidance work. What has to be added here, however, is that any emphasis on one parent only aggravates the emotional burden of that particular parent. If it is the mother, it means that she is singled out for the reproach of parental defeat which the child's need for help implies. Unresolved oedipal attitudes on the part of the woman therapist may have found a vent in this type of child guidance practice. There could be at work also a wish conceived still earlier in childhood to create a better mother than reality provided. It has been noted in the psychoanalytic literature that some individuals in the course of various activities can be seen to pursue in more or less concealed form "the valuable resting place of illusion."[2] Only a pooling of the material produced by child guidance practitioners in their own individual analysis could answer the question whether such unconscious motivations really are at work. However that may be, undoubtedly it has brought upon the mothers the heavy burden of carrying primarily the responsibility for the difficulties of their children. Whatever the reasons for this tendency of female child guidance workers to prefer association with mothers in clinical contact may have been, their continued

[1] Bornstein, Berta, "Emotional Barriers in the Understanding and Treatment of Young Children," *American Journal of Orthopsychiatry,* vol. 18, October, 1948, p. 692.

[2] Winnicott, D. W., "Transitional Objects and Transitional Phenomena," *International Journal of Psycho-analysis,* vol. 34, part 2, 1953, p. 94, note 11.

existence need not be assumed for the present in order to explain the persistence of the mother's being singled out in practice as the parent to be treated. Once such a phenomenon has started—for whatever reason—it has a tendency to persist because of still another law of perception. "Analytically, we may say that perceiving begins with an expectancy or hypothesis . . . we not only see, but we look for, not only hear but listen to. In short, perceiving takes place in a 'tuned organism'. . . .

"A basic property of hypothesis is what we shall refer to as *strength.* There are three theorems that are contingent upon this concept of *strength:*

"(1) The stronger a hypothesis, the greater its likelihood of arousal in a given situation.

"(2) The greater the strength of a hypothesis, the less the amount of appropriate information necessary to confirm it.

"(3) The greater the strength of a hypothesis, the more the amount of . . . contradictory information necessary to infirm it."[1]

In other words, once social caseworkers and child psychiatrists were attuned to looking for the mother as a predominant factor in the etiology of emotional difficulties of a child, the more likely were they to perceive facts confirming their hypothesis. The stronger the hypothesis became through the experience of apparently confirming data, the fewer factual data were necessary to reconfirm it. And the greater the strength of the hypothesis became, the smaller grew the chances of anything suggesting counter evidence to impress clinicians believing in the hypothesis. Once perception of the mother-child relationship as the outstanding factor to be considered in child guidance work was established, perceptions of other factors were apt to lose weight.

In summary, this chapter has suggested on a hypothetical basis to be verified by further research that the divergence between theory and practice in child guidance is unlikely to be the result of mistakes in professional performance. Majority

[1] Bruner, Jerome S., "Personality Dynamics and the Process of Perceiving" in *Perception:* An Approach to Personality, edited by Robert R. Blake and Glenn V. Ramsey. Ronald Press Co., New York, 1951, pp. 123, 126.

patterns sanctioned and frequently initiated by professional leaders, even when appearing in questionable light, can hardly be so explained. The proposition is advanced that these mistakes were "lawful" mistakes, necessary in view of the impact of our principles of perception upon Theory and Practice in their traditional stage of conceptualization.

IX. Trends of Practical and Theoretical Reorientation

ULTIMATELY ALL THEORIES are bound to be proved erroneous if they fail to grasp the essentials of reality. Theories which are not immediately related to any sphere of practical effort, may have a relatively long period of immunity. In cases of directly practice-related theories, however, the exposure of their flaws can be expected to come soon. In the child guidance field, this process seems to have started in the forties and appears to be gathering momentum at the present time.

Apparently singularization of pluralities and the concomitant fractionalization of the environment led to failures in practice and to failures in scientific elaborations of existing theory which were soon discovered and caused concern in some quarters. Rationalizations of patient selections which appeared to be based on the emotional needs of therapists more than on the treatment needs in the individual cases seem to have produced similar results and similar concerns.

In 1942 a staff member of the Jewish Board of Guardians, Mildred Burgum, made the following observation: "Occasional murmurs about the father as a factor in child guidance treatment echo through the field. The fact that the mother is the person most involved in responsibility for the child and his difficulties, and also most accessible in terms of her own time and agency working hours, tends to focus attention on her both in diagnostic and treatment considerations. The father is not entirely neglected, yet the full significance of his role in the treatment situation is rarely adequately realized. My attention was drawn to this problem by an unusual phenomenon occurring in four cases. On inquiry I found that similar situations had occurred with other workers though they had not paid much attention to their significance. It was likely that the number would be further increased if several cases which gave evidence of following the same pattern had not been prematurely terminated for other reasons. The phenomenon occurred frequently enough to merit description and discussion of its meaning, as well as possibilities for a solution. Briefly it is this: the mother gets better, the father gets worse."[1] Here we have an instance where an important category of failures in practice is recognized and presented as a problem requiring remedial attention while the theoretical position to which these failures can be traced remains basically unquestioned. Still, this paper is one of the first signs of a negative reaction to the exclusive emphasis of diagnostic and therapeutic concern with the mother-child relationship. As far as the writer was able to ascertain, however, this paper got little if any response in the field.

It was only as recently as in the late forties and early fifties that something like a group phenomenon of reaction and reorientation began to appear. From 1947 on, a small but distinctive group of publications has indicated that consistent efforts are being made at liberating practice from the shackles of inadequate conceptualizations and unconscious therapeutic motivations. These publications seem to come mainly from a few professional leaders, such as John Bowlby, Gordon Hamilton, Nathan W. Ackerman, Peter B. Neubauer, O. Spurgeon English, and Stanislaus A. Szurek. They take exception to the limitations of perception which we have found to dominate large areas of child guidance practice and start several trends of reorientation. Seen in terms of numbers and apparent impact upon routinized practice on a broad scale, they still appear as pioneer expressions and exceptions rather than as statements representative of the main stream of current theory and practice.

CRITICISMS OF PRACTICE

A review of this part of the professional literature reveals, first of all, a number of expressions which criticized certain as-

[1] Burgum, Mildred, "The Father Gets Worse: A Child Guidance Problem," *American Journal of Orthopsychiatry*, vol. 12, July, 1942, p. 474.

pects of therapeutic practice as such. Our first report has made reference to the fact that the soundness of an exclusive emphasis of clinical child guidance work on the child and his mother had been frequently questioned within the agency itself and by persons connected with it.[1] In a paper read at the Thirty-seventh Annual Meeting of the American Psychopathological Association, held in New York City in June, 1947, Dr. Nathan W. Ackerman and Dr. Peter B. Neubauer expressed their opinion regarding this practice as follows:

"The fundamental closeness of child to mother is a recognized factor. Nevertheless, this is one example of oversimplification which sometimes leads to failure in treatment. If the therapy of the environment is to be child-oriented, the primary need is an intimate knowledge of the relationship between the parents, and the relationship of each parent to the child. The father's personality, as well as the mother's must be understood, and the emotional interaction between these two persons must be dealt with. Often, the father must receive treatment as well as the mother, if adequate results are to be achieved. It is necessary, of course, to recognize the practical obstacles which often stand in the way of such a program. Nevertheless, the relevant issues must be clearly seen, if success in therapy is to be assured.

"In most cases, since the mother is usually the one who brings the child, it is possible to achieve earlier and easier access to her problem than to that of the father. Therefore, one may easily overlook the pathology in the father."[2]

Similarly Gordon Hamilton, in her study of the principles of psychotherapy as practiced in the Child Guidance Institute of the Jewish Board of Guardians, expressed herself in favor of bringing fathers and siblings more actively into the treatment relationship. "Treatment of the parental situation . . . has become not merely one angle for treating the child, but an integral part

[1] Pollak, Otto, and Collaborators, *Social Science and Psychotherapy for Children*, pp. 39–40.

[2] Ackerman, Nathan W., and Peter B. Neubauer, "Failures in the Psychotherapy of Children" in *Failures in Psychiatric Treatment*, edited by Paul H. Hoch. Grune and Stratton, New York, 1948, pp. 86–87, 88.

of the therapeutic process. Theoretically, both parents should be brought into the treatment relationship, but in the American culture, since the mother, especially when there are young children, is most involved, it is usually she who is most actively engaged in the process. In the family guidance of the future, more effort must be made to bring fathers actively into treatment. Siblings come into focus both as individual patients and as an environment for the chief patient."[1]

A more general discontent with the development of therapeutic practice in the field of orthopsychiatry was expressed by Dr. Lawson G. Lowrey. In the survey volume *Orthopsychiatry, 1923–1948:* Retrospect and Prospect which he edited, the introductory note to the "1930 Symposium on Treatment" included this statement: "These papers and the discussion they evoked at the time present leads regarding therapy and its teaching which have never been properly followed up so far as I know. . . ."[2] Dr. Lowrey's remarks have received by no means the attention which they deserved. Apparently nobody has paused to ask how it could happen that in a field as energetic and imbued with the spirit of experimentation in practice as orthopsychiatry, leads regarding therapy which were considered still important eighteen years after their pronouncements had never been "properly followed up." Here a phenomenon worthy of the attention of a research scientist seems to have been left unattended. From the angle of our interest here, however, it might suffice to point out that the "1930 Symposium on Treatment" contained among others Charlotte Towle's already quoted paper in which she expressed concern about an insufficient involvement of the father in child guidance practice.[3]

[1] Hamilton, Gordon, *Psychotherapy in Child Guidance.* Columbia University Press, New York, 1947, p. 282.

[2] Lowrey, Lawson G., "Orthopsychiatric Treatment" in *Orthopsychiatry, 1923–1948:* Retrospect and Prospect, edited by Lawson G. Lowrey. American Orthopsychiatric Association, New York, 1948, p. 542.

[3] Towle, Charlotte, "The Social Worker" in "Symposium: The Treatment of Behavior and Personality Problems in Children," *American Journal of Orthopsychiatry,* vol. 1, October, 1930, pp. 21–38.

CHANGES IN PRACTICE

Over and beyond these expressions of criticism and concern regarding the existing state of affairs, the literature of the mid-century period also contains reports which suggest that here and there actual changes in practice were beginning to occur.

Dr. John Bowlby read a paper at the International Congress on Mental Health in August, 1948, in which he described developments in child guidance practice at the Tavistock Clinic as follows: "First, we do not nowadays undertake systematic, individual treatment of a case until we have made a contact with the father. To those of us who hitherto have not done this as a routine, the experience is a revelation. In the past many of us have tended to leave the father out until we have got into difficulties, and then have sought to bring him in. But by insisting that everyone relevant in the case should have an early opportunity of making his contribution, and of finding out whether he wants to collaborate with us, we find the way towards collaboration much smoother. These first steps in a case are vital and repay very careful study."[1]

Similar reports began to appear in this country. We find for instance a report by Dr. S. A. Szurek and three of his associates which indicates that at the Langley Porter Clinic in San Francisco the case of a thirteen-and-a-half-year-old girl who alternated between overweight and cachexia was handled by therapy with the adolescent and both her parents. This paper showed in addition to its departure from routinized practice also a theoretical reorientation. Abandoning the emphasis on one specific interpersonal relationship, the authors hoped that by reviewing the various courses of therapy with three family members, they might contribute to "a further understanding of the intrafamilial nature of conflicts which may be expressed in the symptoms of a child. . . ."[2]

It might be of interest here to note that the therapy of the

[1] Bowlby, John, "The Study and Reduction of Group Tensions in the Family." Adapted from a paper read during a Specialist Meeting of the International Congress on Mental Health, August, 1948.

[2] Berlin, I. N., Maleta J. Boatman, S. L. Sheimo, and S. A. Szurek, "Adolescent Alternation of Anorexia and Obesity: Workshop, 1950," *American Journal of Orthopsychiatry*, vol. 21, April, 1951, p. 387.

father in this case was not readily accepted by the junior members of the therapeutic team, who "were only slowly becoming convinced of the validity of the director's belief that all significant members of a family should be included in therapy."[1]

Two years after the report from the Langley Porter Clinic, a few remarks made by Dr. Frank J. Curran in discussing a paper given at the 1952 annual meeting of the American Orthopsychiatric Association revealed that at least for diagnostic purposes fathers were seen routinely in the clinics at Louisville, Kentucky, and Charlottesville, Virginia.[2]

Roughly at that time, the Child Study Center at Psychiatric Institute, Pennsylvania Hospital, in Philadelphia, also established interviews with the father as a part of intake routine.

In 1950 J. Franklin Robinson wrote a paper on trends in child guidance clinics, in which he indicated that there is a widening of clinical concern beyond the mother-child nexus but that instances of it are relatively few. "If one parent comes alone," he said, "some clinics endeavor to include the other parent so that it may become an undertaking in which they are both involved."[3]

The widening of perception regarding the significance of multiple familial influences in the causation of emotional disturbances of children expressed itself also in the introduction of new interviewing techniques. In the paper referred to earlier, Dr. Bowlby reported an experience gained in joint sessions in which all parties were brought together and problems were examined from the point of view of each.[4]

In this country similar attempts at freeing existing techniques from the fetters of singularization have been made. Joint orientation sessions with the parents have become established practice of the Child Study Center in Philadelphia, and in at least one case known to the author successful efforts have been made

[1] *Ibid.*, p. 394.
[2] Curran, Frank J., in the discussion of paper by Elizabeth H. Holmes and Joseph P. Lord, "Artie: A Victim of an Inconsistent Parental Relationship," *American Journal of Orthopsychiatry*, vol. 22, January, 1952, p. 48.
[3] Robinson, J. Franklin, "Current Trends in Child Guidance Clinics," *Mental Hygiene*, vol. 34, January, 1950, p. 110.
[4] Bowlby, John, *op. cit.*

by a therapist on the staff of the Jewish Board of Guardians to employ the Joint Interview Technique, not only for purposes of orientation of all participants in one session but for purposes of therapy in a series of consecutive interviews with both parents.

BEGINNING THEORETICAL REFORMULATIONS

Verbalizations of discontent and experimentations with new approaches, however, do not tell the full story. We also find definite signs of beginning reformulations in the realm of theory. The appearance of this trend is marked by the introduction of such concepts as "diagnosis of neurotic marital interactions," "family diagnosis," "family treatment," and "family plan" in the child guidance literature of the midcentury.[1]

It should be noted that from all these concepts reference to one individual as such has disappeared even by implication. The concepts refer to phenomena which involve pluralities. Either they do so on the two-person level as is the case in the diagnosis of "marital interaction," or on the three and more person level as is the case in "family diagnosis," "family treatment," and "family plan." Even more significant is the fact that reorientation does not stop with the introduction of such concepts. We find demands for further conceptual elaborations and a more basic theoretical reorientation.

In their paper "Family Diagnosis: An Approach to the Preschool Child" Ackerman and Sobel stated the problem succinctly as follows: "We believe that the treatment of the young child should begin with the treatment of the family group. However, we find ourselves confronted with the fact that, up to the present time, no adequate criteria for family disturbances, as group disturbances, have been found. Until such criteria are formulated . . . we have no frame of reference for the treatment

[1] Ackerman, Nathan W., and Raymond Sobel, "Family Diagnosis: An Approach to the Preschool Child," *American Journal of Orthopsychiatry*, vol. 20, October, 1950, pp. 744–752; Ackerman, "The Diagnosis of Neurotic Marital Interaction," *Social Casework*, vol. 35, April, 1954, pp. 139–147; Sands, Rosalind M., "Family Treatment in Relation to a Disturbed Preschool Child: A Case Presentation," *Journal of Psychiatric Social Work*, vol. 33, June, 1954, pp. 189–200.

of families as groups, despite the claim of many child guidance clinics to the contrary. Although the trends in child guidance are toward family orientation, the child and the mother, but not the family are treated."[1] And in the same paper the reader notes the statement that "it is necessary to treat the person and the environment as a continuum."[2] With this denial of a boundary line between the two phenomena, the practice of focusing clinical attention upon the individual as the core of the environment has been put clearly under attack. And this attack has been made not only from the angle of effectiveness but also from the angle of a basic theoretical reorientation. In essence, a start has been made toward a homogenization between the individual and the environment.

A similar search for a more adequate theoretical foundation in the struggle for the formulation of a family diagnosis was expressed in 1951 by Jules Henry and Samuel Warson. They proposed the visualization of a child's household situation as a field of forces composed of several interaction systems which could be determined and counted with relative rigor. They presented this scheme, however, as an approach to research in psychodynamics rather than as an immediate guide to practice.[3]

These various lines of reorientation quickly began to show a promise of significant gains in substantive knowledge regarding the psychodynamic structures of family situations. In 1952 S. R. Slavson described important intrapsychic phenomena in both parental figures, fathers as well as mothers, and identified a series of distinct interpersonal relationships resulting from these intrapsychic phenomena.[4] Papers written by Dr. I. Peter Glauber in 1953 and Rosalind M. Sands in 1954 added substantive knowledge of the same type.[5] And at the National Conference

[1] Ackerman and Sobel, *op. cit.*, p. 744.
[2] *Ibid.*
[3] Henry, Jules, and Samuel Warson, "Family Structure and Psychic Development," *American Journal of Orthopsychiatry*, vol. 21, January, 1951, pp. 59–71.
[4] Slavson, S. R., *Child Psychotherapy*. Columbia University Press, New York, 1952, pp. 68–109.
[5] Glauber, I. Peter, "The Nature of Stuttering," *Social Casework*, vol. 34, March, 1953, pp. 95–103, and "The Treatment of Stuttering," vol. 34, April, 1953, pp. 162–167; Sands, Rosalind M., *op. cit.*

of Social Work held in Atlantic City in May, 1954, Dr. O. Spurgeon English presented a survey of the psychological meanings of the various social roles which the father plays in the family and stressed the need for further research in that area. Significantly enough, with the inclusion of his roles and their psychological impact upon the emotional atmosphere of the family in scientific scrutiny, came also indication of a reevaluation of the father's social importance and a call for his self-assertion. Said Dr. English: "Father is a definite entity psychologically as well as in reality. He should be more conscious of what his role is and play it with greater pleasure and distinction."[1]

Still another expression of these trends of reorientation in the child guidance field came from Frances Gitnick King, one of the reviewers of our first report on the liaison project. It took the form of a constructive criticism of our own first efforts at reorientation and expressed its affirmative concern with this trend by a demand for further work which we tried to meet during our project's second phase, in principle if not always along the specific lines suggested.

Expressing concern similar to that voiced by Dr. John P. Spiegel in his critique of *Mid-century Psychiatry*, Mrs. King took exception to the idea that an addition of concepts from one discipline to another in and by itself would produce interdisciplinary synthesis.

"The mere addition of social science concepts to the psychoanalytic theory of child therapy does not answer such questions as: Is there a dichotomy between psychodynamic and social? What is conditioning—does this suggest that environment simply frustrates or encourages the development of the human organism, or is there an intrinsic causal relationship between the organism and environment through the ever-active socialization process? While Dr. Pollak and his collaborators make it clear that they are not attempting a systematic reformulation of theory in order to arrive at synthesis, I feel that true syn-

[1] English, O. Spurgeon, "The Psychological Role of the Father in the Family," *Social Casework*, vol. 35, October, 1954, pp. 323–329. Quotation from p. 329.

thesis is impossible without a systematic examination and reformulation of theory. The method of maintaining the independence of each discipline negates synthesis. It seems to me that we must try to arrive at a new theoretical foundation that truly reflects the living synthesis of man and society. I would like to suggest that our first responsibility is to see whether psychodynamic thinking and the social science approach are theoretically and empirically compatible."[1]

It is important to note that these trends of reorientation are not confined to the area of clinical work with emotionally disturbed children. They can be traced also in the fields of social casework and marriage counseling. In the former we find a growing acceptance of Helen Witmer's observation that with the recognition of the importance of psychological factors "individuals rather than families came to be regarded as clients."[2] Statements to that effect are usually connected with expressions of regret and suggestions for change. It is of special interest to note that almost all these critics of practice refer to the need for conceptualization as a condition for change.

Again only a small group of pioneers seems to be actively concerned in this area. Their publications also follow one another in relatively close succession, showing the vitality of the concern which they express.

In 1951 M. Robert Gomberg expressed the desirability of formulating a diagnosis of the family as a unit and suggested some criteria such as the nature and the quality of interaction between significant members of a family, their behavior and their expectations of each other.[3]

At a panel discussion of the South Pacific Regional Conference of the Child Welfare League in May, 1952, Helen Harris Perlman, referring to the first report on the liaison project be-

[1] King, Frances Gitnick, "Review of *Social Science and Psychotherapy for Children*," *International Journal of Group Psychotherapy*, vol. 3, October, 1953, pp. 462–463.

[2] Witmer, Helen Leland, *Social Work:* An Analysis of a Social Institution. Rinehart and Co., Inc., New York, 1942, p. 175.

[3] Gomberg, M. Robert, "Principles and Practices in Counseling" in *Diagnosis and Process in Family Counseling*, edited by M. Robert Gomberg and Frances T. Levinson. Family Service Association of America, New York, 1951, p. 22.

tween Russell Sage Foundation and the Jewish Board of Guardians, analyzed the situation as follows:

"There has been a rather troubling trend in social casework in recent years. One hopes that it is symptomatic only of a temporary phase of our development—perhaps one of those excessive 'swings' which may be found in the late adolescence of a maturing person and also of a maturing profession. It might be called an 'intra-psychic-mindedness,'—a kind of concentration or obsession with problems of emotional or personality malfunctioning and with methods and schemes for casework treatment of these. That this is a proper and vital area of our concern no one would deny, but the trouble has been that another proper and vital area of concern has at least temporarily been neglected or cast aside as unimportant. This is the area of concern with what is maladjusted or sick in the interpersonal person-to-group, social living of our clients and with the enriched development of understanding and means by which the realities of the person's everyday living may be so modified or changed as to affect, benignly, his internal unhappiness."[1]

In a paper given at the National Conference of Social Work in 1953, Frances H. Scherz described the development as follows: "Family agencies, particularly, have kept the family and its needs in the foreground. But family agencies, perhaps motivated by the zeal and enthusiasm characteristic of the total social work profession, from time to time have strayed into bypaths that, while constructive, have led us away temporarily from our major concern with the family as a unit."[2]

In the light of our proposition that the perceptual consequences of the principle of figure ground articulation apply also to the relationship between theory and practice in social welfare work, the reformulation and reconceptualization proposed by Frances Scherz deserves particular attention. It should be noted that she found it necessary to buttress her efforts of securing consideration in social casework of the family as a

[1] Perlman, Helen Harris, "Putting the Social Back in Social Casework," *Child Welfare,* July, 1952, p. 8.

[2] Scherz, Frances H., "What Is Family-Centered Casework?" *Social Casework,* vol. 34, October, 1953, p. 343.

unit with the new concept of "family-centered casework." Evidently, she found that designation of the focus of diagnostic and therapeutic concern in theory determined the area of perception in practice.

Significantly enough, both 1953 and 1954 are years which bring also editorial expressions of this theme of concern and reorientation in the leading professional journal of the social casework profession. The comments which came from that quarter in 1953 have been quoted in Chapter I of this report. It will be remembered that they are similar to the statements made by Frances Scherz in that they stressed that concern with environmental forces after a period of eclipse in the field of social casework was beginning to be emphasized again.[1]

In 1954 the editor of *Social Casework* entitled her Notes in the October issue "Focus on the Father" and had this to say:

"As the problems of child rearing have come under clinical scrutiny in recent years, the father of the family has been placed in the glare of an unfamiliar spotlight. How uncomfortable he is in this exposed position is difficult to determine. It is true that modern urban life has tended to remove him from the home for long hours of the day and that his role in the family is radically different from the one he played fifty years ago. Today, 'life with father' does not involve the children or the wife in an endless series of skirmishes about their day-by-day activities. Modern life has forced him to surrender many of his former prerogatives as head of the family, and as educational mentor for the children. Willingly or not, he has turned most of the tasks and problems of child rearing over to the mother.

"In line with this cultural trend, clinics and social agencies have tended to work largely with the mother, or with the mother and child, in problems of child disturbance. Practical factors, such as the father's working hours, have reinforced the pattern of engaging only the mother in a treatment relationship. Even in family agencies, where the problems generally are disturbances in intra-family relationships, this one-sided approach still operates more frequently than it should. There is evidence,

[1] "Editorial Notes," *Social Casework,* vol. 34, October, 1953, p. 354.

however, that a corrective trend is at work, and that an understanding of the total family and of the interaction of its members is coming to be considered basic to sound diagnosis in any setting.

"Little is yet known about the nature of the psychological forces that operate within the family as a constellation, or about their relative positive and negative effects on the mental health of the various members. That further study of this complicated process is needed goes without saying. Social workers and psychiatrists, however, have an obligation to study, apply, and test whatever findings are available if such knowledge is to advance. Family-centered treatment, which has come to be a new cliche in social work, can have little substance unless the principles of family interaction are carefully studied and elucidated.

"It would seem, judging from records and reports, that fathers are not any more reluctant to become involved with social agencies than are mothers. This shift in focus from one client—or from the mother-child entity—to the total family obviously increases the complexity of the diagnostic and treatment task. Doubtless the increase of general knowledge about psychology, human relations, and child rearing has contributed to the more widespread use of treatment and guidance resources by all segments of the community, and by men as well as women. The lag, therefore, in drawing fathers into contact with agencies, when such action is appropriate, seems to be related more to the attitude of the worker or to patterns of agency operation, than to general resistance on the part of the male population.

"We are pleased to carry as the lead article in this issue a paper by Dr. O. Spurgeon English presented at the 1954 National Conference of Social Work in which he analyzes the psychological role of the father in the family. We are sure that Dr. English's clear formulation of the specific functions of the father, both in relation to the mother and to the children, will be of value to the field. It should stimulate us to take a new and more encompassing view of the total family both in diagnosis and in formulating treatment plan."[1]

[1] "Editorial Notes: Focus on the Father," *Social Casework*, vol. 35, October, 1954, pp. 354–355.

Similar concerns, shifts in practice, and attempts at liberation from unsatisfactory theoretical formulations appear at about the same time also in the field of marriage counseling. Quite apart from its intrinsic interest, this development must be noted because it shows how widespread the tendency toward diagnostic and therapeutic reorientation is beginning to be. In 1951 the Marriage Council of Philadelphia arranged for its annual meeting a symposium devoted to a discussion of the question whether one marriage partner can be successfully counseled without the other. In the course of the discussion perceptual problems were raised by Dr. Kenneth E. Appel and Dr. Abraham Stone and both stressed the importance of seeing both marriage partners for purposes of acquiring the proper perspective for an understanding of the situation. There were also reports by Dr. Robert W. Laidlaw and Dr. Emily H. Mudd on the advantages of joint sessions with both clients showing a significant parallel to the experience gained with the technique of joint sessions in the child guidance field. Attention was paid to the difficulties which are created when counseling cases are divided. And finally, it has to be noted that a conceptual reformulation was proposed by Dr. Laidlaw and Dr. Stone. They suggested that it was the marriage which was the patient rather than either partner to the marriage.[1]

In summary, child guidance, social casework, and marriage counseling show signs that we are on the eve of a great period of reorientation. There are expressions of dissatisfaction with routinized practice. There are expressions of dissatisfaction with traditional theoretical formulations. And most significant, there are expressions of dissatisfaction already with the attempts to correct this practice and to reformulate these theoretical positions. The concern is expressed that they have not gone far enough and a call is made for research to carry on and fulfill the task of reorientation.

[1] Saul, Leon J., Robert W. Laidlaw, Janet F. Nelson, Ralph Ormsby, Abraham Stone, Sidney Eisenberg, Kenneth E. Appel, Emily H. Mudd, "Can One Partner Be Successfully Counseled Without the Other? A Symposium," *Marriage and Family Living*, vol. 15, February, 1953, pp. 59–64.

X. The Problem of Theoretical Reformulation

THE VARIOUS EFFORTS of practical and theoretical reorientation described in the preceding chapter seem to have been directed at the achievement of one overall goal. They give the impression of having been aimed at a *widening of perception* with regard to elements of reality significant for the performance of the helping task.

Accounts of the observations which led to this widening of perception suggest that they were stimulated by experiences of failure in the treatment effort. Phenomena which had remained unconsidered in traditional practice had at least to a degree vitiated its results. Apparently situational factors of sufficient power to counteract the helping effort had been disregarded.

THE "INTERNAL" NATURE OF "EXTERNAL" PHENOMENA

The nature of these factors furnishes a ready explanation of their influence upon the outcome of the effort to help the client or patient. First of all, they almost always are to be found in the reactions of other human beings to the treatment effort. These other human beings invariably appear to be persons who participate in the group formations of which the client or patient is a member. Thus, they are individuals involved in interactional relationships with the person at whom the helping effort is directed. Seen in this perspective, however, the essence of their power over the result of the helping relationship becomes easily identified. It seems to lie in their own intrapsychic problems and in the effects which the manifestations of these problems have upon the intrapsychic problems of the client or patient. If that is so, however, to consider these persons "external" factors in a client's situation becomes theoretically untenable.

The phenomenon of social interaction siphons expressions of the intrapsychic problems of others into the nexus of thoughts and feelings which occupy the client. Correspondingly it siphons expressions of the client's intrapsychic problems into the nexus of thoughts and feelings which occupy these other persons. In the process both the intrapsychic problems of the client or patient and those of the persons who meet him in group memberships are influenced by one another. They may be maintained in their strength, may be aggravated, or alleviated. Ideally it may be possible that as a result of social interaction the impact of one person's intrapsychic problem may solve the intrapsychic problem of the other and vice versa. No matter, however, what specific outcome the phenomenon of social interaction may produce in the members of a social group, we are faced with a complex of interlocking phenomena which cannot be divided into "internal" and "external" categories. The "client and his environment" indeed form a continuum and have to be treated as such. All the various efforts at practical and theoretical reorientation which have begun to agitate the field of clinical and social welfare practice represent attempts to do just that. In doing so, however, they have run across practical and conceptual difficulties which indicate that the process of reorientation so far has remained incomplete. It is very likely that the core of these difficulties has to be sought in the fact that an ambitious and all-embracing tendency of reorientation was accompanied by a hesitant and only partial effort of reformulation.

CONSEQUENCES OF INCOMPLETE REFORMULATIONS

In retrospect, this seems to have been one of the major sources of the difficulties which we encountered in the second phase of the liaison project. In the first and deductive phase, considerable emphasis had been put on the situational approach as a general orientation of our efforts. In order to buttress this approach, we had proposed a number of social science concepts for incorporation into the theory underlying child guidance practice. These concepts, however, had been limited in number and had not covered all aspects of a truly situational approach. Furthermore, although relatable and in our application actually related to psychodynamic concepts, they had been proposed for incorporation in an additive rather than in an integrative mood. The effort was made to add something new but not to disturb the old. In that respect, Frances G. King's critical comment that "maintaining the independence of each discipline negates synthesis"[1] identified an essential weakness of our approach.

In our actual case discussions during the two years of practice testing in the experimental treatment team, we never quite overcame this weakness, although the Director of Casework Services, Miss Frederika Neumann, had stressed the need for doing so after the experience of the first year. During the whole period we never freed ourselves completely from certain perceptual prisons which resulted from a failure to complete our conceptual reorientation by an extensive as well as intensive theoretical reformulation. The encumbrances of our thinking and acting which resulted from this delay in reformulation were numerous. To analyze them in detail would demand the writing of still another book. A few essential observations, however, may be sufficient to give an impression of the problems which we encountered. It is likely that they will convince the reader of the desirability and importance to complete a reorientation in practice by an all-embracing reformulation of theory.

It can be stated that most members of our experimental treatment team agreed on the basic soundness of the situational approach to problems of diagnosis and therapy in clinical child guidance work. It can be stated also that this agreement was maintained throughout the whole two-year-period of our practice testing. In spite of this, however, a reader of the minutes which we kept of our seminar discussions might easily gain the impression that no such agreement existed at all, or that if it existed on occasions, most of us were prone to forget it. Such a person might point out that we spent a great deal of time discussing such questions as the desirability of seeing a

[1] See Chapter IX, Trends of Practical and Theoretical Reorientation, p. 227.

father, the permissibility of seeing a mother in treatment before seeing her child, the feasibility of having parents who had expressed a wish to be seen by the same worker really so seen, and the appropriateness of a mother's having occasionally direct contacts with the therapist of her child, after she had been assigned to a therapist of her own. The reader might comment that all hesitations and questions of such a nature obviously were incompatible with an acceptance of a situational approach.

SICK SITUATIONS INSTEAD OF SICK INDIVIDUALS

It is probable that many of these controversies were due to the fact that we retained the concepts of "client" or "patient" as terms referring to individuals. If we had redefined them as terms referring to situations, we would have drawn the correct conclusions from our general reorientation and avoided many unproductive discussions. It was only in studying the minutes of the seminar discussions that the writer became aware of the extensive amount of postproject conceptualization and theoretical reformulation which our work in the project's second phase implied. Our continuation of the term "patient" as referring to an individual, and in terms of the Clinic's tradition, as referring usually either to the child or his mother, created considerable confusion. Any suggestion of including other family members in therapeutic contacts ran the risk of encountering the argument that such a person was not our patient. And once overcome, the worker's seeing those persons in therapeutic interviews was likely to be justified in terms of its helpfulness to the child originally referred, that is, in terms of helpfulness to "our patient."

Clinicians will probably agree that it is unlikely to find one or two emotionally sick persons in a family otherwise composed of emotionally healthy people. If children are affected in their emotional development by the emotional health of their parents, it is highly unlikely that the emotional disturbance of the mother will affect selectively only one child and not her other children. If it is true as seems probable in the light of many clinical observations, that emotionally sick persons show a tendency to get married to persons with complementary emotional disorders,[1] then it is unlikely that the father of a referred child is well and only the mother sick. In consequence, a reformulation of theory in terms of sick situations rather than in terms of sick patients would not only have the advantage of inherent harmony, but also the advantage of properly reflecting the essential plurality of the phenomena which it is designed to explain. At any rate, if we had seen the need to so reformulate our theory that our clients were situations which seemed to adversely affect child welfare, the question as to which of the persons involved was to be seen and for whose sake very likely would have presented a much lesser problem.

CHILD WELFARE FOCUS INSTEAD OF CHILD FOCUS

Another failure to reformulate our theoretical basis consisted in our continued utilization of the term "child focus" in our team discussions. Reference to the difficulties which this attempt to retain a term incompatible with our situational approach created in our diagnostic and therapeutic thinking has already been made in the explanation of the postproject introduction of the term "child welfare focus" into this report. What remains to be done here is to elaborate on and explain these difficulties. The widening of our perception for the factors which seemed to counteract healthy emotional development in the children who were referred to us suggested in almost every case diagnostic contacts with, and therapeutic involvements of, other persons. As far as the mother was concerned, this had become accepted practice before our project had been initiated. Her involvement in the nexus of therapy had never appeared to be in contradiction with the idea of child guidance work. However, when we began to become really concerned with the intrapsychic difficulties of the father, not only from a diagnostic but also from a therapeutic angle, the term "child focus" began to present difficulties. Since intrapsychic difficulties in both

[1] Mittelmann, Bela, "Complementary Neurotic Reactions in Intimate Relationships," *Psychoanalytic Quarterly*, vol. 13, October, 1944, pp. 482–483; Waelder, Robert, "The Scientific Approach to Case Work with Special Emphasis on Psychoanalysis," *The Family*, vol. 22, October, 1941, p. 181.

parents were likely to create marital problems as well as develop mental problems for the children, we began to concern ourselves with the question of differentiation between family welfare and child guidance cases. In our search for an answer, we were plagued by the question as to what seemed dominant on a case-by-case basis. Was it the marital conflict or the emotional difficulties of the children?

Another problem which the continued use of the term "child focus" seemed to pose was the justification for the indirect treatment of a child. Could we really reconcile it with our character as a child-focused agency to see for a while only the mother or perhaps even predominantly so without having direct contact with the child? Over and beyond these questions as to who could be seen in therapeutic contact, we frequently were preoccupied with the question how far we could go in the treatment of parents and still retain our child focus. Workers became uncomfortable when the parents showed a tendency to discuss their own problems rather than that of the child. They began to worry how deeply they should get involved with them.

In the end we managed to resolve our conflicts to a considerable degree on a case-by-case basis. In retrospect, however, a study of our discussions and therapeutic decisions shows that our situational approach succeeded only in those instances in which we geared our focus in fact though not in technical formulations to "child welfare" as a social problem expressed in a particular complex of circumstances, rather than to the child as a person. Seen from that angle, it was always possible to reach a meaningful decision as to who had to be seen, whether he be father, uncle, family doctor, or brother-in-law. Similarly, it presented no particular problem as to who should be included in our therapeutic efforts. Finally, it presented no particular problem to decide how far we wanted to go in the depth of our treatment of anyone whom we felt we had to involve in therapy. An orientation to the social mandate of furthering child welfare seemed to furnish meaningful and, incidentally, operationally possible answers to all such questions.

If we had reformulated the concept of child focus from the

beginning of our testing period to *child welfare focus,* much insecurity, many discussions, and many failures to carry through our principles of reorientation could have been avoided. In essence, this reformulation would have helped us see that in all instances it did not matter whom we saw, whether we saw him alone or not, how frequently we saw him, or to what degree of depth we permitted our therapy to go, as long as we kept our clinical concern geared to his role as a family member of the child or the children involved and to the impact of his intrapsychic difficulties upon that role.

ORCHESTRATION OF THERAPIES INSTEAD OF DIVISION OF CASES

Finally, it would have been meaningful if we had realized during our seminar discussions that the concept of "dividing cases" was as such incompatible with the situational approach. On the one hand, we believed in the essential unity of a situation affecting a child and aimed at a coverage of all the essential factors in the situation in diagnosis as well as in therapeutic planning. On the other hand, a fragmentation of the situation by dividing it into two cases or more did not impress us on grounds of purely theoretical consistency as questionable. Our failure to reformulate our theory in that respect left us practically without equipment to deal with the disharmony created by a pursuit of the situational approach and a continued acceptance of the concept of a division of cases. The best that we could achieve under these circumstances was a pragmatic decision to keep cases undivided until some practical difficulties suggested a division. Although this was a reversal of the existing practice, which suggested a division of cases as soon as more than one person became involved in therapy, unless there was a special reason for having them treated by the same therapist, our decision did not go far enough. It retained two basically incompatible positions and reversed only their mutual relationship. We delegated the former arrangement to the status of an exception rather than to that of a rule, but failed to free ourselves from the impact of the earlier approach.

This lack of mental liberation expressed itself, for instance, in questions about the lines of contact between the individuals treated and their therapists. Some of us were of the opinion that the child's therapist would have to see the parents at least occasionally in order to know what was going on in the child's life. Others were of the opinion, however, that this was not necessary since the parents had their own workers. They maintained that the workers could be relied upon to inform one another of significant information that they had gained in the sessions with the persons whom they were treating. There ensued then discussions whether transmission of information from one worker to another, however frequent, could ever give the receiver of the information the same perceptual gain as a direct contact.

If we had been able to abandon the concept of a division of cases completely and to replace it by the concept of orchestration of streams of therapy carried on by different workers, such discussions might not have arisen. Such a conceptualization in all likelihood would have increased our insight into the desirability of facilitating all contacts which were likely to increase the perception of the situation as a unity by the people involved. Proprietary motivations of the therapists, as well as the operation of fragmented perception, would have been kept in better check. Looking at the possible impact of such a therapeutic reformulation, it can be visualized that it may even have an influence on the practice of supervision. At present, it can occur that the division of a case brings it under the impact of two workers who in turn are under two different supervisors with potentially different ideas as to how to proceed in the case. If the concept of orchestration of therapeutic effort were to be accepted, assignment of different workers to different family members may still be made without making it appear permissible to split up the case also on the supervisory level. Who ever heard of an orchestra with two conductors?

INTEGRATIVE RATHER THAN ADDITIVE WORK

Our experiences suggest that a conceptual reorientation is unlikely to produce smooth operations and satisfactory results as long as this reorientation is additive rather than integrative and partial rather than complete. They suggest further that productive research along the lines suggested by the introduction of new concepts in a body of theory depends similarly on the degree of reformulation which is attempted. It is now by and large accepted doctrine that the nature of a theory determines the research that will be pursued. "Theory may be defined as an integrated system of concepts and hypotheses. . . . This definition highlights the fact that a theory implies more than a series of propositional statements. There is the prior assumption of a particular set of constructs which dictates the selective organization of experience. In other words, a theory implies a particular way of perceiving the world. . . .

". . . The development of a conceptual system may make possible the perception of phenomena that otherwise would remain unobserved. From this point of view, a theory may be of great value even if it does not contain a single testable hypothesis but merely suggests a new way of looking at things."[1] However, a theory frequently can do more. It can also open up possibilities of checking on its appropriateness. "The aim of theory in empirical science is to develop analytical schemes of the empirical world with which the given science is concerned. This is done by conceiving the world abstractly, that is, in terms of classes of objects and of relations between such classes. Theoretical schemes are essentially proposals as to the nature of such classes and of their relations where this nature is problematic or unknown. Such proposals become guides to investigation to see whether they or their implications are true. Thus, theory exercises compelling influence on research-setting problems, staking out objects and leading inquiry into asserted relations. In turn, findings of fact test theories, and in suggesting new problems invite the formulation of new proposals. Theory, inquiry and empirical fact are interwoven in a texture of operation with theory guiding inquiry, inquiry seeking and isolating

[1] Bronfenbrenner, Urie, "Toward an Integrated Theory of Personality" in *Perception:* An Approach to Personality, edited by Robert R. Blake and Glenn V. Ramsey. Ronald Press Co., New York, 1951, p. 208.

facts, and facts affecting theory. The fruitfulness of their interplay is the means by which an empirical science develops."[1]

In order to perform these tasks of directing perception and verification, however, theory must free itself from the incongruities and disharmonies created by interdisciplinary efforts in the additive stage. It is unlikely to realize its potential, if it permits a proposition as challenging as that of the "continuum between individual and environment" to stand side by side with the old dichotomy of "the intrapsychic and the extrapsychic."

It is equally incongruous to do away with the dichotomy of individual and environment but to retain the dichotomy of social and psychological phenomena. Once it is accepted in its logical ramifications that the psychological makeup of an individual is based on his experiences with others, "the psychological" becomes social and "the social" psychological. Recognition and consideration of an individual's "social" environment as a composite of carriers of psychological configurations akin to his own will make it untenable to continue the utilization of such terms as "psycho-social diagnosis" or "psycho-social structure."

Thus, it appears as one of the most challenging tasks of further interdisciplinary effort in the field of child guidance work and probably in the whole field of psychotherapy as such to attempt a reformulation of theory in its totality. Such a reformulation would have to gear all its conceptualizations to the same level of abstraction. It would have to eliminate old conceptualizations which appear incompatible with the new propositions. And it would have to strive for a consistency which would permit bringing apparent differences in kind into a scheme suggesting differences in degree. It would have to make an attempt to describe phenomena in terms of a continuum rather than in terms of a juxtaposition.

In essence, such a reformulation would have to abandon the dichotomy of individual and environment. Psychotherapy might

[1]Blumer, Herbert, "What Is Wrong with Social Theory," *American Sociological Review*, vol. 9, February, 1954, p. 3.

have to experiment with a theory which would not know sick "people" and be concerned only with sick "situations." A patient, in the singular, would have to disappear from theoretical discussions. Accepting theoretically that the environment of the individual is at least partly human, the reformulation would have to express persistently that the most important part of the environment is composed of the internal experiences and reactions of others. Once this is recognized and adhered to in expression, a significant part of an individual's environment, its human part, would lose its distinctiveness and would become like the individual and actually part of him. We would not have sick husbands or sick wives but sick marriages; not sick children or sick mothers or sick fathers, but sick families; not sick teachers, or sick students, but sick school situations; not sick inmates, sick guardians, or sick administrators, but sick institutions, and so on. Essentially theory might be experimentally rewritten in terms of the emotional climate of groups rather than in terms of the emotional climate of individuals.

In order to make a beginning in this direction, it might be an interesting experiment to rewrite experimentally the child guidance literature contained in the *American Journal of Orthopsychiatry* during the years 1948 to 1952 in such terms. Those were the years of ferment in which new conceptualizations were attempted and reorientations expressed. Apparently they were also years in which completeness of reformulation had not yet been conceived of as a necessity. A comparison of the formulations as they then stood and a total reformulation into which they could be developed might prove to be a theoretical venture of far-reaching implications for practice and empirical research.

XI. Needs for Further Research

In the preceding chapter the proposition has been made that only a complete reformulation of the theory underlying child guidance practice would permit research the full utilization of the reorientations so far achieved. Many research questions implied in these reorientations may not yet be fully identifiable because the perceptual conditions for such an identification have not been sufficiently developed. Still, certain problem areas can be outlined at this time as having become apparent during the course of our project. In the following pages an attempt will be made to present these areas against their background of project history so as to show the circumstances which caused their identification.

DIVERGENCE BETWEEN THEORY AND PRACTICE

It has been the fate of this project to operate in a twilight zone created by a divergence between theory and practice. Early in its development it became directed at exploring the question whether liaison between social science and child guidance could aid in a change of practice which appeared to be desirable to people who knew the situation. To this purpose, conceptual aids for child guidance practice, taken from the social science field, were proposed. When the propositions were published, the need for these conceptual aids was denied under reference to previously expounded theory. As has been shown in this report, however, it is at least hypothetically possible and supported by a respectable body of research findings in the field of Gestalt psychology, that it might be the theory which is at fault and not the practice. Further research will be necessary to prove or disprove this hypothesis. But it should be stated now that because of the connection between theory and practice and the concern with both which dominated this research project, the whole problem area of divergences between theory and practice was discovered as a potentially fruitful field for research.

Dr. Spiegel's observations that interdisciplinary research has frequently basted together concepts of unequal degrees of abstraction[1] and Ichheiser's work on failures in perception in human relationships[2] may well prove to be reference points for a new type of research effort which would use practice experiences as checks for the adequacy of specific concepts and their combinations as aids for practical perception. That theory may aid practice through perception is established doctrine. That practical discoveries may require reformulations of theory is common experience. That practice and theory may be officially wedded but privately live in divorce has been suspected. *That the reason for such a situation may lie in the theory rather than in the practice is the proposition which in view of our experiences should be added to the problems of scientific research.*

It will be recalled that the divergence between theory and practice in clinical child guidance work seemed to hinge on the differential between the attention paid to the child and the attention paid to his environment. Our exploratory efforts were directed at equalizing these two foci of attention. The amount of significant phenomena which we found in the environment of the child over and beyond his mother suggests that such equalization of attention may be fruitful for diagnosis and therapy. Theoretically, this was never questioned; practically, it was only infrequently done. It might be an interesting research undertaking to test experimentally whether a reformulation of theory could not aid practice in the establishment and maintenance of such equalization.

It is this area specifically in which problems of phenomenol-

[1] Spiegel, John P., "Critique of Symposium" in *Mid-century Psychiatry*, edited by Roy R. Grinker. Charles C. Thomas, Springfield, Ill., 1953, p. 181.

[2] Ichheiser, Gustav, *Misunderstandings in Human Relations:* A Study in False Social Perception. Special issue of the *American Journal of Sociology*, vol. 65, September, 1949, part 2, p. 2.

ogy might be fruitfully investigated from the angle of basic as well as from the angle of applied research. The existing discoveries of Gestalt psychology have been pursued vigorously through tests and retests ever since they were made. This affirmatory and elaborate research effort, however, has been confined to the field of sensory perception. It is true that Ichheiser attempted to adapt phenomenological principles to the field of social perception, but as far as this writer's information goes, experimental verification of his propositions has not yet been attempted. In the field of the relationship between theory and practice, finally, the potential fruitfulness of phenomenology does not seem to have been recognized at all.

The experimental psychologists might find an interesting field of liaison between the work which they have done in the area of perception and the phenomenon of disregard of theoretical postulates in practice. It might well be worth investigating whether it is not possible to design models which could be submitted to rigorous laboratory tests and still would have immediate relevancy for clinical or agency practice in the social welfare field. The hypotheses, which were proposed and elaborated in Chapter VIII, Principles Operating in the Divergence Between Theory and Practice, might provide a start in that respect. *In essence, they amount to the proposition that the organization of elements of theoretical statements govern the perception in practice of the phenomena to which they refer.*

If this nexus of hypotheses should be corroborated and a reformulation of theory be completed which would take account of these principles of organization, any divergences between theory and practice which would then continue to exist would provide a much safer area for the testing of psychoanalytic and sociological explanations than this problem area has offered up to the present time. In summary, an investigation of the question whether the application of theory to practice is determined at least partially by the organization and structure of the theoretical formulations themselves, might provide a significant extension of the principles of Gestalt psychology. At the same time it might provide psychoanalytic and sociological investigations with an area free from the beclouding impact of a variable which so far has been overlooked.

THE STUDY OF GROUP PHENOMENA IN THEIR TOTALITY

In recent years the disciplines of psychiatry and of social casework have shown a pronounced increase of interest in the emotional structure of groups. This interest as such is of relatively long standing. Like almost anything that is of importance in human relations, it received attention from Mary Richmond: "One who has learned, in the details of a first interview, to keep the 'combined physical and moral qualities,' the whole man, in view, will appreciate the importance of applying this same view to the family. The family life has a history of its own. It is not what it happens to be at some particular moment or 'in reference to some particular act,' but it is what it is 'on the whole.' What will help to reveal this trend? What external circumstances over which the family had no apparent control, and what characteristics of its members—physical, mental, temperamental—seem to have determined the main drift?"[1] This postulate formulated by Mary Richmond, however, was difficult to satisfy. Interest in the individual, his unconscious motivations, his mechanisms of defense, and his emotional discomforts dominated the scene during the decades which followed Miss Richmond's writings. Furthermore, the knowledge of psychodynamics accumulated during these decades appears to have been necessary to meet this demand. In consequence, the need for a study of the emotional structures of the family group was voiced again roughly thirty years later. This time the demand for it came from psychiatric quarters. In 1949 Franz Alexander had this to say on the occasion of the annual meeting of the American Orthopsychiatric Association. ". . . For us psychiatrists it remains to increase our knowledge of the dynamic forces by which the structure of the personality is molded. This problem can be divided into two parts. The one is the intimate knowl-

[1] Richmond, Mary E., *Social Diagnosis*. Russell Sage Foundation, New York, 1917, p. 138.

edge of those early family influences which determine the emotional orientation of the growing child. . . . New knowledge will come from further, more precise study of what may be called the emotional structure of the whole family. In the past studies, the center of attention was the child as he is influenced by his relationship to the members of the family; psychodynamic understanding of the total configuration of the family still wants for further investigations. The promising studies of Drs. Adelaide Johnson and Stanislaus Szurek and others in this field will have to be further pursued."[1] Apparently the time has become ripe to fulfill this persistent postulate. That it can be done on a case-by-case basis, is suggested by the work of Ackerman, Glauber, Sands, and our own experiences in the project. This type of effort, however, would have to be extended to a systematic study which transcends the individual case analyses so far undertaken. Before such an extension is made, two preparatory phases of research may have to be performed. First of all, it is necessary to extend our research interest to the intrapsychic problems of family members other than the mother and the child, and to the impact of these intrapsychic problems on the interrelationships between those family members and others or the interrelationships between these others. This has not been done so far. The omission is not difficult to explain. Owing to their traditional emphasis, both psychiatrists and psychologists as well as social caseworkers had to approach any study of the emotional climate of groups with the perceptual equipment of an essentially individual-focused profession. It has been pointed out at considerable length in this report that this equipment probably was the cause of considerable fractionalization and singularization of pluralities which we have encountered in the field of child guidance. At any rate, we are now faced with almost the same imbalance of knowledge regarding the various members of the family group as we were twenty-five years ago. It was noted by Charlotte Towle as early

[1] Alexander, Franz, "Looking Ahead in the Fields of Orthopsychiatric Research, Symposium 1949," *American Journal of Orthopsychiatry,* vol. 20, January, 1950, p. 77.

as 1930 that because of the more frequent contacts of child guidance workers with mothers more was known about them and about work with them than about fathers.[1] Twenty-four years later, Dr. O. Spurgeon English had to repeat this observation and to voice again the need for research regarding fathers. ". . . Effort to define the psychological role of the father brings up certain questions for future investigation. So far in the study of the psychodynamics of mental disease we have described the pathological factors under the name of environment, family, and parents and we have talked of rejecting mothers and stern fathers. Little effort has been made to *quantitate* the role of the father psychologically as follows:

"1. How much of the psychopathology in a given case has been due to the absence of the father?

"2. How much of the psychopathology in a given case has been due to the indifference of the father to the mother even though he was devoted to the child?

"3. How much of the psychopathology has been due to the favoritism of the father for a certain child in the family?

"4. How much of the psychopathology of a delinquent child can be shown to be due to the indifference or unwise management by the father of the child himself?

"Since the mother plays such a large role during feeding and toilet training, she undoubtedly is a crucial factor in producing some of the health or psychopathology of that period. But, as we hope we have shown, the father's influence is definitely not absent even then, and he plays an increasing role as time goes on. If a mother, for instance, is sufficiently orally depriving to produce alcoholism or schizophrenia in her progeny, could the father, if he knew enough, prevent this catastrophe, or could he mitigate its severity, and if so how would he go about it? These areas of family living need some good research work, utilizing the psychiatrist, social worker, and psychologist. Such quantitation of the father's role in abetting the production of

[1] Towle, Charlotte, "The Social Worker" in "Symposium: The Treatment of Behavior and Personality Problems in Children," *American Journal of Orthopsychiatry*, vol. 1, October, 1930, pp. 26–27.

illness may indicate how much more seriously the American father must take his role in family life."[1]

In spite of the tremendous interest in the phenomenon of sibling rivalry and its impact upon personality development, attention has been largely directed upon the sibling who is jealous and hardly ever on the sibling who causes rivalry. Perhaps it is an oversimplification to assume that the mere arrival of another child or the preferential treatment of a sibling by the parents alone causes sibling rivalry. It might be a productive field of research in interpersonal relationships to find out what the personality and behavior of the envied sibling really are before hypotheses about the impact of sibling rivalry upon emotionally disturbed children are formulated.

Similarly, the frequent occurrence of parent substitutes in our society with its high incidence of the employment of mothers and with its high incidence of divorce would suggest that there is a need for extending research efforts also to the intrapsychic phenomena existing in the spouses of divorced parents, grandparents, aunts, uncles, and housekeepers.

Greater attention will have to be paid also to the psychodynamics operating in extrafamilial factors. We live in a period in which the family has lost a considerable part of its childrearing functions. This process is still going on. Familial functions are being taken over by persons who are not biologically connected with the child and who also do not form a part of the primary group of his home. Reference is here made to the members of the child-rearing professions and occupations, such as nursery school teachers, camp counselors, and perhaps in a sense also baby sitters, if the last named are employed on a more or less permanent basis. The members of the child-rearing professions undoubtedly spend a great deal of time with the child during his formative years and color the impact of his familial experiences upon him. Apparently they do this in earlier and earlier periods of the developmental process. The time

[1] English, O. Spurgeon, "The Psychological Role of the Father in the Family," *Social Casework,* vol. 35, October, 1954, p. 329.

has passed when one could assume that a preschool child's personality-forming contacts are confined to the members of his family. Day nurseries, nursery schools, cooperative child-care arrangements among young mothers on a neighborhood basis may introduce into the child's life extrafamilial factors of determining influences at an age as early as three years, or even earlier. *Against this panorama of social change in child rearing, the range of people who might exercise significant influence on the development of the preschool child appears wider indeed than is frequently assumed in clinical practice, and to a considerable extent extrafamilial. The collection of a large body of data regarding these categories of persons seems to be the first condition of an approach to the study of the emotional structures of groups.*

A second preparatory phase would be the collection and categorization of a very large number of *family diagnoses* and also of *life sphere diagnoses.* The term "life sphere diagnosis" is here introduced to suggest that the emotional structure of family groups may have to be accompanied by a study of the impact of extrafamilial factors on these emotional structures in order to achieve an understanding which approximates the complexity of child development in modern society.

The difficulties which any such study is likely to encounter have been suggested by the case examples presented in this report. It also has been pinpointed theoretically in the literature. As already mentioned, Bossard's Law of Family Interaction states: "With the addition of each person to a family or primary group, the number of persons increases in the simplest arithmetical progression in whole numbers, and the number of personal interrelationships within the group increases in the order of triangular numbers."[1] The difficulties which here are expressed in the symbolism of mathematics have found expression also in a medium more familiar to the clinician. ". . . The interpersonal dynamics in the family group are far from being simple. Family relationships are always multilateral, which is

[1] Bossard, James H. S., *The Sociology of Child Development.* Harper and Bros., New York, 1948, p. 146. See also note on p. 80.

sometimes referred to as the primary triangle—father, mother, and child, each forming an apex. Actually, the emotional network is much more complex. Relations would be triangular if each related to the others exclusively as individuals, but in the family, as in all groups, each relates also to *the relation* between and among the others. Thus, the child relates to his mother and to his father as individuals, but he also enters into and affects the relationship of his two parents. Similarly, the father has a relation with his wife and his child as individuals, but he affects and must consider the relationship of the two and his place in that emotional constellation. This applies to the mother as well. In the same way, each sibling has to deal with the relations of his parents and their relation with every other sibling and the relation of the siblings to one another, and his relations to the parents as individuals and as a couple.

"This vastly complicates the network of emotions and their ebb and flow in a family group."[1]

This complexity is likely to discourage the researcher. It need not, however, if it is recognized that all effort of human understanding is geared to finding simplicity behind complexity. To be sure, the task of formulating a family diagnosis or a life sphere diagnosis has to be based on the perception of an ever-increasing number of factors. It is unlikely to be solved unless that increase of perception of the determinants of emotional group conditions is accompanied by the recognition of organizing principles. Our case studies have shown that the concept of "social interaction" might serve to furnish such a principle only in situations comprising a relatively small number of persons. Our project experiences, however, have also suggested that more complex family situations might be studied under utilization of the concept of "social roles." Other concepts may suggest themselves as the efforts of analyzing the emotional structures of groups embrace more and more cases of relative complexity.

From the beginning of this project, it has been stressed that

[1] Slavson, S. R., *Child Psychotherapy.* Columbia University Press, New York, 1952, p. 86.

concepts are not only perceptual, but also ordering devices.[1] Their use as identifiers of organizing principles in the understanding of a larger number of items of perception will require systematic elaboration. After this is done, it will become a more easily manageable proposition for clinicians to diagnose and treat the problems of pluralities which comprise more than two persons. Theory in liaison with empirical research will have to forge the tools for the fulfillment of Mary Richmond's and Franz Alexander's postulates for an understanding of "the whole" or "the total configuration" of the family.

As far as theory is concerned, the problem seems to be one of finding and elaborating concepts which would permit the clinician to give an identifying and qualifying description of the group phenomenon in its emotional dimension.

It will be the task of theory development and empirical experimentation to test further whether the concepts of social interaction and social role can fulfill the promise of describing the emotional structure of the family as a totality.

Such a continuation of effort might profit from the spadework done by Leonard S. Cottrell, Jr., in proposing a conceptual schema for the analysis of situational fields.[2] This schema deals with the phenomenon of social interaction between two persons. Its importance lies in its conceptualization of a phenomenon which by definition transcends the one person emphasis of all psychological schools which emphasize the individual. The basic unit of analysis, "the interact pattern," is bipersonal. This is not the place to recount all the theorems proposed in this schema. It is important, however, for the analysis of the emotional structures of the family or other groups to extend the conception of the interact pattern from one designating a series of reciprocal behavior items between two persons to behavior patterns which over and beyond being reciprocal have an effect upon the behavior of persons who are not partners of the original interact. This "long distance" effect may be

[1] Pollak, Otto, and Collaborators, *Social Science and Psychotherapy for Children*, p. 33.

[2] Cottrell, Leonard S., Jr., "The Analysis of Situational Fields in Social Psychology," *American Sociological Review*, vol. 7, June, 1942, pp. 370–382.

direct or indirect, that is, behavior between A and B may cause behavior of C or behavior of either A or B toward C. In the triad, for instance, of parents and child, the behavior of the father interacting with the mother may not only cause a certain response of the mother to the father and of the mother to the child, but also of the child to the father or of the child to the mother. The mother's response to a stimulus provided by her child may not only create a response in the child, but also in the father. Parental behavior thus does not only affect child behavior, but also spouse behavior. Spouse behavior does not only affect spouse behavior, but also parental behavior. It may also cause child behavior.

All these reciprocal and long-distance response patterns may become family interaction patterns of relative permanence.

Any attempt to utilize the observation of these interact patterns for purposes of group analysis would have to be concerned with the identification of concordant or discordant effects upon the membership. In the emotional dimension, for instance, the clinician would have to answer the question whether a role played by one family member in an interact pattern creates similar emotions in all members of the group or different emotions. In the first instance we have emotional concordance, in the other emotional anomie. Care would have to be taken not to confuse emotional concordance with emotional comfort. The interact pattern between two spouses may not only make them anxious, but also the children.

The possible consequences of interact patterns in the family may thus represent a continuum of emotional constellations. There may be concordance of positive emotions—the loving family; there may be emotional discordance—love and hate; and there may be negative concordance—the hate-ridden family and the anxiety-ridden family. Still, neither positive nor negative emotional convergences may be taken as expressions of health or pathology as such. It is not the content but the appropriateness of affect which determines mental health.

After family diagnoses, using these or other concepts as organizing principles, are accumulated in large numbers, the identification of group syndromes and their categorization will have to be undertaken on a comparative basis. Together with the crystallization of the results of efforts to study the emotional structure of groups, attention will have to be directed at studies concerned with their causation and their consequences. Every one of these structures will have to be conceived as having a history. At the same time, it will have to be conceived as presenting at least part of the history of other emotional structures.

Our project gave interesting hints of the research potential existing in these areas and in one instance a start has been made to carry out research along the lines suggested here. In one of our cases the child presented the syndrome of transvestitism.[1] In the seminar discussions of this case it appeared that there were also a few other cases of transvestitism in treatment at the agency. Furthermore, the psychiatrist on our team, Dr. Maurice R. Friend, also happened to have such a case in his private practice. Gearing our discussion to Dr. Phyllis Greenacre's work on fetishism,[2] we gained the impression that this form of perversion may be the result of the influence of a special combination of social factors in the pregenital phase of child development. Pursuing this impression, Dr. Friend and a number of associates began to work up the available cases from this point of view.[3] In other cases, we gained the impression of a definite destiny pattern of emotional climate repetition from one generation to the next. The readers of this report will recall to what degree the case of Steven M. showed dramatic repetition in this respect. Another aspect of the study of the emotional structures of families and other primary groups would be the evaluation of their impact upon the functioning of the group from the viewpoint of society. It will be recalled that the presentations of family diagnoses in this report included institu-

[1] Because of the severity of the pathology involved, this case was not included in the case presentations of this report.

[2] Greenacre, Phyllis, "Certain Relationships Between Fetishism and Faulty Development of the Body Image" in *The Psychoanalytic Study of the Child*, International Universities Press, New York, 1953, vol. 8, pp. 79–98.

[3] Friend, Maurice R., Dorothy Dunaeff, Betty Klein, Louise Schiddel, "Observations on the Development of Transvestitism in Boys," *American Journal of Orthopsychiatry*, vol. 24, July, 1954, pp. 563–575.

tional analyses. These institutional analyses attempted to evaluate the emotional pathology of the family groups against the perspective of the family as a social institution.

The institutional analyses of the emotional family structures here discussed have been geared essentially only to the concepts of association and dissociation in terms of the relationships between the spouses and in terms of the relationships between the parents and the children. Other conceptualizations of the institutional aspects of family life may be found useful in this type of work. In essence, such evaluation of identified syndromes of family pathologies or other group pathologies would determine therapeutic goal-setting in relationship to social needs. They will become necessary to furnish an organizing principle for the orchestration of the various lines of therapeutic effort which will suggest themselves increasingly as a result of the reorientations occurring in the child guidance field. These various lines of treatment effort will present a special need for orchestration if they are to produce family health rather than family disintegration.

Social evaluations of emotional group structures which show pathology may well be applicable also to institutions other than the family. There is always a danger in work with emotionally disturbed children that the temporarily unsettling effect of therapy is not sufficiently recognized in its impact upon the demands of social living. Institutions cannot be run on the principle of catharsis in the form of acting out. In the future, a way will have to be found by which the emotional liberation resulting from psychotherapy can be geared to the demands of institutional effectiveness and of social competence. Institutional analyses of sick situations will have to be integrated with the psychiatric analyses of their emotional structures.

SPECIFICITY OF PROFESSIONAL SUBCULTURES

Institutional assessments of the impact of family pathology on the fulfillment of the social functions of the family are always in danger of being blurred by the tendency of many clinicians to project their specifically professional value systems on the community at large. These institutional assessments are also endangered by the ethnocentrism developed in every culture which makes those who belong inclined to think of those who do not as deviants. It is very likely that in a successful contact between a child guidance worker and persons in the life sphere of an emotionally disturbed child a certain amount of acculturation has to take place in terms of diagnosis, the formulation of a treatment plan, and the setting of a treatment goal. This acculturation process may vary in degree and in intensity from case to case, but it is likely to be achieved more easily and more frequently if the professional person involved is aware of his own professional value system as a phenomenon relative in time and place.

Psychiatrists and social workers have specific professional training experiences which make them qualified to gain such awareness of the specificity of their own professional subculture. In both disciplines a high degree of self-knowledge is considered essential equipment for the performance of the professional task. The concern with phenomena of counter-transference in psychoanalytically oriented therapy is perhaps only one of the most dramatic expressions of this general concern with self-awareness in the helping professions. In the past this demand for self-awareness has been directed largely at the intrapsychic problems of the specific individual involved. As mentioned in Chapter I, the proposal made by the writer to extend this tendency of self-study from the intrapsychic of the individual worker to a cultural self-study of the profession as a whole has been well received by social workers. Some promising attempts at self-study have been undertaken among the ranks of that profession. Significantly enough, one of these efforts encountered considerable controversy after the publication of its findings. This controversy is likely to push the findings of the study into the realm of untested but hardened opinion instead of utilizing these findings as propositions which can be tested by further study.[1]

[1] Letters to the Editor regarding Helen Padula's paper "Some Thoughts About the Culture of Social Work," *Journal of Psychiatric Social Work*, vol. 24, October, 1954, pp. 56–60.

It seems to be necessary, therefore, to utilize the interest of social workers in this aspect of their professional existence for a professional self-study planned on a nationwide basis. Such a study, of necessity, should be carried out with the assistance of social scientists in the research design as well as in the preparation and analysis of the paper. Very likely the study might have to combine the essential viewpoint of anthropology with the quantitative emphasis of modern sociology. Nonetheless, it should remain a self-study in terms of planning. The study's accuracy, validity, and acceptance might be jeopardized if it were to treat the social workers as a tribe being observed by an anthropologist from another part of the world.

Other professions active in the child guidance field, notably those of psychiatry and clinical psychology, might gain also through similar self-studies. It should be noted, however, that until now they do not seem to have expressed the same interest in an investigation of their professional subculture, as have the social workers. At any rate, these specific studies of the various subcultures represented in the child guidance field should not be seen as the final aim of this line of research.

The increasing specialization of professional competence in our time and the resulting need of teamwork has brought the three professions of psychiatry, social work, and clinical psychology into daily working contact. The experience of practically everybody involved in this type of cooperation suggests that teamwork which is so much praised in our society is not without difficulty or at least not without problems of its own which require effort to solve. Since cooperation is one of the great values on which there seems to be widespread agreement, the experience of the three professions with the team approach should be of great interest to the professionals involved, as well as to the representatives of all behavior sciences. It should also be of greatest interest to the community at large.

The three professions involved have the advantage of being trained in diagnostic thinking and self-perception. Caseworkers in particular have developed special skills in recording which could be of great assistance in the collection of pertinent data.

If members of the three professions turned these capacities to the study of a working arrangement which becomes increasingly necessary also in many fields other than their own, significant scientific gains might be made from a societal point of view.

THE ECONOMICS OF THERAPY

What has been discussed so far has been presented as research possibility without concern for the practical implications in terms of the economics of therapy. Although conceived in a child guidance clinic and permanently practice oriented, the research stimulations resulting from this project should not be fettered by concerns of therapeutic efficiency. Questions such as laws underlying divergence between theory and practice, the impact of theoretical formulations upon perception, and questions regarding the nature of the emotional climates of groups in which children play a part during the process of their development have research value whether they lead to more economic procedures of therapy or not. On the basis of pure logic one might argue that the more one knows about a case, the greater becomes one's power to achieve curative success. However, this may well be a generalization which may not hold true in practice. It is by no means yet established that therapeutic procedures of the past have not been in many cases equally successful and less expensive than the procedures suggested by this project would be. This also would require further research. It might be begun, however, too soon. As long as fuller perception and the means of achieving it are contested and opposed by groups of workers owing to the values which they have come to accept in the course of their professional training, as long as lack of experience prevents security of operation, fair measures of differential efficiency cannot be expected. The question of deciding whether it is more economical and in the overall picture more efficient to concentrate on the mother-child relationship in child guidance practice will become accessible to an answer only after a practice which pays attention to all family members has been tried and mastered. This would be the applied research which child guidance practitioners may want to follow in response to the question raised by the liaison project.

Such research, of course, might have many ramifications. It might, for instance, have to come to terms with such questions as to whether weekly interviews are a necessary routine in treatment, whether office time of one therapist can be allocated only to one person involved in a sick situation or simultaneously to several persons. Experimentation of workers seeing parents together, parents and children together, and siblings together might open a fruitful field not only for the development of new techniques but also for a new consideration of the economy factor in therapy.

If these research suggestions are to bear fruit, they will have to be taken up by the child guidance field rather than by one agency. As a matter of fact, differential reactions to the findings reported by us, if they are undertaken in a climate of research rather than in a climate of emotional controversy, may provide opportunities for comparison and control situations which only the child guidance as a whole field can provide.

PART FOUR

THE AGENCY LOOKS AT THE PROJECT

HERSCHEL ALT
Executive Director, Jewish Board of Guardians

PART FOUR: THE AGENCY LOOKS AT THE PROJECT
Evaluative Comment by Herschel Alt

Dr. Pollak has invited me to comment on the demonstration described in this book from the standpoint of one of the co-sponsoring agencies whose clinical service constituted the laboratory for the project. The questions may well be asked:

> How far have the original purposes of the project been achieved?
> How has the demonstration influenced the evolution of the agency's treatment orientation and practice?
> What of the interest of the agency in the continuation of an ongoing relationship between social science and child guidance practice?

The original demonstration, as has been indicated in Chapter I, focused on two important objectives: (1) fuller recognition in practice of the value of the situational approach, and (2) utilization of social science concepts by the practitioners as operational tools in diagnosis and treatment. The publication of the first report engendered a good deal of controversy over whether the broader approach which the project embodied was new or already a part of current casework philosophy and practice. This is a debate which would be difficult to resolve with any dogmatic assurance. Dr. Pollak's analysis of the literature relating to the treatment of fathers provides one relevant index.[1] Perhaps the only answer possible to the question of newness is that it is a matter of degree. Social work may have always emphasized the situational approach but may have frequently neglected it in practice.

It may be relevant to point out that there are situations in

[1] See Chapter VII.

which the distinction between differences of degree and kind loses its meaning. It has been held that when you get a difference in degree of sufficient extent you may, in fact, be getting a difference in kind. If the difference in degree is sufficiently marked to differentiate activities, you have, in fact, a difference in kind.

While no objective case-by-case evaluation in our agency has been undertaken to assess the impact of the project upon our practice, and we have not isolated other dynamic factors within and without the agency which may have also influenced our work, we are left with the clear conviction of the positive value of the demonstration for the agency and the field in which it functions. The clinical practice of the agency reflects the influence of the project in many tangible ways, and it is important to point out that these changes have occurred without any formal mandates or decisions to modify practice but purely through the educational process flowing from the project itself.

As Dr. Pollak points out, one of the social science concepts which proved to be most useful in the attempt to integrate sociological and psychodynamic thinking in child guidance practice was that of the *family of orientation.* Recognition of the meaning of this idea had the effect of extending diagnostic perception and therapeutic planning to all members of the household in which the child who was referred to the Clinic was growing up. It provided a permanent challenge to strive for psychodynamic understanding of all the members of the family, to see the social interaction among them as based on these individual psychodynamic pictures, and to base therapeutic planning on such understanding. While retaining its focus on the child's difficulties, it helped to shift the orientation from child psychotherapy alone to family psychotherapy and to explore procedures which such an orientation demanded.

As a result, we are now treating more fathers and siblings than before the inception of the demonstration. We are making more home visits. We are seeing more members of the immediate family as well as the "family of orientation"—parents, siblings, grandparents, aunts, and housekeepers. We are seeing more doctors and teachers. This broadening and intensification of treatment effort is taking place in spite of extreme pressure upon the agency for service to a greater number of children and families—an index of the quality of our conviction as to the value of the more intensive approach. It is likely that the agency will move ahead with a fuller implementation of these trends as funds permit.

The meaning of the project becomes clearer when we see it in the perspective provided by the stream of experience within the agency as well as within the field of casework and clinical practice generally. While it was carried on in one division of our own agency, it was influenced by and in turn affected thought and practice in the agency as a whole. What is true of our own agency is also true of the field of clinical service in general.

The establishment of the project is no accident, as clearly outlined by Bertram J. Black in his introduction to *Social Science and Psychotherapy for Children.*[1] The project grew out of the conviction of the professional leadership of the agency that the time had come for reformulation of the scientific basis for its child guidance practice. By 1940 the child guidance services of the agency had evolved from a practice relying primarily on the tools of social casework to a child guidance service in a clinical pattern. This was accomplished by efforts to maintain as full a degree as possible of unification of social and psychological aspects of treatment. While, on the one hand, there was an emphasis on differential diagnosis as the basis for treatment planning, at the same time there was continued concern that the environmental factors in child guidance practice be given full consideration.

The experience of the one brought increased sensitivity to social issues as well as a heightened recognition of the impact of external events upon people's lives. We were led independently to ask a number of questions about the agency's basic approach to its task. One result of this interest was an invita-

[1] Pollak, Otto, and Collaborators, *Social Science and Psychotherapy for Children.* Russell Sage Foundation, New York, 1952, pp. 9–19.

tion to Gordon Hamilton to undertake a descriptive study of the agency's child guidance practice, which appeared in 1947 as *Psychotherapy in Child Guidance.*[1] The next was the cooperative arrangement with Russell Sage Foundation to undertake the demonstration, the latter phase of which is described in this book. Another was a clarification of the agency's treatment focus, which resulted from a conference held at Asbury Park in 1949. This conference was called to take a look at the practice of the agency, the way in which treatment was organized, the professional skills required, and the agency's program for training of personnel.

The conference was attended by the senior members of the various disciplines included in the professional staff. Psychiatrists, psychologists, psychiatric caseworkers, and other special consultants from all the major divisions of the agency were present, as was Dr. Pollak.

The group gave expression to the need for a broad conception of child guidance problems, one that went beyond consideration of intrapsychic factors alone; a conception that embraced clinical diagnosis, broad environmental factors, as well as interpersonal relationships beyond the primary ones involving the parental figures. That this broad concept of etiology had great implications for a treatment program and consequently for training in the agency was affirmed.

A few concrete expressions of this interest within and without the agency added to the meaning and the future potentialities of the project itself. The development of various forms of group therapy, dating back twenty years, carried with it something of the same emphases on interaction on a broader stage, on the relationship between the individual and the group, and members of the group to each other. The impact of these approaches was further heightened by what was taking place in the Council Child Development Center, as well as in our full care residential treatment projects.

At the Council Child Development Center, which is a spe-

[1] Hamilton, Gordon, *Psychotherapy in Child Guidance.* Columbia University Press, New York, 1947.

cialized facility for the study and treatment of preschool children and includes within its resources both a child guidance clinic and a nursery school, we find first a blending of not only the usual clinical disciplines, but an integration of those with education. Treatment is not seen as limited to psychotherapy or even to psychotherapy of the child and the parents, but embraces the child's living experience for the greater part of the day. It is significant, too, that in a treatment center of this sort not only are both parents involved, but often siblings as well. But this trend toward what I call total treatment has been given the fullest expression in our residential treatment projects. Here we find not only the fullest degree of utilization of all clinical and social service skills, but also education, group work, and planned life experience. What is perhaps significant is that all the disciplines involved undergo a certain kind of adaptation as they become integral elements in a total treatment function which in itself is specifically designed to study and treat a particular kind of child.

A good deal of impetus for a broader approach to clinical procedures derives from activities focused on evaluation of treatment. Thus, Ackerman and Neubauer, some years ago, analyzed some of the reasons for failure of treatment of children in our child guidance services.[1] It became clear that treatment primarily focused on the child alone was insufficient, and, to be effective, needed to embrace a much wider area, including the treatment of one or both parents as well as siblings. In addition, it was necessary to take into account the interaction of the changes occurring in the patient and their effect upon others in the milieu. Subsequent to the establishment of the Center in 1947, Dr. Nathan W. Ackerman, then its director, undertook an extensive investigation, in which he is still engaged, to develop a systematic diagnosis of total family function as well as therapeutic methods concerned with the family as a unit.

Dr. Ackerman, although no longer a member of the agency staff, has continued his efforts to formulate a scheme of family

[1] Ackerman, Nathan W., and Peter B. Neubauer, "Failures in the Psychotherapy of Children," *Failures in Psychiatric Treatment,* edited by Paul H. Hoch. Grune and Stratton, New York, 1948, pp. 86–87, 88.

diagnosis which would identify the basic psychological problems the partners bring into the marriage and to their life together which may lead to family conflict and disintegration.

Outside of the agency itself, perhaps the most important trend in casework practice is that which is broadly described as "family-centered" casework, and includes several related but distinct treatment projects.

A general characteristic of all these special treatment efforts is the search for a more systematic family diagnosis and a more comprehensive family therapy. All emphasize the more complete fusion of sociological and psychological factors, both in etiology as well as in treatment. They seek to incorporate into study and treatment procedures as much as possible of the total life experience of the individual. Beginning with the totality of personal relationships within and outside the family, they take account of environmental factors within the family setting and outside it. Some seek to utilize authority as a positive force in treatment, recognizing the interplay between the individual and external forces, and dealing with both his resistances as well as his adaptations. These new approaches to family treatment are also bringing renewed emphasis on social relations.

The newer practice emphasizes the formulation of a comprehensive picture of total family living before undertaking any delineation of individual personality structure. Thus, the diagnostic exploration may begin with the physical attributes of the home, with the neighborhood, with the relationships of the family with other families in the community, and continue with the ways in which the physical setting and the neighborhood factors play a part in the social adjustment of the family. Then it moves on to the social conflicts, the values, and standards of the family. As far as possible, treatment of the individual is planned so that it will contribute to the betterment of the group situation. More consideration is given to the strategy of the total treatment plan before any particular individual family member is selected to receive psychotherapy.

In our demonstration project, this more comprehensive and

more fluid approach yielded a new synthesis of therapeutic methods which proved more effective in dealing with reality and interpersonal problems than earlier forms of therapeutic effort. In my opinion, in the future it can be expected to do the same in other instances of application.

A review of the influence of the project within the agency, taken together with other trends in clinical practice within and without the agency, shows that there are a variety of efforts seeking to utilize the situational approach as exemplified by the treatment of families at the Council Child Development Center, the utilization of planned living experience at our Hawthorne Cedar Knolls School and the newer residential projects, and family centered casework. There is little question that these and many other similar activities with the same objectives will continue. Within our own child guidance services I would like to see more attention given to fuller preparation of families for treatment. I would like to see how far changes in the child's personality can be brought about through modification of parental attitudes and the environmental situation without direct treatment of the child.

As we have just indicated, the social science project has proved to be a valuable experience for the agency. It is now in order to look ahead and see what bearing it may have on the relationship between the social science disciplines and child guidance practice and on the possible participation of the social scientist in a child guidance agency.

Both social science and child guidance are broad concepts, and the experience described in this book undoubtedly lends itself to different kinds of evaluation. Every child guidance worker and social scientist will draw his own conclusions. We in the agency which participated in the project are clear as to the contribution which an individual social scientist, acting as a consultant to the functional clinical team, achieved in our own agency. Although the agency has not, through its leadership group, staff, or trustees, formulated any definitive attitudes with respect to the role of the social scientist in child guidance, I myself will here attempt to outline a few of the specific possibilities for a fruitful cooperation between social science and child guidance.

If we conceive of the social sciences as constituting an empirically demonstrated body of knowledge about social behavior, and see clinical practice as an art based upon it, obviously the relationship of the two would be direct and would be continuously cultivated.

Even though we are still far from this kind of ideal situation, the social scientist, together with other scientists, has an important part to play in collaborating with the clinician in formulating a cohesive frame of reference for child guidance practice. This is a pressing need because no frame of reference so far devised encompasses all the factors operative in the totality of the living situation.

Perhaps the most important operational concepts, from the standpoint of clinical practice, which Dr. Pollak develops are "family diagnosis" and "family therapy." In giving greater specificity to these concepts so as to make them useful in clinical practice, he draws on still another theoretical aspect of social relationships—cohesiveness. In spite of considerable thoughtfulness and imagination which enter into the illustration of how his ideas of family diagnosis might be applied in practice, I feel we are still left with very broad categories which are perhaps insufficiently specific for practical purposes. The same may be said of the development of the concept of "family therapy." As we have already seen, an operational frame of reference for family diagnosis and family therapy would be of inestimable value to the clinical field.

Perhaps some questions about the order in which the various stages in this kind of effort might be projected would be helpful in clarifying the problem. Should we move from social science concepts, many of which are logical constructs and generalizations applicable to mass phenomena, and proceed to test them in individual situations; or should we begin with the phenomena as they appear in clinical case studies? In the case of the project, we moved from social science concepts such as "family of orientation" to the specific case. This carried with it steps in the adaptation of the concept to the practical situation. The other alternative would be to move along both paths, from the general to the particular, as well as from the particular to the general.

In the demonstration described in this work, the social scientist was not only an objective observer and involved in the description and analysis of data, but a member of the clinical team. One obvious question is whether this is an appropriate role for him. Would this be a desirable permanent arrangement for all other clinics, or is it merely worthwhile for a transitional demonstration or educational period?

In formulating a reaction to these questions, one has to distinguish between the social scientist as an individual professional worker with certain skills as a person and as a scientist, and the general theoretical concepts of which he is the bearer. As a participant in a clinical program, he finds himself in the role of middleman compelled to weigh strategic considerations involved in a cooperative enterprise as well as to interpret theoretical concepts. Much of the value of our project is due, we believe, to the personal gifts of the consultant as well as the professional point of view which he brought.

Judging from our experience, the social scientist in a clinical setting, while not himself involved in the actual treatment, has to be able to see how the special concepts of his field are related to other scientific concepts as well as practice. He has to see how they fit into their proper relationship in the treatment process. In other words, he has to be able to adapt theoretical concepts to the solution of practical problems. He must also be on the alert to see how far these concepts are sufficient to cover clinical phenomena in themselves and in their combinations. Intelligently pursued, the testing of concepts in clinical situations should not only lead to clarification of the concepts themselves, but to a recognition of their limitations and the beginning of formulations of new ones.

The positive achievement of our project was also in a great measure the result of the keen critical faculty and wisdom of the consultant. His unremitting insistence on the avoidance of a sharp differentiation between individual and environment was instrumental in ensuring that this became part of the professional orientation of the staff.

Whether a social scientist from a discipline such as sociology, social psychology, anthropology should be involved continuously as a member of the clinical team is open to difference of opinion. There is no question, however, that there is a place for the social scientist in a child guidance agency as a teacher and consultant and research worker, and as a builder, with other scientists and clinicians, of a scientific base for practice.

In weighing the various considerations for his inclusion as a member of the clinical team, positive as well as negative values suggest themselves. Perhaps the greatest value of such an arrangement is the added assurance of being able to deal with complexity. In practice as well as in scientific research, the principle of least effort frequently is at work. This may mean the reduction of complexity to simplicity, even at the price of oversimplification. The social scientist, just because he is not directly involved in treatment, is freed from the temptation which may confront the practitioner, of avoiding further complications of the difficult therapeutic task. His participation is guided by his concern for group concepts and thus safeguards the broader perception which the practitioner needs to utilize. On the other hand, being forced into contact with workers strongly concerned with intrapsychic phenomena, he is protected by them against his own pitfalls of oversimplification, which is to exclude depth of affect and the power of unconscious motivations from his purview. Seen from that angle, both clinical practice and social science research stand to gain from his inclusion on a clinical team.

Such an inclusion, however, may present an additional burden on the caseworker in a clinic, who already has to perform his professional task under the considerable stress and strain of psychiatric consultation, consideration of the test results furnished by the clinical psychologists, and supervision from within the ranks of his own profession. It must be a question of concern to the administrator of a clinic how many forms of outside influences upon the individual worker's judgment can be reconciled with the maintenance of professional self-esteem, initiative, and morale on the part of the caseworker.

Furthermore, it would be misleading to assume that social scientists, ready and able to meet the professional requirements of the middleman described above, can be found in adequate numbers to recruit them for many clinical teams. Many graduate departments of sociology and psychology are not sympathetic to the psychoanalytic orientation. Also, clinical sensitivity is rarely a requirement for a social science degree.

The practical solution may be the establishment of pilot teams from which the influence of the broader approach could be carried to the staff through the channels of supervision, and thus be transmitted to other clinical teams operating in an agency.

Many clinics may not find it possible, for financial and other reasons, to include social scientists as members of the staff, even on such pilot teams. In many instances, it may be possible for clinics to join together to work out such arrangements or to do so in connection with educational institutions.

It is my opinion that the project disproves the view that theoretic bases for clinical practice and social science belong in different logical spheres, and, as such, efforts devoted to their synthesis are wasted. The project experience and Dr. Pollak's suggestions as to further research, taken together, point to many fruitful possibilities. The task ahead is a two-sided one—the fashioning of a theoretic base for child guidance practice, and appropriate operational procedures which would integrate such theoretic concepts in practice. Child guidance, social casework, and other arts involved in modification of human behavior will grow soundly to the extent that their operational concepts and methods are grounded in empirical science. As these are expanded, they not only will provide a larger and sounder scope for clinical practice, but in turn contribute to an empirical basis for social and biologic science. The scientist, biologic and social, and the clinician must collaborate in the forging of such a conceptual frame of reference which, while based on empirical facts accessible to the clinician, must also meet the tenets of the logic and philosophy of science.

INDEX

Index